One Man's Garden

Books by Henry Mitchell

The Essential Earthman
Washington: Houses of the Capital
One Man's Garden

One Man's
GARDEN

*Henry
Mitchell*

HOUGHTON MIFFLIN COMPANY

Boston · New York · London

For information about permission to reproduce selections from this book,
write to Permissions, Houghton Mifflin Company, 215 Park Avenue South,
New York, New York 10003.

Library of Congress Cataloging-in-Publication Data
Mitchell, Henry, date.
One man's garden / Henry Mitchell.
p.   cm.
Includes index.
ISBN 0-395-63319-2
1. Gardening.   2. Gardening — Washington Metropolitan Area.
I. Title.
SB455.M57   1992   92-11090
635 — dc20   CIP

Printed in the United States of America

Pen-and-ink drawings by Susan Davis
Book design by Robert Overholtzer

The material in this volume originally appeared,
in slightly different form, in the *Washington Post.*

AGM 10 9 8 7 6 5 4 3

For Edna and Caryl Haskins

CONTENTS

JANUARY

N O GARDENER needs reminding that life depends on plants. No plants, no life. Very simple. This rough and real fact is the basis for the gardener's awe of plants, and from this fact springs the gardener's anxiety about pitching out any green thing.

I have often advocated chopping down Norway maples, hemlocks, and other noisome trees that convert gardens into dank wastelands, so I am well aware that not every green creature should be cherished and preserved. All the same, we owe our life on this planet to plants, and there is no need to forget it.

There is no need for every American to be lured into gardening. It does not suit some people, and they should not be cajoled into a world they have no sympathy with. Many people, after all, find their delight in stealing television sets; others like to make themselves anxious with usury and financial speculation; still others rejoice in a life of murder. None of these is very good material for a gardener.

All I require of society, in the matter of gardening, is a decent awareness that gardeners have a greater stake in society than others, and an occasional reflection that no life is worth living without a vine and a fig tree.

❖ Names from the Garden's Guest Book

A dear person, assisted by another dandy woman, gave me twenty-two plastic trash bags of horse manure for Christmas, and in last week's mild weather I got it spread on particular treasures in the garden. Ten roses on their arches had first claim, followed by the planting site of ten forthcoming tomato seedlings, then a dab for a crinum that should have bloomed in the summer but didn't, and a handful for the Princesse de Sagan (a red rose sitting all by herself), and a bucketful for what I hope is a hardy palm. Like youth, horse manure goes all too quickly. Before you've got started good, it's gone and you wonder how it went so fast.

This is the time to remind ourselves that we have our most beautiful skies in the winter. This sunrise the horizon was thundery dark gray-blue, surmounted by a broad band of orange salmon, then a band of turquoise, and above that a wide band of coral-rose. Above all that the sky was robin-egg blue with a few puffy clouds touched with light red. Of course only steady, wholesome folk (which includes gardeners) are awake to see it.

Many gardeners like to support wildlife in the garden, at least on a small scale, and this may be difficult, as the easiest fauna to attract in a city garden are rats. I once made a brush retreat (as recommended in a wildlife book) but had to remove it, as rats from a dozen counties soon applied for shelter. But I do keep bird feeders going, using only sunflower seed and suet (the suet in hanging wire containers), and as a result have many birds and of course squirrels. At first my peasant nature rebelled at the cost of feeding squirrels, but when I saw their ingenuity, determination, and general invincibility and then considered my own laziness, I saw that I would have squirrels forever and therefore resolved to love them. Things have gone smoothly since.

I put up a flicker nest box, which was taken over by starlings and then by a single squirrel, so I consulted books and built two nest boxes for squirrels. For two years they have ignored them, but on December 22 a pair moved into one of them, though it is only nine feet off the ground, and squirrels prefer to nest much higher. They carried in a lot of dried clematis stems for a couple of hours, and as they are just outside a bedroom window, we have an excellent view of their coming and going.

This past week squirrels have entered the second nest box, and several other squirrels have explored the first box. They stick their heads in until the occupant sticks his head out. A new black squirrel has investigated both boxes, and I only hope all this activity will not cause the original occupants to say nuts to it and move out.

Once we had a chipmunk, but not now. In a rotted maple we found a mother possum with five youngsters the size of oranges, but she was just passing through and stayed only two days. We had a raccoon who left dusty paw prints all over a newly painted wooden gate, and another one that came and destroyed a white water lily imported from Africa, after which we set a trap, but we only caught a neighbor's cat. He was greatly put out when released but has continued to come back all the same, and through some unknown good fortune the coons have not.

We usually have at least a couple of pairs of birds nesting — chickadees, Carolina wrens, cardinals, and mockingbirds. We also have eight mourning doves who come to feed. Usually a pair nests in the spring on a four-by-four wooden lintel, but the two eggs always fall off and the parents go elsewhere. Their nests are a disgrace, consisting of perhaps six twigs dumped at random, but they must be doing something right, as we now have the eight regulars and there were none when we moved in some years ago.

Nothing is better for wildlife in the garden than a fish pool. Counting sparrows, which we may as well since we have them coming out of our ears, we must have more than one hundred birds a day flying in to drink. Near us sea gulls feed at a grocery store, and I am just as glad they don't come to us and eat up the goldfish. Grackles I think do; I once saw one make off with a baby sparrow. Crows never came until the last year or two. I never catch them fishing but have seen them fly off with the glass thermometer that floats in the pool. Fortunately, I like to hear crows making a racket early in the morning, and love to hear the mockingbirds singing all night in May.

Butterflies abound in the summer, though no rare ones that I am aware of. It's said that if you take a big clay saucer, such as you might set a twelve-inch pot in, and fill it with mud kept constantly wet, you attract more, especially if a bit of horse manure is mixed in, but I have not yet tried it. Hummingbirds, I have learned, prefer several separate feeders, as they are bullies, and one will keep others from feeding.

A great sight is the pileated woodpecker that we have had visit on several occasions, once honoring us by looking at the rotted maple. Purple martins used to send scouts to look at the martin house but always flew on to the country, so we gave the house away. They do not like trees or tall shrubs near their house, and require plenty of space to whirl about in.

No foxes, nor, for that matter, tigers, but what we do have are agreeable occupants of a routine town garden that give great pleasure.

❖ *Architecture to Make the Garden Glow*

Architecture is the mother art of gardens, not because a garden needs to be (or should be) cluttered with architectural gewgaws, but because the stuff of architecture — the tension between differing volumes, the fall of light and dark, the rhythms of texture — is the essence of a garden.

Nobody can begin to grow one fiftieth of the plants that it is possible to grow in this or any other climate, and it is well to understand that to begin with. The gardener should resign himself to what is, after all, the paltriest ambition to grow everything. This does not mean he should not grow about four times as many different plants as he is growing at the moment. But the temptation to devote every square foot to growing another plant should be resisted, for the excellent reason that other approaches will make the gardener happier.

You have only to look at the most admired gardens — Sissing-hurst, Hidcote, Bodnant, even Dumbarton Oaks (which ought not to be limited by designer Beatrix Farrand's surprisingly limited taste in plants). Each of them is notable for its architecture, not only in the buildings that form so prominent a background but also in arbors, summerhouses, stairs, balustrades, mosaic pave-ments, and canals or pools. Often in England and France, when I have admired some garden, I have subtracted the walls, arbors, pavements, and other architectural features and found myself left with relatively unimpressive scenes. The beauty of plants — lilies, agaves, you name it — is enchanting in itself, but the placing of them all together in a setting of some splendor will quadruple their effectiveness.

Needless to say, a garden need not be formal, with one side balancing the other; the garden may be a woodland or a combina-tion of meadow and copse. The great garden at Sheffield Park, which relies so heavily on its magnificent trees and lake, is an ex-ample of a highly architectural garden, in the sense I mean, how-ever informal it seems at first.

In small town gardens ("small" has come to mean less than a quarter-acre, not less than five acres, as formerly), it usually is easier to adopt straight walks and geometrical forms, but there is no reason the small city place should not be given almost entirely to a copse of dogwood and sourwood or a huge informal pool fringed with peltiphyllums and reeds, overlooked by a mossy arbor of cedars. Almost any gardener will at first balk at enclosing the garden with hedges or shrubs or walls; the realization usually comes later that the space occupied by these things is well worth the price of giving up a collection of wild irises or fifty additional peonies, or whatever tempts the gardener in the way of flowers.

Few walks should be narrower than five feet. When the cost of bricks or other paving is at first considered, this seems an extrava-gance. Like a good furnace, it is not an extravagance in the long run. And a good investment is a batch of poles of various heights — tree limbs will do if you have them after a great storm — that can

be moved at will to form an idea of heights, well before the ultimate shape of the garden is decided on. My impression is that
gardeners are at first terrified of heights. They think four feet is
high. If they look at the gardens they most admire in pictures or in
the flesh, they will find the volumes of those gardens are often
twelve or twenty feet, not waist-high.

In any case, the gardener should not be afraid to plant large
shrubs or tall hedges or even trees, merely because the garden is
small. In back of a row house, I would rarely plant a tree if the
place were mine, but would build a little pavilion dedicated to a
grapevine or other creeper or shrub, giving a fine bulk of noble
foliage without the disadvantage of overwhelming shade. But a
wild persimmon or sassafras or red cedar or other small tree would
do; so would a willow, which could be made manageable either by
confining its roots or by sawing its branches from time to time.

Water is urgently important, for the good reason that nothing
else in the garden will so delight the gardener, whether he knows
it or not. But the critical thing is to visualize this before everything
is in concrete. Graph paper is possibly the chief invention since the
wheel for gardeners who do not have a strong architectural sense.
Remember always that if things must be either too big or too small,
they should be too big. Until experience teaches the lesson, the
garden designer will invariably make everything too small, too
complicated in outline, too fussy, and the result will not please.

One wide paved walk, one lily pool as large as can be managed,
one border as wide as feasible, and an enclosure of shrubs notable
for foliage and texture and flower or fruit (the viburnums, small
magnolias, nandinas, photinias, yews, hollies, come immediately to
mind, along with such creepers or vines as the grape, actinidia,
akebia, and campsis), and the bones are cast, as you might say.
Within this framework of bulk and light and shade, you then consider the mini-site (what are you to do with this four-foot strip in
dappled shade, say) and decide what you would like best from
among all the things possible. For example, you might fill the
dappled strip fairly solid with white Japanese anemones for the
fall, or anemones and bugbanes, or anemones and a few tall lilies,

and maybe edge it with one clump of blue hostas and a patch of catmint.

But what an error to get into specifics here. The point most important to make is that one's delight in the garden depends far more heavily than one thinks at first on the effects of sunlight and shadow, on massive bulk and relative emptiness contrasting with each other, on the effect of light on water, on the texture of brick and wood and stone.

Generally, ornaments do not give the pleasure one expects. In the small garden, possibly one sculpture will do, provided you ever find one you think is incredibly beautiful and you can afford (after forty-five years I actually purchased a bronze Siamese lion-dragon-dog), but usually it works better to use a plant as orna-ment — a fat box bush, a willow in a tub, a winter cherry, a clipped yew, a handsome pot or urn with plants spilling out of it (but not concealing its shape).

I would hardly cite my own garden as an example to be fol-lowed, because I have the severe vice of wanting more plants than is aesthetically right; but then, I am writing this not for pigheaded folk who know precisely what they want but for those who are not quite sure how to make the place beautiful. And if that is your aim, as it is for most sensible people, the most important advice I can give is to think of architecture, think in terms of bulks and voids, in terms of light. Colors and other minor things can be filled in later and changed at will.

❖ Oops! There Goes Another Rubber Tree Plant

I now pay for amaryllis sloth last summer. There are several bulbs, some of them eight years old, that I grow in pots, where they flower every January or February. Last summer, instead of turning the bulbs out of the pots and planting them in a good sunny spot to build up strength, I stood them outdoors in their pots, giving no new soil, no humus, no fertilizer, nothing, not even water.

The first bloom stalk this month had only two huge flowers instead of the usual four. Some of the bulbs, which are old enough and large enough to flower, are not flowering at all, because they made so little growth outdoors in the cramped pots, with utter neglect. They reproach me sorely every time I look at them. Next summer I shall do better by them.

Another house-dweller is the agave, that grand succulent creature resembling a yucca descended from Genghis Khan. It is native to dry, warm parts of America. I fell heir to one that was tossed out in the alley a few years ago, not so large then, and since I am not quite sure I can kill a plant without suffering trauma, I took it in, and it began to grow. It sent up some offshoots. I put it in a large clay pot, which it soon broke with its expanding roots. Then I put it into a hexagonal redwood tub, and it might have been all right for another year in that, except the bottom rotted out.

It now sits precariously in the living room, in the one spot that, I hope, is far enough out of traffic that nobody will be speared by its sharp spines. In the summer I trot around with rose shears cutting off the sharp tips of the swordlike leaves, but there is not much I can do with the fierce teeth that completely line the leaf edges. The agave and its babies in the tub are three and a half feet high, I would say, and four feet wide, maybe more. How I will get it out in the spring? Well, spring is a way off.

If I dared, I'd plant it out in good deep rich earth in April, but I know it would grow so vigorously it would be almost impossible to dig up next fall. And where will it go next fall? Already I am meeting resistance to putting it near the washing machine, the oil tank, the paint shelves, the bathroom, or almost anywhere else. It will have to go somewhere, I don't know where, and it will have to be in some container without a rotted bottom, though I don't know what.

The trouble is — one trouble is — I like agaves, the bigger the better. Well, these things work themselves out. Sometimes the gardener gets hit by a truck before he has to face the fact that the house won't hold but so many cubic feet.

There are several subtropical beasts like monsteras and certain philodendrons that start off looking neat in a smallish pot. The roots start going over the edge and the gardener thinks that the least he can do is provide a bigger pot, so he does this. These are the same plants that grow up trees in Madeira and other warm places. I have always known that, and I know that if you keep them rather starved in poor soil and refuse to give them larger and larger pots and tubs, they will stay semimanageable for years. On the other hand, you do like to see them flourish mightily.

Rubber trees are a common problem, though not with me. They go right up to the ceiling and then want to go through to the next floor. I have solved this. I grow mine, one of the kind that develops bronze or green-red leaves, in a large plastic pot a foot or so across. When it started getting too big, I let it almost die of thirst. That helped. Then in the summer I set it in a new place, out in the open, where it got all the winds of heaven. Every three or four days it blew over. It is now only about seven feet tall and a bit ragged, but its fight for survival has kept it from going through the ceiling.

Nothing is simpler than cutting the top out. New growth springs from the old stems. The part cut out makes fine cuttings, and new plants root easily. But I do not cut out the tops. I am afraid I'd root them, and then, within a few years, instead of one rubber plant too big for the dining room, I'd have a dozen.

Fooled it.

❖ Maintaining Your Garden and Maintaining Your Sanity

Pamela Lord at the Garden Book Club said something awful. "I've been thinking a lot about it," she said, "and I'm tired of hearing so much about maintenance-free gardens. If you aren't going to get out there and live with it — including taking care of it — then what's the point of gardening anyway? This year," she continued, "I'm going to order fewer new things and concentrate on taking care of what I have. I've decided maintenance is almost everything."

She's right, of course. People who say disgusting things are often right. In fact, however, it turned out (as Ms. Lord chatted along on the phone) that she is acquiring a number of plants new to her, and I doubt she spends her winter weekends grubbing out briars and straightening fences, for all her high and mighty talk.

Some years ago I resolved that nobody would ever work in my garden but me, though of course my splendid companion goes out there occasionally to pull up a clematis or two, and fills a lot more body bags with weeds than I do. Because we have no hired help, and because I am sloppy by nature, the garden usually looks terrible except when the spirit enters and I dash about for four days in a manic fit to straighten things up. Then the garden looks fairly okay for a week.

I attribute this state of things to a virtue I happen to possess (and not to the clear fact that I am lazier than most people), which is a fondness for digging. The more you dig, the greater mess you make, and if you consider digging the Great Good Occupation of Adam's Sons, of course you have to budget your time. Which means you dump everything on the walk and tend to that pile of pruned stems from the grapes "later." You can be sure the phone will ring or a hurricane will come up or it will be time to do something else urgently, and the prunings will stay where you dump them. On later excursions into the garden, a good many of these can be kicked under a yew or otherwise semidisposed of, and the dogs are good at picking some of them up and wandering off.

You don't dig far in Washington without encountering massive roots. I never knew such a place for tree roots, and as for pokeweed, nowhere else in the world do pokeweeds grow so quickly or make roots so enormous. I have two hatchets and two axes. It's dirty work, but somebody has to do it, as I say before plopping down with a grunt after an exhausting forty-minute session.

Some people are clearly better at maintenance in their gardens than others — the same ones, probably, that keep files of birthdays and jokes for all occasions and have neat desks. The world in general admires them, and I in general stand in awe of them. In moments of transient bitterness and sarcasm, I say, *Of course they are neat, since they haven't got anything to be messy about.* The truth, however, is simply that they are better organized than I. They know that sooner or later the grape branches are going to have to be picked up (it takes them literally years to rot away) and cut up and hauled out to the trash, and it's more efficient to do it promptly than to do it "later."

They are right, which makes the whole thing more annoying. I read an anecdote about some Lady Rothschild, a woman with a flawless garden where nothing was ever undone that ought to have been done, who was visiting another garden in the fall. There were some brilliantly colored leaves on the grass paths, and Lady R. exclaimed over them: "How gorgeous. I suppose you import them?" She had never seen a stray leaf on the paths at her own place.

We need not go as far as the Rothschild garden, of course, but some of us — certainly I — could do better in the way of general maintenance. We must try.

❖ Tomato or Tomahto: Tips on Types to Plant

The gardener's attention is now riveted on the tomato, because (a thing others will think odd) although tomatoes are not planted out in Washington until May 10, January is the proper month to ago-nize over which tomato to grow.

If the plants grow well, two plants per adult will yield enough for most people. Your typical gardener commonly plants more than that, on the theory that things will not go well at all. One false economy usually practiced by city gardeners is to jam in as many plants as possible, but sober experience will show that better re-sults come from spacing the plants at least two feet apart, and preferably three.

The best scheme for most gardeners is to grow them in cylindri-cal cages twenty-four inches in diameter and five feet high — you just plant the infant tomato seedling in the center and as it grows it's supported by the cage. You make these easily from reinforcing mesh or any heavy wire fencing, but be sure the mesh is large enough to let you reach in and gather fruit.

There are well over a thousand varieties of tomatoes in America, and perhaps three hundred of them are being grown fairly widely. But with limited space, a gardener naturally wants the perfect tomato. There are commercial tomatoes that are bred for supermarket sale or canning. These are best left to the great firms for which they were bred, and are generally a poor choice for the home garden. The home gardener does not need a variety that can be shipped and handled roughly, nor the varieties that all ripen within a few days, then produce no longer.

Still, even the poorest tomato is improved beyond recognition if allowed to become dead ripe on the vine. One great reason that many grocery-store tomatoes are dismal is that they are picked completely green and artificially ripened.

In Washington I hear many complaints about early varieties of tomatoes, those that are supposed to produce fruit within sixty days or so of being set outdoors. In general they lack the high quality of the later varieties, and the gardener often discovers that they do not ripen any earlier than high-quality later sorts. Henry E. Allen of Bethesda, Maryland, commonly called Mr. Vegetable, says he has never found an early variety he likes. With him they ripen no more than a week before the late kinds, and many of them not only give up after the first few tomatoes ripen, but also often simply collapse once our warm weather arrives.

There is a debate, at least among picky gardeners, about hybrid tomatoes. These are produced by crossing two established strains to achieve a variety stronger, better, more loyal, courteous, kind (on my Scout's honor) than the older varieties. They are more resistant to a wider assortment of diseases, and when well grown with ample sun and water in rich soil, they yield heavier crops; at least that is what most gardeners think. But others insist that non-hybrid varieties have richer flavor and less tough flesh. If there is room to give each plant at least four square feet, the gardener can grow both hybrid and older standard types and see which he prefers.

❖ *Sowing Beauty in Beastly Surroundings*

Perfection is not required and certainly need not be expected in any field of gardening. Often when visiting famous gardens I have been urged to admire the placement of some mountain ash or yew and invited to marvel at the foresight of the planter some two hundred years ago. The truth is, I am delighted the great tree is in just the right place, but foresight my eye.

The way it works is, a gardener plants stuff all over the place. Much of it dies and much is chopped out. Taste changes; new owners develop strange enthusiasms for rhododendrons or winter hazels. Economics change, and the emphasis on glasshouses vanishes. Where there were twenty-six gardeners, now there are three, and farewell to the box-edged beds filled with ranunculus. What one sees now is what remains after all the hazards have occurred over the years, and what remains physically and economically possible.

It is the same in the small town garden. The garden is a process, not a sculpture or a painting that once given form will stay that way. The trees grow and shade out the water lilies, or the trees fall in storms and that's the end of trilliums. An ugly shed is erected or a fine old hedge is removed, or similar things take place to change the character of the garden remarkably. A garden is ephemeral. Few are the gardens that have lasted more than forty years, and even in that time they usually have changed character beyond belief.

It surprises me, after all these years of poking about, to see how rarely visitors notice that what they truly admire in great gardens is old brick walls, luminous pools and ponds, a beautiful architectural background — it can help a garden no end to have a Roman temple or a medieval tower at the end of it — and these things, marvelous as they may be, have little to do with the poor gardener's skill or lack of it. What the ordinary town gardener has to do is make the most of what he cannot change. He can obscure, with a locust tree or a vine arbor or anything else of appropriate size, an ugly warehouse or a parking lot. He can cut down a locust and remove an arbor that hides a beautiful building or a superb view.

Suppose (and it is the usual thing) a city garden has surroundings that are ugly and cannot be hidden. Suppose a ten-foot wall of mellow brick would be a great help but cannot be acquired, for any number of reasons. Even so, it is possible to have a beautiful garden. The eye can be directed away from the grossness that cannot be demolished and focused instead on a small summerhouse in the center of the garden or a small pool for fish and perhaps some lush and graceful roses on high posts behind the pool. A mass of flowers can be concentrated in the foreground, and nothing dazzling allowed to be seen in the direction where the worst view is.

Suppose there is a long range of unbroken cinder-block wall or the backs of commercial garages at one side of the garden. It will usually be impossible to block them from view, but much can be done to diffuse their otherwise insistent massiveness and length simply by planting a small tree in front of them. An examination will show that most of the crud is still visible, but the fact that the long stretch is broken by the interruption of a tree or two will do much — almost everything — to take the curse off. It is a principle of camouflage that if there are blobs to break an outline, the thing will no longer be seen, or at least it will not so insistently assert itself.

With a small garden, at least there is the comfort that it is much easier to design than a large garden, and much more can be done (merely in terms of dollars) to correct the unfavorable site. Grape arbors and pools, big pots, handsome pavements, and striking specimen plants are far more feasible in a garden back of a row house than they are in a large garden.

I always felt sorry for owners of huge gardens with vistas on such a scale that the nearby village really had to be demolished to make the garden look right. We in crowded towns at least do not have to think what it costs to raze fifteen surrounding city blocks. We are not so expansive and we have no such power. We surrender to the inevitable and find in the installation of some four-by-four posts with grapes or other vines, and in the introduction of a fat box bush or a stone plinth or a wooden railing just here, that we have done much to transform what at first seemed a hopeless jumble or urban blight.

There is another approach, quite valid, to the question of surrounding ugliness, and that is simply to ignore it and to concentrate on neat rows of beans, superbly cultivated roses, or whatever the gardener prizes most. There can still be a place for the gardener to sit and admire his asparagus or whatever. A wooden sentry box, open to the magnificent view (twenty by sixty feet) of the cabbages, is not beyond the means of anybody who has a garden at all.

You have only to look at allotment gardens (those strips side by side in which a number of gardeners may grow ten tomato plants or two hundred gladioli) to see how worthwhile even a tiny garden can be, even without such dream fixtures as clipped hedges and limpid pools with red fish and blue water lilies. Relax, I suggest, and waste no further time muttering about the absence of ceanothus-clad walls of salmon brick with the tower of St. Phlomis-atte-Puddle for a backdrop. Dig that hole. Fetch that leaf bag full of horse manure. Plant that bush. A vine, after all, and a fig tree are enough for any mortal to rejoice in, and more than most men nowadays can have. The world would be vastly better if every human had a grapevine.

A useful book for anybody facing the challenge of a small garden in the city is *The City Gardener's Handbook* (New York: Random House, 1990), by Linda Yang, noted garden writer for the *New York Times*. The author has faced the horrors herself — not all that awful, when you get down to it and figure what has to be done — and will save the novice many false steps. The photographs, moreover, are highly reassuring of what the result can be.

❖ *The Gardener's Lot*

The life so short, the craft so long to learn. This was said about literature, but it really fits gardening better. Poetry, after all, is learned extremely early as a rule, if it is learned at all, but gardening is the province of old crocks past the age of twenty-eight.

Why does it take so long to learn? Partly because books contain endless errors, and partly because the craft is so close to the real world. A poet could write the same thing, I would think, in Seville or Bald Knob, Arkansas, but a gardener must deal with weather, with soil, with sun that varies madly.

Take the Italian arum. *Arum italicum* is a plant valuable for small gardens in town, since its beautiful dark green marbled or veined leaves appear only in October, when other things are in decline. It is fresh and fine all winter and spring, dying down with warm weather.

It used to be a common enough plant. I saw it often as a kid in Tennessee. I do not see it so often up here, and although I found one company that sold it in New York, it was not the beautifully marked form I wanted.

When a buddy of mine went abroad and said he wanted to bring me back something, I said, "How about some seeds of the Italian arum?" He came back with a small bare root an inch long, with no leaves or rootlets. He stole it from a famous garden. I said I might have to have him put in jail. But first I waited to see if it would grow. If it didn't, I might need this guy to steal another one on the next trip.

It took a year for the root to make two leaves, one of which was broken off, probably by the same wretched dog that keeps watering my best box bush. The year after, it put up two leaves again, and they did fine. The third year there were four leaves, the largest of which was broken. The fourth year there were finally about five leaves and the plant bloomed and set seed.

Ah. This plant is easy from seed. I often grew it from seed in the past. The seed finally ripened to its proper scarlet on the spadix (that spike you find in the middle of the calla or the jack-in-the-pulpit or this arum), and I cut it and brought it indoors to dry thoroughly. I intended to plant the seed this past October and (counting chickens) expected twenty nice little plants next spring. Because the seeds were few and precious, I set them on the mantel in the living room. They ripened along nicely.

One day they were not there.

This may be the place to say that nothing is accomplished by roaring up to one's wife. Even if she has in fact thrown out some treasure, she will never admit it, and the years have shown me that after considerable righteous bellowing on my part, it usually turns out that I moved the seeds myself, or planted them and forgot them. Things like that.

In this case, we believe the spadix fell off the mantel and got chewed up by our young terrier, Max. The seeds, I suspect, are poisonous. Come to think of it, Max was mysteriously ill one day. Anyhow, no seeds. And yet this arum is a plant I would like to raise plenty of, and to spread around.

What is it now, five years? This is precisely the kind of delay you encounter in gardening. With better luck, I could have had flowers and seeds the first year, and nothing really is simpler than raising an Italian arum, getting seeds, and growing them as easily as radishes. All the same, however simple it is, it may take a sixth year.

At some effort, I imported a plant of equal merit in the winter, the big-leaf bergenia called 'Ballawley Hybrid', since I could not find it in America. That doesn't mean it isn't grown. There are lots of wonderful nurseries that can't afford to advertise nationally, and doubtless there are commercial sources for the plant in America, but I couldn't find them.

A disgusting thing you will encounter in your gardening life is this sort of sentence: "The bergenias are planted far too often. They are fairly boring plants, though 'Ballawley Hybrid' is probably as good as any, if for some reason you feel compelled to grow a plant so dull and routine." You always see such a thing in print at just the time you have knocked yourself senseless acquiring the plant and coddling it along. To crown it all, the dull, worthless plant you have finally got at enormous effort and some expense will die on you, as mine did — just in time for you to read another comment: "One of the worst things is that these bergenias spread about in a tiresome way and have to be weeded out."

If, as I believe, gardeners are the elect of the earth, cured in humility and grace and other good things, it is because Nature herself hammers in upon us the lessons of patience, and reminds us far too frequently how little our skill and experience are worth. The next step, needless to say, is to see a garden in which there is nothing but a forsythia bush, a large terrace for cocktails, and (gasp) a huge patch of 'Ballawley'. The owner always says, "Oh that. It's something somebody planted. Don't look like much, does it?"

I once planted a rare evergreen oak from Burma and was prepared to pray over it for some years. Instead, it grew as well as a plain water oak, and never gave me a minute's worry. I loved (in those days in that garden) to show it to people, and if they seemed impressed, I always said, "Well, it grows like a weed. Can't think why anybody ever has any trouble with it," knowing perfectly well that the gardener would go home, order it and plant it, and struggle along for ten years to get the blasted thing going. Cursing me the while, of course.

It takes no time to fall helpless prey to the delights of gardening, and nobody should be put off by thinking it is difficult or takes forever. Even oaks from acorns grow with astounding speed. Yet it is true that you can spend most of your life gardening before it finally dawns on you what you think is most worth growing. And the rest of your life (as Gertrude Jekyll once observed) puzzling out how best to grow it.

I think the best summation of the gardener's lot was spoken by a fellow in London who, against all odds, wound up with a beautiful garden out in the country. "This garden," he used to say, "was made by doing impractical things that we could not afford at the wrong time of the year."

FEBRUARY

IF GARDENERS SPENT less time running about doing things they think they are supposed to do and more time contemplating the beauty of the world's plants, they'd get more out of their gardens and be less of a pest to the civilized world.

I have a useful rule of thumb for judging garden books: whenever I see charts in which you read down one side, then across, I know the book was written by some idiot whose learning and whose love are exhausted by a three-word summary. Thus, there will be a chart of useful flowering shrubs, and you read down the side till you get to Rose; then, reading across, you find such items as Height, Season, Color, and so forth. You will read under Height, "Variable," and under Season you will be informed "Spring" or "Spring through fall," and under Color you will find "Various: white, yellow, red, etc.," so you wind up knowing nothing about any rose.

This approach, however, pleases many book publishers, staffed as they are by people who cannot get honest jobs and who imagine that such a worthless chart represents taut, crisp acumen when what it really represents is abysmal ignorance of the subject. Such books abound in "calendars" in which you are exhorted to run out and do something every week or every hour of the year: "December is the time to chase field mice out of the barberry bushes" and so on. By punching a computer key, all the dumb advice of the centuries can be belched up and recycled for a new work. All too often the poor gardener discovers that since he is learning nothing about roses or any other plant, perhaps he should get busy on the field mice, as that is the only specific thing he can find in the book.

What we really want to know is which flowers are most worth growing in the succeeding seasons of the year, and whether there is any trick in growing them (almost always there is not), and which varieties are acknowledged by experienced gardeners to be most worth the space and effort needed to grow them. Sooner or later most gardeners will die, to put it cautiously, and the question then is whether the gardener has spent his time and resources fidgeting about with fungi, moles, bugs, and evil squirrels or has gloried, year by year, in the snowdrops.

Gardening is full of mistakes, almost all of them pleasant and some of them actually instructive, and it all turns out right at the last, provided the gardener's attention remains fixed on the marvelous things available to be grown rather than on tasks urged by ignorant puritans, such as chasing mice or pestering starlings.

❖ *Sowing Seeds Indoors, and Other Poppycock*

A friend, having made a note that I have never raised poppies with any success, thoughtfully invited me to view her Shirley poppies in bloom in February. Not outdoors, of course. She is the rankest amateur, she is fond of saying, and just raises a few things in her basement under lights, including these poppies, which are — she scarcely knows how — growing like gangbusters. But then, any fool can grow them.

So go ahead, don't pay any attention to me, plant your seeds indoors in October or January or early February. Any fool can succeed, as my friend likes to remind me. But I am here to say that the one gardening operation that brings the most grief to the greatest number is this sowing of seeds in the house before mid-March.

People tell me what they do, and I know it anyway, as I have often done it myself. They rev up and buy ten bucks' worth of seed from a catalogue, and there they are on January 10 with the seed in their hand, the Styrofoam cups on the windowsill, and what joy there is when, on February 1, all kinds of wee green sprouts make the heart leap. It is far otherwise on March 10, when the few surviving spindly pale green shoots lean desperately toward the light. Outside there is a snowstorm. The gardener reads that he should "harden off" the seedlings by exposing them to greater light and cooler temperatures outdoors, then bring them back inside for a few days. Very well. It's hardening-off time, not that the spindly seedlings are going to survive either outdoors or indoors, but the gardener hesitates to harden them off in a rain of sleet.

After about three years of this, the gardener says nuts and sprinkles the seeds outdoors in fall or late winter, hoping a few will grow. A few do, but they cannot compete with the late winter weeds, and commonly no flowers result, not even one. Then the gardener says nuts again and waits till April 1, searching garden centers for the very first flats of geraniums and alyssum. These are borne home in triumph, planted out, and they too perish in a late freeze, or even without a freeze they die in windy, damp cold.

Nuts again, says the gardener (we are now up to about the tenth year), and he learns to wait till late April or May to plant out those semimythical "sturdy, thrifty, well-hardened plants" that the books keep talking about. And sure enough they grow and bloom, so the gardener concludes that the way to do it is to wait until full spring is here and then plant out the best and costliest young plants he can find.

But suppose he wants a certain variety of petunia or verbena or zinnia or whatnot, and knows he will not find it at any garden center. The only way to get it is from seed. He then has two choices.

He can wait till mid-May and plant the seeds outdoors, in a well-prepared (which means tilled and weed-free) soil in friable condition — which means work, so don't just race over "well-prepared" as if your soil already were dreamy — and give them protection from emerging weeds, from strong winds, and especially from drought. When the seedlings emerge, you should transplant them to stand about a foot apart, except for things like poppies and cornflowers, which often die when transplanted.

The other method is to proceed on St. Patrick's Day, in the Washington area, exactly as the foolish gardener did on January 10, with your Styrofoam cups and soil (or whatever you use), and you will still have the joy of beholding the tender green sprouts. Except that this time they will live. The light is strong; the temperature is milder. If it snows you don't care, because your seedlings are safe indoors. They don't dry out, because you water them, and they don't suffer from wind or slugs or the usual hazards of God's great outdoors. They grow up sturdy, because on mild sunny days you put your flats or pots of seedlings outdoors, then bring them in at night. Their leaves are really green, not pale, and their stems are sturdy, not etiolated.

Depending on how fast they grow, they go outdoors in permanent positions in the second half of April or early May, if the varieties are pretty hardy, or after mid-May if they are tender. In either case, it is warm (or hot) outdoors, and you will really take time to get the weeds out of your seedlings' permanent planting sites. Your plants will be tough and in the first great flush of youthful strength, well able to withstand a bit of buffeting in the great rude world.

Although some gardeners can manage it, for most of us it is difficult to raise good seedlings in the house on the windowsills. The solution, short of a good cold frame or a reliable greenhouse (and greenhouses are a pain in the neck, if you want the truth), is fluorescent lights, the cheap kind that are called shop lights. No need for more expensive tubes.

It's said you can install them anywhere, but the obvious place for those who have basements is down there. At my house there is a workbench, the surface of which is made of four-by-fours (when two-by-fours would have done) and which, needless to say, I have never used except to store old fire screens, broken tile slabs for baking, and other important things I'll need someday. I have cleared such stuff off, moving it all to a space above the twenty-year-old cans of paint. I have installed a shop light.

Just here I should say that I take seriously the warning not to use adapters to change a two-prong plug to a three-pronger. Naturally, before I read the warning on the box of fluorescent tubes, I bought an adapter. I went back and bought an orange ten-foot exterior extension cord. The average hardware store will inform you that such cords are not available in less than twenty-five-foot lengths, but that is not so. Demand your rights.

The fluorescent light comes with a little foot-long cord. There is no outlet in the western world a foot from any known place for installing the lights, so you need an extension cord. Remember that houses burn down every day from improperly used extension cords. If it is not clear to you, call an electrician. It is cheaper than a new house. And call a good electrician, I might add.

Once the light is set up, make sure the soil in which the seeds are to be sown is sterile. Some potting-mix soils are nearly sterile enough to be used right out of the bag. Otherwise, and with all soil you have dug from your garden, sterilize it by heating it. I have used a great stew pot and put in the dirt with an inch or so of water above it and boiled it for half an hour or so. Or you can use the oven: spread the soil thin and bake it for half an hour. Sometimes there are objections to these procedures, but the point is, you want the soil to be free of both weed seeds and evil fungoid organisms that prevent the seedlings from growing up sturdy.

Different plants need different amounts of light. For tomatoes, sixteen hours a day has been recommended (though imperfection is a rule of gardening life), and the tops of the little plants as they grow are kept only two inches below the tubes. A successful grower tells me that he keeps his four to six inches below, then lets the plants grow till they actually touch the tubes. As a novice at this, I intend to keep mine two inches below.

In planting seeds, the gardener rarely plants uniformly. Some are half an inch deep, others right on the surface, and such haphazard methods bring haphazard results, which is all the poor gardener has ever expected. There are books on seed planting.

I was well into middle age before I learned that petunia seeds are sown right on the surface and that they need light to sprout. Ah so. Forty years of failure explained in a sentence.

❖ The Imperfect Gardener

The commonest bad mistakes made by gardeners, as I judge from my own experience, are these:

• Failing to enclose the garden with shrub screens, hedges, walls, or fences, with the result that the scene never looks finished, no matter how well things are growing or how many things are in flower.

• Planting too closely. No gardener thinks time will pass and plants will grow. Even slow growers like box increase in bulk surprisingly, in surprisingly few years.

• Ignoring the tremendous effect of small flowers massed. Instead, the gardener too often plants varieties with large individual flowers that show up far less well than varieties with much smaller flowers but more of them.

• Being unable to focus on one thing at a time. There are only so many weeks a year, and most shrubs flower for at least two weeks, so the task of planting the most beautiful or interesting things for each season is not too burdensome. But the gardener will not focus on such seasons as, say, early July, then plant things together that look fine then.

• Hoping always to find varieties that bloom the longest. Thus, the gardener must have roses that bloom from May to November, and deplores peonies, lilacs, fall crocuses, and other flowers that come in one great burst, then shut up shop for the rest of the year.

I say nothing of many other faults, such as letting the fence lean instead of repairing it promptly, or leaving empty pots at the side of the walk instead of storing them neatly in the garage.

One of the most startling demonstrations in all gardening is Americans prowling about the celebrated gardens of England. They moan and croon and say they could never achieve such effects back in America, because the English climate is so favorable, so mild. In this they are totally wrong. England has a dreadful climate, hardly any sun and, surprisingly, not enough rain either. Plants grow slowly there. It is July before things truly get going, and they peter out in September. Most of the plants admired in those island gardens are readily grown in Washington and other moderate regions of our country, and even in the Plains states, luxuriant effects can be had from quite hardy plants.

I have seen Americans in England falling into fits over such roses as 'Seagull' or fainting in Paris over a similar rose, 'Thalia'. The trouble is not that such things grow better abroad than here, but that here the gardener would not dream of planting them. The gardener here plants some climbing rose, brand-new, that is supposed to be showy and constant, then wonders why, a few years later, it does not really give the effect he wants. Such roses as 'Seagull', with flowers only an inch or so wide, come in great clusters and emit heady perfume. They make a tremendous show for two or three weeks. They do not bloom again till the following spring, and this is argued against planting them.

Then why do Americans have such fits over English gardens, where such roses are as common as they are rare in America? I could understand someone's not liking 'Seagull', or any other particular rose, but I do not understand why the gardener refuses to plant it here, then goes off his rocker when he sees it abroad.

❖ Nature vs. Nurture

Often I surprise myself at how little I notice in a flower, and the reason for this is haste and excitement with the flower as a whole. The beauty of an iris, say, is so great that it was years before I paid much attention to its structure. Eventually, when I bred irises in a small way, I marveled at the elegance of the style arms, the stigmatic lip, the wonderful tight way in which the stamens curve to fit the curvature of the arm.

The casual viewer, who may admire the beauty of the iris as

much as any fanatic iris fancier, will wonder how the dedicated gardener can tell the name of every iris among, say, five hundred kinds in the garden. But it is easy if you know and love the flowers. Of the five hundred, there will be only one hundred yellows, perhaps. They vary greatly in the size of flower, the placement of blooms on the stem, the marks or little stripes on the haft of the lower petals, the shape of those petals, the degree of arching of the top petals, whether they touch the other petals or arch up without touching. They vary in fragrance, in texture — some being satiny, some velvety, some waxy — and in substance — some being thick-petaled and some thin like tissue paper.

We have no trouble naming one hundred different people, who vary in looks less than irises do. It is simply a question of noticing obvious things — obvious, that is, if one cares to notice differences among the blooms. The one great thing I learned with my years of playing about with irises is that it is far from easy, even after watching particular seedling plants for several years, to tell which aspects result from inherited genes.

I soon learned that once a seedling blooms, the flower does not change much over the years. When I was new to irises, I would have said they never changed at all, but then I discovered there can be exceptional years in which the blooms quite outdo themselves. The substance can be greater than usual, the flare of the petals can be more beautiful and noticeable than usual, the color can even be slightly more luminous than usual. But these are small variations, and there is never a year in which one variety looks like another variety, not to the careful ordinary observer. Certainly it never happens that an iris changes from one color to another, no matter how old and no matter how different the environments in which it is grown.

If a particular iris variety has eight little marks on the narrow part of its lower petals, it will forever have them. Nothing in the way of cultivation (or prayers, for in past decades we hated those marks and stripes that interfered with the broad color expanse of the lower petals) ever changed those marks. The leopard does not change his spots.

Yet I saw that if for several years a certain iris bloomed on eighteen-inch stalks, I could not assume it was a dwarf grower. In experiments I was shocked at how often a dwarfish plant, when transplanted to another spot, would bloom on forty-inch stems. It is easy to look at irises growing together and to assume that one common environment affects them all, and that is often incorrect.

If a seed is planted and then transplanted when three inches high, and is grown along for a year until it blooms, one of the tiny plants may start off with a bit more water, a bit more sun, than a neighboring plant, and such tiny differences may get one seedling off to a great start, in which every genetic possibility will come to perfection, while a nearby seedling will remain a runt, at least until it is moved and given a new start without competition.

Once in a litter of basset hounds, one was a runt, one was a giant, and five were in between. It annoyed the bitch a little, I think, for me continually to switch pups to different nipples. I gave the runt the best nipple and the giant the least favorable one. In very few weeks, all the pups were the same size. When I took them in for temporary shots, the vet said he had never seen a litter in which all the pups were equally well fed, their weights identical.

So it was with irises, and I learned not to assume too quickly that a small iris plant was genetically small. Often it was only environmentally small. But if the iris has the genes for smallness or for great height, nothing will change those genes, and when the environment is wholesome, the plant will be the size it is genetically programmed to be, never mind how different it may have looked in an unfavorable environment.

Such things are commonplaces to anyone who ever bred irises a few years and watched them. But a visitor, seeing a starved iris, will hardly believe that the flower on an eighteen-inch stem will bloom on a forty-five-inch stem elsewhere in the garden.

My point is that even such elementary observations are not common among gardeners, especially young gardeners new to the game. But even old gardeners, who may observe the iris carefully, rarely regard their other plants carefully. I grew common wild primroses and cowslips for years and never noticed the first thing about them except that they bloomed like mad every spring and became dormant with hot summer weather. I did not even experiment to see if they would stay green all summer (they will) if given more shade and water. And as for the remarkable behavior of the stamens, I never even looked at the stamens, except in a casual way.

I have again been reading a book I find fascinating, *Darwin and His Flowers,* by Mea Allan (New York: Taplinger, 1977). I can hardly believe the wonders that Darwin discovered simply by close observation. Anyone could have seen the same things, conducted the same simple experiments that he did. He had no computers, no fancy laboratory, no laboratory of any kind. He just took time, and he asked questions. How do vines climb? That was one of his questions, and he found the answer. The rest of us never dream there is an answer, we just go plodding nicely along admiring our wisterias, never thinking to ask, never dreaming we might learn something.

Really, it is hilarious to think of it — thousands of years, and nobody bothered to ask questions or bothered to examine plants carefully, not as Darwin did. He was a great lover of plants; he caressed flowers, and he knew nothing of botany at first. He said he knew no more about the plants he collected in the Galápagos Islands than the man in the moon. And yet he became the most important botanist of the world. Beyond that, plants, not birds or mammals or insects, were the impetus for Darwin's view of life on the planet, culminating with the *Origin of Species.*

The man had a brilliant intelligence, but the things he learned about plants did not require more than ordinary intelligence. He asked the questions that we might have asked as children (how do vines climb?) but no longer ask once we grow up and become stupid. One minor lesson of the past century is that you start asking questions about primroses and you will bring down the whole civilized world. What terrible chaos, what grief, sprang from Darwin's simple experiments and endless careful notetaking. And, of course, what miracles of new freedom, new knowledge, and old truth that nobody before him had bothered to discover.

❖ *Happy Returns*

A friend has returned a glass pickle jar I forgot I gave him (it had small goldfish to get him started with his fish pool), and I am delighted to have it back. A simple gallon-size pickle jar affords the possibility of a superb mess. I put mud in the bottom, add water, and raise water lilies. As I do not have either light or temperature properly controlled, these attempts often come to nothing, and during the winter, as I investigate progress or add water, I seem to slop things about a good bit. I feel that the pickle jar is better than the enamel laboratory tray for my African water lily, the one that has leaves no more than an inch wide and flowers no more than half an inch. It is hard to pull it through the winter indoors. It is not doing nearly so well (virtually dead but two leaves still, and spring is not far off) in the enamel pan as it did previously in the glass jar.

Like most gardeners, I do not care about plastic pots, whether they are returned or not, unless they are the big ones that hold three gallons or more, but I do miss clay pots, glass jars, and other Containers of Importance that I sometimes send a plant in. Another thing that upsets gardeners is giving away a plant with good soil on its roots. Most gardeners work hard to shake every atom of dirt off a plant they give away, and of course it looks stingy because it is stingy. It's hard to say, "Here's the plant in its ball of earth, but be sure you drop by a bag of equally good dirt next time you're in the neighborhood."

Those new to gardening should know, however, that most gardeners hate to part with dirt, clay pots, pickle jars, really good labels, stakes, tarred twine, and any kind of wooden box. They do not mind giving a plant that sells for $40 if they have an extra one, but the other stuff (which may be worth a dime) it tears the heart to part with.

I cannot imagine why I gave away the pickle jar to begin with. I certainly did not expect it to be returned. And I am overjoyed to have it back.

❖ The Cypress, Belle of the Bald

The train trip from Washington to New York is depressing except when passing by swamps and inlets. Mile after mile of junk and chaos, empty warehouses and so forth, give no idea how beautiful this countryside once was. But as I looked out on a recent journey, I saw a great bald cypress rising above a lower story of general ugliness, and my spirits soared. It was leafless, of course, but still had its architectural conical beauty, and I wondered how on many trips I had managed not to see it.

The bald cypress is called bald because in old age the top of the tree is blown out by storms. In this respect it resembles the yellow poplar or tulip tree, which almost invariably loses its crown. White oaks, in contrast, rarely lose their top branches even in old age.

I once read that everybody should have some mental vision of a beautiful scene to be called up in times of despondency, and I have two. One is of a blue iris in bloom, and the other is of a bald cypress shimmering in August heat, the branches laden with white egrets motionless except for an occasional trembling of the plumes.

I should say that these visions have not done a great deal in times of unhappiness, but then they have done no harm either. Sometimes, when I am quite content, I think of the two scenes before going to sleep, and as I go to sleep about two minutes after I hit the bed, I need something quick and simple.

The cypress (not to be confused with evergreen cypresses) is a great ornament of gardens, and I wonder why people plant it so rarely. In the wild, in the lowlands of the lower Mississippi, it grows in standing water in swamps, but it also grows where roses and tomatoes grow, where an oak or an ash would grow.

There are several forms of this native bald cypress, some of them more weeping or pendent than others, and some with more billowy branches, like fat plumes, than others. In the fall they turn yellow-ish, not very colorful, before the needles drop. This tree, like the larch and the ginkgo, is one of the few conifers that drop their leaves every winter.

A nice thing about it is that the shade is soft and light. I knew a garden where daylilies were grown right up to its trunk. In a town garden it would be hard, I guess, to arrange for the egrets in the branches. You could learn to settle for starlings, probably.

The usual form of this tree is a cone, but if you like to play around with saws, as many gardeners do, you can make it into a more horizontal outline. I think the natural shape is impossible to improve upon.

Often gardeners ignore some of our most beautiful wild trees — persimmons, hawthorns, sassafrases, deciduous hollies, sourwoods — in favor of foreign trees. Almost the only native tree widely planted in gardens is the dogwood. Unlike the other native trees mentioned, the cypress grows as tall as any forest giant, but it can always be trimmed back, and in any case it will make a billowing, feathery mass of light green foliage for many years before it assumes its final massive stature.

There is a famous bald cypress near the highway at Tunica, Mississippi, that is said to be centuries old. Its trunk rises like a great redwood to a tuft of green branches, the crown long since disappeared. A poetic lady of the region once wrote an enthusiastic ode to it, a mighty centennial, as she said.

There is another famous one in Arkansas, said to have been a landmark when Hernando de Soto passed through in 1541. It grows in dense forest. I knew an admirable photographer who wrote a magazine article about it, with illustrations, but the tree could not be photographed as a whole. The photographer therefore shot the bottom of the tree, then backed off and shot the top. A body of type ran between the two pictures on the page and the effect was fine.

Other cypresses are quite different. The Italian cypress, slender and columnar, is hardy here, at least against a wall, but it has a bad way of toppling over in the winter if ice weighs down its branches. It has a rather modest root system and the whole tree goes over. The same is true of the Arizona cypress, in my experience. The

Arizonan has beautiful gray-blue needles. It is perfect for forming arches over a walk, but there should be a steel framework or something of the kind, which the cypress will soon cover. I once made arches of this cypress without a framework, and very beautiful they were till the first bad winter; then they all hit the dust like the Italian cypress.

The bald cypress, though, not only is utterly hardy but is not damaged by anything our climate offers. It grows wild as far north as Maryland, perhaps farther, and certainly grows all right into southern New England. The bald cypress should be planted in spring, say April, and given plenty of water its first summer. I have never seen or heard of any bug or bacterial pests on it.

❖ A Screen of Shrubs

Here is a problem I envy: how to plant a shrub border or screen for two hundred feet along the edge of a suburban lot, curving along the front and sides, with a good-size lawn between border and house. At first the owner thought of a hedge, until it dawned on him that he probably couldn't talk his wife or kids into clipping it. He also considered an unclipped hedge, which might do well enough, until I suggested that he think of a mixed border of shrubs to provide small pleasures throughout the year. The shrub border or screen that we are considering has an outer row of large bushes nearest the sidewalk and an inner row of smaller shrubs nearest the house but separated from it by the lawn.

A thing worth considering is how the border will look at different times of the year. The plants suggested here have the merit of looking fairly good through the year, but some are evergreen and cheerful in winter, while others flower at specific seasons. It would seem only sensible to consider how many of the shrubs should be evergreens, and where in the border they should be placed. If, for example, the approaching headlights of cars shine into a downstairs bedroom, a little thought can correct that.

The outer row might include such virtuous subjects as *Viburnum plicatum,* 'Maries' variety, which makes a nice rounded shrub perhaps eight feet in all directions, with tabular branches strung with single flowers of dazzling white about the time the dogwoods bloom. Unfortunately, its foliage is not gorgeous, though perfectly all right in its way, and sometimes it colors salmon to red in the fall. The shrub sets great crops of blue berries on red stalks, but these never last, since the mockingbirds eat every last one in June. It is bare and not especially attractive in winter, but when all things are added up, it is one of the most desirable of garden shrubs.

A rather similar viburnum only with much better foliage is the Japanese snowball bush, with (not surprisingly) white flowers like tennis balls all over it in spring when the irises bloom. It is similar to, only handsomer than, the plain snowball bush (*Viburnum opulus* 'Roseum'), which kids have torn off and thrown at each other for some centuries.

Viburnum setigerum makes a ten-foot shrub, sometimes compact but sometimes shooting about like a fountain, especially when young, that blooms inconspicuously in the spring but enters a period of glory in August and September, when weighed down with scarlet berries.

There are other viburnums that might be explored, all of them fine in a shrub border, though some get rather too large to suit today's problem of the suburban screen. *V. tinus,* which is evergreen and which flowers off and on through the winter, is for some reason ignored, but is lovely with its rose-flushed clusters of white flowers even before the camellias bloom. It is not ironclad hardy, but should do nicely as far north as Zone 7.

For winter cheer, there surely might be a few hollies. A good one for today's purpose is 'Foster No. 2', which is sold as *Ilex × attenuata* 'Fosteri'. It is upright rather than globular, has beautiful smallish leaves and heavy crops of berries — one of the best garden hollies.

A shrub of dull foliage but with the merit of incredibly bountiful crops of pinkish red fruit in the fall is *Euonymus* 'Red Cascade'. Mine does not fruit; I suspect it needs a pollinator such as the plain

European spindle tree, *E. europaea,* of which 'Red Cascade' is merely a garden variation chosen for its spectacular fruiting habit.

Another fine euonymus for this outer border is *E. alata* (not the form called 'Compacta', but the plain *alata*), which makes a plant nine feet high and maybe twelve feet across. It has most re-markable corky ridges on its branches, attractive all winter, and (the crowning glory) pinkish scarlet fall foliage. Where there is space for it, nothing is more beautiful in late October, and few things rival it.

If a conifer is thought desirable in the border, nothing is better than a spreading yew, of which there are many garden forms. *Taxus × intermedia* is the name, and you simply ask for one that will grow as wide as it does high. It is a beautiful rich black-green in winter, and it is nice to have one for cutting.

One of the few shrubs to cast fragrance on the air in October and early November is that form of the evergreen elaeagnus called *Elaeagnus pungens* 'Fruitlandii'. It wishes to sprawl by sending out long willowy shoots that arch about. Its flowers are papery, small, off-white and barely visible, and the scent is like sweet olive. Birds greatly like to nest in it, and mockingbirds like the small, hard, olivelike fruit in the spring. It is just as well, by the way, if you want a particular plant, to be sure you get it and not something vaguely like it. 'Fruitlandii', for example, is not the same as *Elaeagnus pungens,* and 'Red Cascade' is not the same as another euonymus.

A good broadleaf evergreen that may reach eight or nine feet, more or less round, is a hardy sweet olive called *Osmanthus* 'Gulf-tide', which looks like a neat, densely foliaged holly but has scented flowers in October and November when it feels like it. For some gardeners it flowers madly every year; with me, it rarely flowers, but is handsome enough in its glossy leaves.

A rather shapeless shrub that might be included is butterfly bush, or *Buddleia,* in one of its good garden forms, such as 'Ile de France', which has wands of violet flowers in the summer. It is much loved by butterflies and, alas, bumblebees, though I should say that while terrified of bumblebees, I have never been stung by one, even though everything I seem to grow is a great favorite of theirs. My place draws bumblebees from six counties. There are other kinds of buddleias, some with neon black-purple flowers, or off-white or rose-violet. They are cut almost to the ground every spring when the daffodils bloom, so you want to stick in the buddleias among shrubs that have more monumental character, such as viburnums, euonymus, hollies, and so on.

Nothing equals the hybrid Asian witch hazels (*Hamamelis* × *intermedia*) for delight in late January–February–early March, depending on the weather. There are curly little flowers made of narrow strap-shaped petals. Usually, as in the variety called 'Jelena', they are orange-bronze in effect and surprisingly showy.

The only crab apple I would use here is Sargent's (*Malus sargentii*), with blush-touched scented white flowers in spring and small reddish crab apples in the fall, and it tends to perform only in alternate years. It grows more slowly than most crabs and is handsomer.

I cannot sign off without mentioning both the crape myrtle (*Lagerstroemia indica*) and *Hydrangea paniculata* 'Grandiflora'. The first makes a shrub twelve or fourteen feet high with the most beautiful woody stems imaginable, neat foliage that colors well in the fall, and, of course, spectacular sheaves of flowers (white, several shades of pink, rose, watermelon, and red, depending on the variety you choose), starting in mid-July. It can be damaged in zero-degree winters, but is grossly neglected in gardens here, and it should be everywhere. There are new sorts nowadays that do not strike me, and I mean no disrespect, as triumphs. The hydrangea is the one with white flower clusters like a moderate hornet's nest in August. A well-developed plant is impressive, however common the species may be.

If you like them, you might include a forsythia for its early-spring blast of yellow and also the common lilac for its irresistible smell in April.

Lesser shrubs, planted five feet inside the line of the outer row of larger shrubs, might include the following.

Abelia × *grandiflora* has neat polished dark-green thin leaves and a dense twiggy habit of growth, with small pink-flushed white flowers for a good many weeks in late summer and fall. These are much visited by butterflies and, needless to say in this favorable climate, bees, wasps, hornets, and the Lord only knows what else. It is not a very showy shrub, but it looks neat and trim in the five weeks before and after Labor Day, which is a merit in anything.

Jasminum nudiflorum, the winter jasmine, is scentless but produces bright yellow tiny trumpets on bare rich-green stems from Christmas on. In the open it flowers in early spring, but where sheltered it blooms off and on in winter, and moreover it is useful for its cut branches brought indoors to flower in January. It sprawls, but when there are things to lean on, it hoists itself up a few feet.

Kerria japonica is sprinkled all over with golden nickels just before the azaleas bloom, with a smattering through the summer and fall. Its foliage is undistinguished, but its open habit of growth is pleasant, arching down at the ends of branches, and after it loses its leaves in the fall, the bright green stems are good-looking. I prefer the single form, with one row of petals, but there is a double sort with blooms like small shaggy carnations.

Taxus, or yew, in its dwarf forms will provide a mound of deep green in winter. The one called 'Repandens' makes a weeping hummock. All yews are intolerant of waterlogged soil (as indeed almost all plants are) and should never be planted in a hollow where water stands after rains.

Mahonia aquifolium, whose broad evergreen leaves turn bronze in winter, grows to knee height and sometimes spreads out to form a naturalized grouping of stems running back into the taller shrubs. It used to be despised, because everyone went mad for the taller mahonias like *M. bealei,* but now its merits are again recognized.

Leucothoe axillaris, one of the smallish andromedas or hobble-bushes or dog-hobbles (we were most pleased when one of our dogs stumbled over quite a little plant of this), has stems that arch to the ground with pointed leaves that turn bronze in winter. There are small, pleasant white clusters of flowers that do not look like a great deal in spring. The shrub combines nicely with most larger things.

Viburnum × *juddii,* which often remains at four feet in height, though it may grow into a seven-foot globe (in other words, it could go into either row), is, like all viburnums, a good-looking plant, especially in daffodil season, when it produces pink tennis-ball clusters of small waxy flowers that are intensely scented.

Nandina domestica, the so-called celestial bamboo (though it is a member of the barberry family), is one of the handsomest of all broadleaf evergreens, its fernlike foliage turning bronze in winter and serving as a gorgeous foil to its melon-size clusters of scarlet berries. For all its exceptional beauty, however, it does not blend or combine well with other things, since it is so distinct in itself. You simply shift it about (before planting it, of course) until it seems happily sited to you.

Azaleas in endless variety are possible for the inner small-shrub border, depending on whether you like them. A white one that takes care of itself in mixed company (though this could be said of most azaleas) is 'Treasure', a Glenn Dale variety that, through some miracle or other, is widely grown by nurserymen. Its foliage is half-evergreen and not glossy, but it makes a handsome bush, and its flowers, speckled in the throat with fawn color, are to my mind exceptionally beautiful. I much prefer it to 'Glacier', another good one, which would be chosen by those who love its glossy leaves.

A good scarlet, 'Stewartstonian', usually comes with a mis-spelled label, having a few too many *s*'s and *t*'s for the illiterate to cope with. It has the uncommon merit of extreme flower-bud har-diness, so that it blooms perfectly even after those occasional out-rageous winters that damage other azaleas. It also has quite rich bronze-red leaves in winter.

Barberries, both the deciduous and the evergreen kinds, are wonderful in their beauty. Most of them fruit heavily, and almost all are, alas, severely thorny. Of course you don't have to run out and pat them every day, but they are annoying in a minor way when it is necessary to get among the shrubs to pull up poison ivy, seed-ling maples, dogwoods, oaks, and so on. For while a shrub border is quite trouble-free, it will be much visited by birds, and an amaz-ing number of trees will try to grow in it without any invitation. Discreet whacking down twice a year will keep them out.

❖ *Timing Is the Key*

When you first start to garden, you usually have no idea what the real delights are going to be. You generally suppose the joy will come from raising the first dahlia bigger than a washtub or the production of a rose seven inches across. These are heady highs, of course. But they overlook the element of time.

Time, you might almost say, is what gardening is about. It's one thing — and a fine one — to see the leaves fall in November and the first crocus in January and the snowdrops on February 4 and the azaleas on April 15 and so on and on, the first year you see all this. It's another and more resonant thing the thirtieth time you see it. A certain daffodil opens on March 4 and you are dumbfounded. Always before it opened on March 15 or 16, not varying year after year. So why is it blooming so much earlier this year? The weather and temperatures give no clue. This makes the flower much more engaging than it would be had you not watched it opening on March 15 for the past twenty years.

The roses come and go. At first you think, when June comes and the bush is out of bloom, that an eternity will pass before next May, when it blooms again. But after a few years you conclude that 'Agnes', say, is worth growing even if it only blooms once a year. It is very like discovering that youth does not last or come round on schedule every year. At first it is a shock. But if you are reasonably lucky, as I was, you like getting older. You don't have to live through all that youthful bother again, and the future may well be novel and more agreeable than the past.

In the garden, at least, you soon grow almost sick of flowers that bloom endlessly. I love the petunias, the wild-looking off-white and pale lavender ones that keep popping up from self-sown seed. They always look cheerful in the heat, they smell just fine, and they never look worn out and bedraggled. Besides, their color is soft and they don't scream at you. But floribunda roses can become boring after a while; so can marigolds. They are nice enough; it's just that after a few months you wish they would look different.

It is otherwise when the snowdrop blooms. Wow. Look at that. Right through the snow. Nobody ever gets bored with snowdrops or crocuses. Or the strange flower of the jack-in-the-pulpit or the marbled Italian arum. It only lasts a few days, then is gone, and is not showy even during the four days it's in bloom. But what a pleasure to see it, when its brief day comes.

Azaleas are an example of a flower that finishes blooming just about the time I get sick of looking at it. For some people, azaleas bloom too long, but for me they hit it just about right. I have never liked those late azaleas of May and June; by then I have had a bellyful. But when April comes round again the azaleas are greeted like long-lost friends. So there is something to be said for not being gorgeous for so long that everybody loses interest.

The coming and going of flowers, the rise and fall of plants, are of utmost importance in the pleasure of gardening, far more than the young gardener might think. That gardener has not lived until he has experienced the death of a magnolia or a yew or a camellia that he had thought would be there forever. What a shock. But after it happens a few times the gardener no longer goes to pieces. It's the way life is, and the gardener learns that life really does go on.

Sometimes you will plant a pecan nut just for the hell of it, and then marvel when a violent storm snaps the crown off it fifty years later and (if the innings hold) a new leader develops and the tree looks none the worse for wear at sixty years. A plant means one thing to you if you buy a house and find a hundred-year-old oak, a wonderful bit of luck. But it means something else if you have an oak from an acorn you planted ages ago. The raging storms, the early freezes, the year the leaves turned brighter red than usual — all that is part of the oak you have raised yourself, or the oak you have watched over many years.

So time does make a difference in any garden. At first you wonder if anything will ever get large enough to count in the general picture. Then you wonder if there is any way to keep it from growing further. For years the little *Cunninghamia* was a favorite shrub, say, then all of a sudden it becomes a small tree, then after a while you start thinking of it as a gnarled and marvelous fixture of the garden, and you can hardly think back to the time before you had it.

The great trick, I am now sure, is to flow with the tide.

MARCH

SNOWDROPS ARE BLOOMING, crocuses are up and so are some of the daffodils, and here and there the grass is quite green. Spring is here.

Of course, it depends what you mean by "spring."

For most gardeners, spring is when things at last start to grow again and snowdrops bloom and buds swell. The witch hazels are out; the new leaves of clematis are half an inch long. For others, spring means no shirt and coffee in the summerhouse. They will never acknowledge spring until April 14. But for us, the die-hard gardeners, spring is already here, even though we may have snow, an ice storm or two, and ground frost for another six weeks.

❖ *Year-Long Lessons*

The eminent Edwardian gardener Gertrude Jekyll wrote in 1900 that it takes "half a lifetime" to decide what's best worth doing in a garden and another half to try to do it. She was a quick study, of course. Most gardeners take a full lifetime to discover what's best worth doing and then run out of time. To sum up enormous wisdom for you in a sentence, the formula is simple (that's the trouble,

it's too simple): grow the most beautiful flowers you have ever seen
or heard of, going through the year.

That is the formula for the best gardens. There are a few corol-
laries, just as in law school you study conflict of laws. Go by the
above formula, however, and temper it as follows.

If some season does not greatly interest you, forget that season
and concentrate your effort on the seasons you like best.

If hard experience shows you that for some reason you cannot
grow good lilies, peonies, lilacs, or irises, then concentrate on flowers that do well for you, even if the ones you give up happen to be
on your list of "most beautiful in its season."

Pay reasonable attention to plants for background that enhance
all others. You may not be madly fond of yew, photinia, box, or
holly, but make room for them anyway, even if it means cutting
down on the roses, azaleas, and chrysanthemums that (let us say)
you like much better.

Resign yourself to usable paths or walkways in the garden. Five
feet is quite narrow, when you consider that plants have a way of
flopping over the edges and when you consider that you will be
trundling along behind a wheelbarrow or setting up sawhorses to
trim fence posts, saw plywood, and other pleasant chores.

Having wasted your substance, as you perhaps feel, on a wide
walk and various evergreens, what remains of the garden? First,
consider a fish pool in full sun but as near the house as possible.
For city gardeners, a concrete pool ten by twelve feet is about as
large as the home handyman can construct by himself. You are that
handyman, and of course can press your wife, good friend, or child
into helping. Over the years you will say it was the single best gardening decision you ever made, even though the sunny site you give
it means that much less space for other flowers. The magic of dark
clear water, goldfish, and water lilies, to say nothing of dragonflies,
justifies almost any sacrifice in other gardening directions. Or, if
you can't build your own pool, you can buy a horse trough of galvanized steel. You can get a circular one seven feet in diameter, set
it in flat on the ground, and cover the sides with what you like if the
metal offends you. Boston ivy will cover the outside in one season,

adhering right to the steel, or you can use fence wire and grow ivy, akebia, kadsura, or anything else that strikes you as suitable.

We have now reduced the garden space further, and still we're not done. Make a place to sit that's big enough for a table and some chairs. Pave that place. There are whole books on paving, so read a few.

Now, with what is left you may want the center open and given to well-shorn grass. Some people adore grass. I do not. Some people like to cut it, usually with those machines that ought to be outlawed along with chain saws and other noisemakers. But if you must have a lawn, then have one and be done with it.

Otherwise, the center of the garden, usually the sunniest part, may be devoted to the best flowers, starting in late winter with crocuses, squills, wild anemones, aconites, snowdrops, millas, and moving right along to daffodils, commencing with the very early dwarf and intermediate-size kinds, and with them various quite early tulips and Roman hyacinths, especially the blue (the white Romans are not hardy). Then come such huge early tulips as the fosterianas, with the main-season daffodils in as wide an assortment as space allows. You will discover gradually which daffodils you like best, and you will concentrate on them.

Then come peonies — you will want very early kinds such as 'Red Charm', which are finished by the time other peonies start blooming. In Washington and similar climates you will give special attention to the kinds called early (though not so early as superearly), such as 'Monsieur Jules Elie' and 'Festiva Maxima', to name two old varieties of utter reliability. You can also have some midseason sorts, but the late peonies are risky in our heat. You may want a few tree peonies, which are not trees but woody creatures four feet high. They do not die to the ground in winter but hold their woody branches, bursting into leaf and flower before the regular Chinese peonies.

Then you have tall bearded irises. They bloom for a month if you grow a number of varieties, and each clump lasts in bloom about two weeks. Not long. But long enough. When I grew some hundreds of varieties, I never regretted the end of iris season.

Among the most beautiful flowers of the season are Siberian irises. Try a few spuria irises also. They grow splendidly for some gardeners, not so well for others, so try them gingerly to see how they do. Later, Japanese irises are among the few garden flowers that may properly be called gorgeous. Try a few, and remember to keep lime away from them.

From April 15 onward for a month you have azaleas. You can have them both earlier and later, but I mention their great month, in which the Kurumes and Glenn Dales bloom. With them you can be as riotous, gaudy, and vulgar as you please, or as delicate.

Then come roses, starting with such early shrubs as *Rosa* × *cantabrigiensis,* with light yellow quarters massed all along its pendent stems. In some gardens the main season of hybrid tea and floribunda roses coincides with the peak of the iris season in mid-May, give or take a week or two. In others, the roses follow the irises, along with Oriental poppies. They have a short flowering season; their main color, fire-engine red, dominates everything else, and they make a gap when they die down soon after flowering. But a clump or two is hard to resist. It's up to you whether you grow some crown imperials and other fritillaries.

We're only halfway through spring and have not considered such shrubs as lilacs. Space is running out, and you probably will need more than half of all available space for the flowers of summer and fall, and perhaps some tomatoes. You can always encroach on the lawn and probably will, which is why I suggest doing away with it to begin with.

❖ Days of Magic

There are magical days in March in which poke, dock, coarse field grasses, and brambles come up easily, with a little help from a spading fork in the case of deeply rooted specimens. These same weeds are virtually immovable if left until settled warm weather.

If you use cow or horse manure you will get a good assortment of bad grasses, the sort that sprout inside iris, peony, or daylily clumps, for example, and that will overwhelm and kill them. Poke and brambles, though, are the gift of birds, which is why you so often see these noxious weeds springing up along fences or beneath climbing roses.

There is usually at least one benighted fellow in every neighborhood who thinks the bindweed is pretty, like a small white morning glory. This terrible scourge (and in this climate I cannot think of anything else so grievous except ground elder) is spread far and wide by seeds that seem heavy enough but that must be borne by the wind anyway. It does have the grace to grow from dazzling white fleshy roots (I grew up calling this weed devil's guts, the name for it in my country), so at least the diligent gardener can spot it when digging about. A great many fragments of root will be left in the ground, and these must be dug out or (for sometimes digging is not possible, next to a favorite rose) pulled up faithfully enough for the weed to be killed at last through exhaustion. Commonly the gardener is exhausted before the bindweed.

Unfortunately, in our highly favorable climate (a virtually ideal climate for gardeners) we get awful rains in March, April, May, and June, and the rains of early spring are the worst, because on the intervening blue and sunny days the gardener is tempted to do other things than spend his time on his knees grubbing weeds. But ideally, the garden should be perfectly weed-free by early April, in order for the gardener to devote all energy to the bindweed, which does not sprout until the weather warms.

❖ The Thin Line Between Nature and Human Nature

Gardeners are much exercised about goo or sticky stuff on flower and leaf buds, and usually it's April before the capital expresses its despair at peony buds that are covered with busy ants, attracted by sweet exudate. It was surprising, however, to have several winter inquiries about this. One gardener, I gather, has a lot of money bet on the question of whether the peony flower buds need the ants to swell and open properly.

They do not need ants. But the ants do no harm that I have ever seen. You might think that anybody with the brains to plant peonies right side up to begin with would have the wits to figure out that if the opening flowers were dipped in a bucket of water the ants would float off, but an urgent question every spring is how you get the ants off before they start falling off and crawling about the dining table or elsewhere in the house. You either knock them off with your hand or wash them off, one way or another. If you use the bucket method, dump the water on the ground. There is no point going through life killing ants that are doing no harm at all.

Many other plants have resin or sweet, sticky films over the swelling buds. People do not ask about horse chestnuts, which are beautifully varnished in the bud. Sometimes (and though I have never seen it myself, I cite Charles Darwin as authority for the fact) flies are stuck on the chestnut buds and perish there. As far as anybody knows, the tree gets no benefit from the death of the flies.

Such instances of varnish, which exist presumably to protect the growing bud to some extent, have nothing to do with the sticky film or glue globules found on sundews or the sticky surface of Venus's-flytrap leaves. The poor insect is simply glued to the glandular secretions of the sundew, and the plant digests the victim. On the Venus's-flytrap, the hinged leaf (very like an oyster shell) snaps shut to trap the insect when it irritates the spines that stick out from the leaf surface. Since the insect is trapped by the sudden mechanical shutting of the leaf halves, you may well wonder why the leaf surface is sticky — no insects are trapped by that stickiness, after all. It is presumed that the point of the sticky surface is to stick to the feet. When the insect exerts energy to free its feet, it blunders against one of the spines that trigger the closing of the trap. Without getting its feet stuck first, many an insect would maneuver without ever touching the spines.

Nature is endlessly ingenious and, of course, unspeakably vicious and barbaric. Any complaints should be sent not to me but to the designer of the universe. I never minded the fact that the whole system rests essentially on death, and who eats whom, but surely a kinder, gentler means of death could have been devised for bugs, bunnies, and so forth.

The only good thing about the system is that from time to time nature is beautiful beyond dreaming, and nothing can be done about it. This may be the place to say, however, that I do not hesitate to interfere with nature on many occasions. I chase off cats trying to catch infant squirrels, and I frequently dip drowning bugs out of the fish pool. The mere fact that it is natural for cats to catch squirrels makes no difference to me; it is also natural for me to chuck rocks at the damned cats. Nature does not hesitate to interfere with me, so I do not hesitate to tamper with it.

In the long run, of course, nature works its cruel ways with all living creatures, and we accept it for the excellent reason that we cannot change it. We yield, in other words, what we cannot keep, and if we have any sense at all, we accept the system as it is, interfering only when we see that we can get away with it (as in fishing bees from pools).

Fortunately, we are able to reassure ourselves that plants, at least, do not suffer as a squirrel does in a cat's jaws. Plants have no feeling. Still, there is much we do not know about plants. It came as rather a surprise to find electrical reactions in the Venus's-flytrap and to be faced with the uncomfortable fact that the trap works very much as human muscles do. The world was more comfortable when we could believe that only humans had any feelings, let alone rights, and most comfortable of all when we could believe that only people of our own race and subgroup need be thought of. It was widely believed in parts of America until a few years ago that Mediterranean and Balkan (and perhaps Irish) people were built differently and did not suffer from inhuman factory conditions, and it was gospel in the South, when I was a kid, that blacks could work endlessly under a blazing sun without feeling it in the least.

As for nonhuman animals, like horses and dogs, it was long believed that they felt no pain. Few sounds are more unnerving than that of a rabbit grabbed by a dog, but I grew up understanding that the rabbit felt no pain, it was just a reflex. So I hope future researchers let well enough alone and do not start discovering that plants suffer too.

❖ Tracing the Roots

You'd think a plant that grows only in some small part of the world would be forever limited to that region and could never adapt to quite a different climate. When the first metasequoia trees were found in the 1940s in western China, they were limited to a small valley, though later some outlying specimens were discovered. The tree is ancient and had been known only in fossil rocks. Once, however, this tree was widespread in temperate climates.

You might guess, therefore, that the world's climates had changed and that now this tree could survive only in the valley, which (you would guess) had a microclimate unique in Asia or perhaps the world. On the contrary, the tree grows nicely in Mississippi, Massachusetts, Missouri, throughout England, France, and elsewhere. It is easily propagated by seed, dormant cuttings, and half-ripe cuttings.

Since it is marvelously adaptable, how did it wind up in such an isolated and limited spot? You can think of reasons, perhaps, but the point is that a tree that seems at first to have the most specialized geographical requirements may flourish almost anywhere, once it's given the chance.

Other plants, rudely called weeds, are well known to us — plantains, dandelions, chicory, and so on, all introduced from the Old World. But you might think that weeds that will grow anywhere would in fact be found everywhere. They were not in America until recent centuries.

We come now to the tumbling tumbleweed. Thanks to C. F. Eckhardt, writing in the *National Tombstone Epitaph,* it is now clear to me that the tumbleweed (*Amaranthus albus*) comes from the steppe country of western Asia and only arrived in our West in the 1880s, brought unintentionally (with seeds of a particular wheat) by Mennonites emigrating from Russia. It is incorrect, then, to show tumbleweeds in movies with settings earlier than that. Tumbleweeds certainly were nowhere about at, say, the struggle for Texas independence, which occurred a half-century before they arrived.

Once I saw a television mystery based on an Agatha Christie story that showed Miss Marple getting off a tour bus at Blenheim Palace. She followed the sign marked "Gardens" to the side and suddenly was in the gardens of Hidcote Manor. This is very like showing a character deciding to visit Washington Monument, then entering Grant's Tomb.

Anyway, once she was in the garden, which is packed with rarities, she said to another visitor, "*Hemerocallis fulva.* I can never get mine to look like that." This is, of course, similar to visiting the National Gallery, sailing past the Duccio, and observing, "Door handle. I can never get mine to look like that." It was not the plain *Hemerocallis fulva* she was looking at in the first place, but the double and rather congested form known as 'Kwanso'. It is a feature of the "red borders" of Hidcote, though it is not red but orange. And if there is one plant in the temperate world besides the dandelion that it is impossible for a gardener to fail with (except in dank shade), it is that hemerocallis. It can be grown by any idiot (or any connoisseur, for that matter, for there is nothing wrong with it as a garden plant), and it looks the same wherever you see it.

What she meant to say, probably, and would have said if Agatha Christie had got things straight, was "Oh, the blue poppies. *Meconopsis grandis.* I can never get mine to look like that." For this blue poppy is not so easy to grow, and Miss Marple almost certainly would not be able to grow it, considering that she is forever snooping about and running off to solve murders instead of remaining steadily at home worrying about the meconopsis. Both are Chinese plants and both grow now in gardens of other continents, but one is virtually a weed while the other is kept going at great effort. I was distressed (heh-heh) to notice during my last visit that the meconopses at Hidcote are petering out, despite all the care given them.

❖ A Word about Worts

"Wort" is the old word for plant, and it survives in such forms as mugwort, sandwort, figwort, and so forth, and it is pronounced "wirt"; in fact, it was formerly spelled "wyrt." It has the same vowel sound as world, worthy, worship, worst, worry, worm, word, work, and there is a great plot in America to make wort rhyme with fort. No. WIRT. It is rude to correct someone's pronunciation in conversation, so I never do that, but it curls my teeth to hear it wrong, and on my more paranoid days I believe there is a conspiracy for every human who cannot speak English to dash up to me and say wort like fort. Truly, the sufferings of a garden writer are vast.

The hogwort (HAWG-wirt) is a splendid weed of precisely the sort I cannot resist, and through incredible good fortune I have been given two young plants. They have basal leaves; that is, each leaf is on a stem rising directly from the earth, which I suppose will soon be pronounced some odd way. The leaves are a foot or so across, somewhat wrinkled, like a rhubarb or gunnera. They are coarse. It is not the kind of leafage you would choose if you were planting around polished marble or wrought bronze, but I have little of either.

The flowering stem in summer reaches six or eight feet and has a great umbel of flowers like cow parsley, and there are said to be 10,000 little flowers in the cluster, which may be four feet in diameter. No, I do not know who counted them. In the garden the hogwort gives much the same effect as angelica, another wonderful creature, the stems of which can be candied and put on cakes, not that I ever knew anybody to do it. Angelica grows easily from seed, which I have more than once bought at herb shops.

Theoretically, when huge plants of angelica and hogwort flower, the plants die and are renewed by thousands of seedlings springing up everywhere. In practice, this may indeed happen. Or it may not.

Commonly the gardener relies on stray seedlings, but one year he wakes up to see there are no seedlings at all. I enjoy saying I had none at all after about the third year, and I enjoy saying this because it suggests that I weed so carefully that no little self-sown seedling has a chance. It is far otherwise. I think the trouble is I have so many weeds that no self-sown seedling has breathing space. In any case, the moral is to save seeds when they are ripe and to plant them the following spring. This way, you always have plenty coming on.

Borage, an excellent and beautiful herb with sky-blue flowers of great clarity, is another great seeder, so the gardener rarely thinks to save seeds, since he is sure (based on the experience of a year or two) that hundreds of young borage plants will turn up next spring. I no longer have borage either.

Mulleins are the same, when it comes to seeding. They are everywhere, and then after a few years you realize that there are none coming along. Mulleins, I have read, are good to lay over wounds from spear points, so one does not like to be without them. Borage is good to float in a claret cup, but if you do not drink claret cups, I am not sure what you do with it. The leaves taste somewhat like cucumbers. Borage flowers are sometimes put in salads. I tried it once and was uneasy with the result and did not try it again.

All biennials that grow from seed in one year but only flower the second year and then die are best kept going by saving the seed, not by counting on natural seeding in the garden. Of course, if you have a patch of gravel or chinks in masonry, you will find plenty of seedlings there, or in any other place you don't want them. But before pulling them out, consider whether they would not look fine growing where the wind sowed them. I often wish I had old masonry walls with chinks where the mortar used to be. Nothing in all gardening is more delightful than growing plants on walls in which little pockets of soil or grit afford home for the roots.

Valerian never grows so well elsewhere as on an old wall. And one interesting thing is that plants are often hardier growing in a wall than on the level earth. Snapdragons and wallflowers, among others, often reach vast size in walls and live for many years, whereas in an ordinary garden bed they die out after a couple of years.

I went to much trouble to get seeds (like chaff) of a little daisy from Mexico, *Erigeron karvinskianus*. It has whitish flowers the size of pennies all over it, and these turn pinkish, so a clump is festive in a moderate sort of way. It is an utter weed, and it has its nerve not being altogether hardy. But on a wall facing south, growing in pockets of rotted stone or earth, it often proves hardy and seeds all over the place. I have seen tall walls completely covered with this small weedy ornament.

I have a spot not quite so large as a playing card, where my stucco work failed (stucco to cover a galvanized steel horse trough), and I am hoping to establish the daisy there. I have worked in a handful of dirt where the stucco fell off, and I am nursing along tiny plants of erigeron, or what I hope is the erigeron. I think the tiny leaves are different from the other weeds I have, and I have most of them, some of which are probably rare except with me.

Suppose I succeed in establishing the erigeron in the face of the stucco, what then? Why, I shall have a patch of weedy tiny daisies covering several square inches, and they will not be much to see. But they will give me great pleasure. Gardeners are familiar with projects like this. They mull about in their heads for two or three years and finally get the undertaking off the ground, and once in a while they succeed, and the visitor — eyeing their triumph — privately wonders why they went to the trouble in the first place. But the gardener beams and basks, oblivious to the visitor, who thinks he is cracked.

❖ *Forgotten Seeds, Surprising Sprouts*

A quart jar of water containing infant water lilies overturned on the bed as I was pawing about with a fork to get them out for transplanting into jars with more space. Many gardening mishaps can be blamed on the dog, but not this. Naturally, I have no idea which water lilies the seeds came from, though I knew at the time I dumped them in the jar last fall.

One should always write on a label what the seed is, where it came from, and when it was planted. Otherwise, months or a year later something sprouts and God only knows. At the moment I have a good-size pot outdoors with seeds of tree peonies in it. They take two years to germinate. The pot is covered with rabbit wire, or hardware mesh as they call it up here, to foil chipmunks, voles, squirrels, or whoever likes to dig up seeds. I do not need to label that pot, as of course I remember all about the tree peony seeds. But when and if they sprout eventually, I'll be quite surprised, most likely.

Once I planted some seeds of hybrid auratum lilies and of course forgot all about them. That was a delightful experience, as the first I knew about those seeds was seeing a great clump of lilies in bloom a few years later. They were in a narrow, utterly shaded strip by an air conditioner, and I almost never go near it. Such an experience gives the gardener the unhappy feeling that seeds would do better if the gardener did nothing — which is not true. Anyway, the point is to label seeds in pots or in the open ground when they are planted.

A kind person wrote a most touching letter, enclosing seeds of a small yellow-flowered member of the poppy family. That person can no longer garden but would like these flowers to keep on, so I shall certainly plant them. When they bloom I'll probably proclaim a miracle, having forgotten their provenance. But in this case, probably not.

Over the years I have found that a mild day in December is the best time to clean out the lily pool, but late March or April does well also. Once in my cleaning I came across the nymph of a dragonfly and of course put it back after refilling the pool. But all such beasts like gunk on the bottom, and I wondered if I had done it in. As a result, I have not done such thorough cleaning since. It works well to remove the loose tree leaves and the withered (and soon rotting, if not removed) leaves of water lilies, sweet flag, and so forth as winter begins. Then a further cleaning in warm weather keeps stuff on the bottom under control without, I hope, unduly alarming the fauna.

Anybody who has a lily pool with fish will find a good net a sound investment. I do not have one, as I have an excellent pole with a wire rim (from an old net) at the end. My wife sews cheesecloth onto it from time to time. Cheesecloth makes an absurd net, offering too much resistance to the water.

This year I thought it well to move a few of the white goldfish into a smaller horse trough. I would remove them after they laid eggs, to see if I would get a fine population of white fish. White, in these fish, seems to act as a simple recessive gene, so from all white fish the first generation should be all white.

Well, the great breeder among them is about seven inches long, a female, and I have been at it off and on for two weeks now, trying to catch her from the big pool. She lumbers about, heavy with eggs, and reminds me of a basset bitch about to whelp. If, however, she so much as catches sight of the net coming in the water, she jets forward like a rocket. Once I have put the net away she resumes her leisurely ways. She is perhaps six years old — I got her as a small creature from a place that sells fish to feed other animals. Her surprising alertness probably accounts for her survival. We have gulls in the neighborhood as well as other fish eaters; fortunately, the sea gulls have not discovered the pool, but of course the possums and coons have. They take a toll, but the fish population has stabilized at roughly two hundred, most of them fingerlings.

❖ *The Simple Secret*

Simplicity, as I suppose you are sick to death of hearing, is the secret of everything in gardens; and my heart is with every city gardener who says well, yes, but one more redwood, surely? Simplicity is all very well when you have fourteen acres or even a half-acre, even a quarter. It is torture when you have forty by twenty-five feet, or even forty by a hundred and twenty feet.

A garden is not merely a beautiful aesthetic exercise. A garden is also the field of battle for the enthusiastic gardener. Certain lapses from correctness may be expected, and certainly must be forgiven, if the small city plot (which could be rather beautiful) is occupied by a fanatical gardener. If he is there, the garden may be interesting — it may even be amazing — but it is not likely to be beautiful.

This may be the place to say that there are higher beauties than mere beauty. The gardener's passion, clearly, is of a higher priority than the simple manufacture of a beautiful garden, which even any architect can make.

The small garden of Washington would almost always be astonishing in its beauty except for the small gardener of Washington, for of no group other than gardeners is it so true that we have met the enemy and he is us. The small patch back of a row house has two surprising effects on gardeners: it is so small that there is no point doing anything at all with it, and (southerners and westerners are especially likely to feel this) anything in the world can be done with it, only on a small scale.

The truth is, the smaller the garden, the more important to plan the space for the gardener's delight. And the truth is that a small plot makes many — most — of the great garden effects impossible, so they should be forgotten to begin with.

❖ *Magnificent Obsessions*

Do not be alarmed if all of a sudden you can't think of anything but crocuses. Or it may be daffodils. This happens to gardeners. The brain is fully infused with some plant or other, and for several days — sometimes as long as six weeks — the mind goes in only one gardening channel. There is no point phoning some gardening friend to talk about daffodils if he happens to be in a dahlia mode. It will pass, and he'll phone to talk about daffodils, but by that time you will be in your peony period.

I shall name the primary obsessions of the gardener, which come in no predictable order. One year I did not even go through peonies, but went straight from irises to water lilies.

Snowdrop (including crocus, scilla, trout lily, and small spring bulbs in general), azalea, iris, peony, rose, daylily, lily, water lily, dahlia, chrysanthemum, and viburnum: these are the main clouds that descend on the gardener. I do not suffer from the chrysanthemum attack, but most gardeners do. Of course, there are dozens or hundreds of other plants the gardener thinks of, but I have mentioned the ones most dangerous for the repose of garden design, since when these truly great seizures come, the garden is promptly redesigned on paper and in the head.

In a daffodil phase, for example, all the chrysanthemums and dahlias come out and the irises are reduced by half. Two large trees are sawed down (in the gardener's mind), and with all this new space suddenly available, 217 new daffodils are ordered and planted.

But then, once the daffodils are through blooming in the real world of April, the gardener is not obsessed with them. The trees are restored; the irises not only come back but extend their realm through the bean and tomato patch. And suddenly the peony fit occurs, in which the irises are reduced by a third, six rosebushes come out, the trees are sawed down again, and all the dahlias go.

Rose fever sets in. The irises are reduced by half, two thirds of the peonies are dug up, all chrysanthemums are abolished, and all dahlias except five are abolished. This permits twenty-two new roses.

Water lilies are excessively perilous. When they enter the head, two rose beds are eliminated, the irises (recently restored) are reduced to seventy-five good clumps, daffodils are shifted to bare-survival status under climbing roses, and for a good two weeks the plan is to construct a twenty-three-by-thirty-one-foot pool. Think of all the new fish. No reason the golden orfe should not be tried again (they do not like small pools and die in the summer heat), and maybe some of the less common kinds of lotus, including our beautiful native yellow variety, which is too vigorous, really, for small pools.

As these enthusiasms come and go, the gardener must remember that millions of people suffer them. The pain of losing a cherished plant in a bad winter is as nothing compared to the pain of realizing that there are at least twenty-three roses that must somehow be added to the garden if life is to be more than one long agony.

And even that is nothing to the pain of seeing the New Garden (the redesign you have done carefully, to accommodate the 178 new irises) fall apart in the harsh daylight of reality. That surge of joy when you saw you really could have all those irises ebbs out again like life's blood as you finally acknowledge that you can have them only if you cut down all the roses. Which you have done, naturally, in your new plan, and been so happy for a few days, until the iris phase passed and the rose phase set in. Then you are horrified to see, in the new plan, so much space given to irises, which bloom only a few weeks.

The important thing, apart from realizing that you are not going to die, is to change the garden slowly. When the rose fit is on, do not act immediately. Do not go out that very day and pitch out the hollies. Remember, the rose fit will pass, and you will soon want those hollies back.

It is the same with all the plants you have mentally sacrificed on behalf of whatever flower has seized your full attention for the moment. Be especially wary of the water lily. If, in your enthusiasm, you build your huge pool, it will be hard to undo it. You will be in trouble when the next iris fit descends, because you cannot then reduce the size of the pool by half.

It is best to endure at least three or four years of succeeding enthusiasms, yielding to each in turn and recovering in time. After several years, you may indeed pitch out the chrysanthemums (or peonies or roses or whatnot) and allow your yearning for sweet peas to flower, but it will not be a precipitous whim, it will be a real decision you can live with.

It is all very like Aeschylus and the grim tragedies of the House of Atreus. After so much suffering, a sort of peace, or an endurable substitute for it, comes to you. You no longer expect all the roses in rose season, all the irises in iris season. You no longer say, "If I pitched out all the rest, I could have seventy-eight camellias." No, child, you know you are going to keep the roses and tomatoes and daylilies. You become more adept at planting things on top of each other and cherishing survivors.

Peace comes to the gardener when at last he has all his flowers in reasonable and sane balance — the day after the undertaker comes.

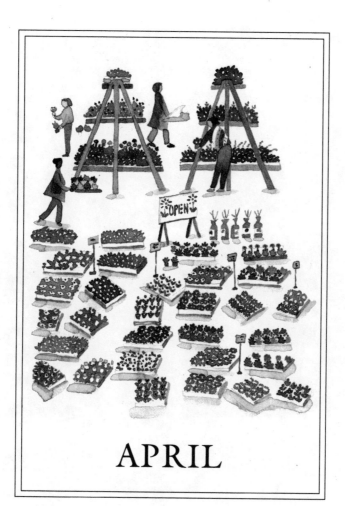

APRIL

T. S. ELIOT SAID, "April is the cruelest month," and I would add March, May, and much of June. What we loosely call spring, meaning the season in which plants grow vigorously and come to flower in a time of nice skies and warm airs, is partly imaginary. In spring the gardener has the sharpest disappointments of the year, as a rule, especially in this capital (so favored as a gardening region, offering the best of both North and South). We have our most terrible storms in spring, as far as the garden is concerned, and although we are wonderfully free of late freezes (compared with England, say), we still have what I call cold weather some-times into the month of June.

As our daffodils begin to bloom in March, our hearts leap up, briefly, but they don't stay leapt up, for all too soon the magical day that so excited us — blue sky, crocuses, snowdrops, scillas, early daffodils, temperature of sixty-five degrees — is followed by a hail-storm or a drop to twenty-two degrees and a flurry of snow or ice, and gray skies that look more somber than any sky of the winter. If we have temperature drops to thirty-two or below — we need to remember that early spring is invariably variable — we always have warmer-than-usual days and colder-than-usual. Nothing would be more surprising than a spring of settled weather.

There is not much to be done about it. The flowers that bloom in variable weather have evolved over the eons to survive in variable weather. A bloom here and there may be doomed, but in general there is nothing to worry about when a freeze "threatens" the crocus or daffodil or emerging tulip. They are born to this.

People who cannot tolerate the anxiety of possible damage to, say, early magnolia flowers should simply not grow them. Normal gardeners, however, soon learn to take the weather in stride. They know that if you refuse to plant anything that may be damaged by weather, you will not have anything at all.

If tender folk go to pieces for fear a plant may be hurt (even before it is hurt, and it usually isn't), then how do they cope with the death of a dog or a person? We are not born to a bonbon-type life, you know.

❖ Flowering Fruit Trees

Flowering cherries bloom about April 4 in Washington, and few trees are so covered with bloom, which is the more striking since leaves have not begun to appear and since the branches and trunk are virtually black. The contrast between the massive structure or architecture of the tree and its ethereal cloud of white or pink blossoms is rivaled only by the pear tree, but only the cherry displays blossoms that hug the outlines of the branches. It is one of the first plants a gardener is likely to be seduced by, and often the gardener regrets it later.

The Tidal Basin is a flawless site for the main planting of the capital's cherries, since they are glorious in bloom and may be ignored the rest of the year. Which is another way of saying the cherry is not a handsome tree except in its four or five days of flowering each year.

At the Tidal Basin the terrible greedy roots of the trees do no harm, since there is nothing else growing down there anyway, but in the garden these roots make it impossible to grow anything else near them. Also, the trees become much larger than the gardener counts on — he thinks he'll be dead and gone before the cherry gets very large — and they cast dense shade. Commonly, the earth beneath old cherry trees is perfectly bare.

The trees never look better than they do with a lagoon or lake to reflect them, and since the trees are large, it helps the effect if any architectural detail is simple, bold, and noble. The Jefferson Memorial is a good thing to put up to enhance the cherry trees, but difficult of attainment in the usual town garden.

The most beautiful of all cherries to my mind is the rosy form of *Prunus subhirtella,* which comes in a weeping form as well. The Tokyo cherry, *P. yedoensis,* which is the main cherry of the Tidal Basin, is more nearly white than pink and may be regarded as equally flawless. You do not see Sargent's cherry so often. It has pink flowers and is upright, at least in youth, and the leaves color in the fall.

The Japanese have many garden varieties, some of them as double as carnations, with varying habits of growth — some have striking horizontal branches. Here you are on your own in choosing varieties. I do not like any of them very much, except in other people's gardens. It is one thing to see a great double white or pink for fifteen minutes, and something else to live with it the rest of your life.

The commonest garden (as distinct from wild) cherry is *Prunus serrulata* 'Kwanzan', with carmine-pink double flowers accompanied by bronze-colored leaves just breaking forth. Unlike some, I love the bronze and carmine together. This cherry, which I would never dream of planting myself because of its great size and possibly overopulent display, is marvelous as a single specimen with plenty of space to breathe in, especially if the setting is rather artificial, as it is in front of a house. It would not be my choice for planting in a woodland, where its lush beauty might seem somehow to violate the proprieties. Still, the gardener may think a little overopulence is just the thing, and if he does, then plenty of garden cherries should satisfy him. I warn merely that the trees cast heavy shade, the roots are greedy, and the flowering season is brief. If these are not serious objections in a particular garden, then there is no reason a passion for cherries should not be indulged boldly.

My own idea of floral perfection is the peach tree, but I do not like the foliage much. In colder countries than ours — England, for example, where it does not get awfully cold but never has any summer heat as we know it — the peach is admired for its long, narrow, curving, shiny leaves. The English think it looks tropical, and they have rather a passion for hinting, in their gardens, that their climate is warmer than it is.

Neck and neck with the peach, in terms of floral beauty, is the pear, which is white instead of pink, and which has clusters or puffs of bloom instead of a steady chain of flowers like the cherry, plum, and peach. The scent of the pear blossom, which reminds some of a dirty fish and chips shop, is to me attractive. It's not something you want to smell for hours (like hay or tea or sasanqua camellias) but very agreeable all the same, probably because I loved pears as a kid.

I often wonder if anybody grows really edible pears here. There is the little 'Seckel', which I know many gardeners manage well, and I hear that 'Bartlett' is feasible. What I want is a 'Doyenne du Comice', and in fact I grow one, but have no illusion that I will ever get fruit that is edible from it. It grows well in the far west. What a joy if someone would write and say that this pear does well in their garden here. I throw this bait out every couple of years, but nobody ever rises to it — probably because nobody succeeds with this pear.

In any case, squirrels probably enjoy pears, and the foliage is the handsomest of all the fruit trees, and the upright, somewhat sparse habit of an old pear tree is ornamental. It is worth growing simply as a flowering tree to accompany early daffodils. The flowers are often frozen, so fruit is not guaranteed, and pears often die of fire blight. But then we all die of something. Such sorts as 'Seckel', 'Tyson', 'Moonglow', 'Doyenne du Comice', 'Stark's Delicious', and 'Kieffer' are generally considered more resistant than others.

I take no pleasure in dampening the enthusiasm of "organic" gardeners, and indeed happily spend some time every summer cutting bugs out of the apples I grow (people sometimes comment rudely on the resultant pie, merely because the hunks of apple are oddly shaped); still, it is only fair to sane beginners to warn that if you expect fruit of the quality you find in a supermarket, you are not likely to get it without spraying every week or so throughout the growing season. It seems to me foolish, and possibly wicked, to imply that the home gardener can grow vastly better fruit than Safeway, say, if he only refrains from chemical fertilizers and sprays. What you get is not superior fruit but a nice collection of worms, mildew of several types, scab, silver leaf, and so on and on.

I do not spray for the obvious reason that it costs money, takes time, and distributes poisons about the place. On the other hand, I do not explode when my apples are wormy, my grapes are full of black rot, and my peaches die of a nice assortment of causes. Since virtually all home gardeners wind up buying their fruit at the store anyway, I wish they'd face the fact and stop spraying haphazardly and for no purpose. Here it is chilly April (liable to turn into blazing hot April at a day's notice), and for ninety-nine cents a pound there are glorious grapes in the grocery, probably from Africa. It is sheer folly to think 'Concord' or 'Niagara' or any of the other grapes, even the ones far better than the two mentioned, are going to be of that quality in the home garden, short of the gardener's spending all waking hours with them and spraying like a chemist gone mad.

❖ Celestial Bamboo

Possibly the most beautiful of modest evergreen shrubs is the celestial bamboo, *Nandina domestica,* which is not a bamboo at all. It is related to the barberry, though you would never guess it.

The Japanese often plant it near their ceremonial teahouses, where (it is said) guests can pick their teeth upon leaving with the slender woody branches of the plant's flower and fruit stems. I have not been able to confirm this, when I have asked Japanese gentlemen about it. Maybe they don't use toothpicks. Besides, I thought you just drank tea in a teahouse, and would not need toothpicks afterward. I do not use toothpicks no matter what, so I have not tested my nandinas for this alleged valuable property, but pass it along for what it's worth, if anything.

Anyway, the plant produces woody stems, usually no more than four or five feet high in Washington (taller in the Gulf regions), crowned with a beautiful plume of highly dissected leaves, not as fine as a fern but suggesting one in delicacy. The new growth is bronzy red and somewhat curled, later flattening out and turning a soft green with a not quite semigloss finish. In the fall the leaves turn dark green and red, very like some oaks, and retain a bronzy cast through the winter. There are also cantaloupe-size panicles of bright red berries rising from the top and arching over — a luxuriant effect. Cardinals often eat these berries, and I think migrant grosbeaks do too, but not ours, a thing I attribute to my wife's annual expenditure of $118,000 or thereabouts on sunflower and other birdseed. The cardinals are all as fat as quail and see no need to eat any kind of berry. Usually, with me (and I see nandinas about town behaving in just the same way), the berries remain intact into the early daffodil season, and only now have lost luster and started falling off.

I am inspired to mention this beautiful plant that has no shocking showiness about it as a sort of antidote to the double-flowering cherries now powderpuffing the capital. Still, I well remember when I first saw such double cherries as 'Kwanzan' as a boy; I thought them the most beautiful trees of this earth. Later I began to notice the tree is not at all handsome when not in bloom, and its roots are uncommonly greedy. Also, as I got older I just leapt from pinnacle to pinnacle in sophistication of taste, so that now the only cherries I like are the single ones, and not many of them. But as we become utterly superior persons along life's highway, we should never let that grandeur hurt other gardeners, or do anything to take away their delight in double cherries.

I remember a dear friend, now with God, who in her old age wanted to plant a 'Kwanzan' cherry in front of her house. Another gardener, very elegant indeed, said 'Kwanzan' was vulgar and not good enough for so prominent a place. The woman approached me on the matter, and I said, "If that's a tree you think beautiful, by all means plant it and to hell with anybody who doesn't like it." This very day I passed by her old house and am happy to say the bright pink 'Kwanzan', weighed down by a mass of pompons, is a thrilling sight, vulgar or not, and is growing like gangbusters.

❖ What Goes On under the Apple Tree

I know tribes have been discovered in which people did not know where babies come from, but it comes as a surprise to learn that many Americans do not know where apples come from. A celebrated art (paintings) critic and a noted fashion (female garments) critic recently told me they were surprised to hear that if you plant a seed of any 'Albemarle Pippin' apple, you will get an apple that may be utterly different from the apple that bore the seed. Good grief. Is sex really such an esoteric subject in our country that grown people are startled by it?

Of course, there is nothing wrong with ignorance; we are all ignorant of most things that might be learned about. It's just that most people, I had assumed, knew that sex involved contributions from two individuals, and knew this from an early age. Since that is a false assumption, I shall speak today of sex in apples and other plants, which operates very much as sex in humans does.

It will be discovered (since it has not been noticed, evidently) that a human child is not identical to either of its parents. Furthermore, if there are five children, say, they will vary from each other, sometimes greatly. That is because at the time of conception, half the chromosomes (on which are lined up the genes) come from one parent and half from the other. The whole point of sex is to prevent filling the world with people exactly like ourselves, and surely this is one of the most comforting thoughts in all of science.

If one parent has blue eyes and the other parent brown, the child has an equal chance of having either brown or blue eyes. Except that some inherited physical qualities are dominant when passed on, while others are recessive. Brown eyes are dominant, blue are recessive. If the brown-eyed parent comes from a long line of brown eyes, the baby will have brown eyes. But if the brown-eyed parent's father, say, had blue eyes, the recessive gene for blue may be present and may combine with a gene for blue eyes in the next generation, thus producing a blue-eyed baby even when one parent has brown eyes.

In any case, sex works the same way in apples. Apples are fruits (babies) produced as a result of sexual activity and the fertilizing of an egg by a sperm. If a thousand seeds are sown and raised from an 'Albermarle Pippin', you will get a range of physical characteristics in the resulting trees (and their fruit), from individuals that are very similar to one parent to those that are similar to the other parent. And in between — apples not like either parent.

Sex is not utterly simple. You may get surprises. You will not always get, from any cross (sexual mating), a range of individuals covering the whole possible spectrum of variation. Some of the inherited genes may be dominant, thus swamping (in the first generation) the recessive genes contributed by the other parent. Some genes may not work together. And there is such a thing as dosage factors, in which a gene is more or less dominant but subject to influence by other genes.

Those unfamiliar with sex at all may then inquire how it happens you can get a tree, generation after generation, that always produces 'Albemarle Pippin' or 'Granny Smith' or some other particular apple. The answer is simple: these trees bypass sex, and are produced by grafting the tissue of a particular apple on the understock of something else. Never mind the understock, for the moment; the point is that the tree grows from tissue of the desired variety of apple, with no contribution from the outside. There has been no sex. As if we were to produce a baby from our fingernails or hair or a bit of skin from our arm. Then the baby would be exactly like ourselves. An apple produced from tissue of the apple — from its hair and nails, so to speak — will produce the identical apple.

If, however, you grow an apple from seed, you are getting into sex. You have not merely the original tissue but a seed produced from two parents, just as we produce human babies. And whenever you do this, you are getting two, not one, donors of inheritance, and the offspring will thus not be identical with either parent.

Someone has asked how certain apples are not bred (by sexual crossing of two different apple trees) but just discovered. This changes nothing. An apple seed may sprout and grow in a woodland, and like an apple grown from a seed anywhere else, it will be a new kind of apple, the result of inherited physical qualities from its two parents. It may be superior to both of them, and this may be noticed and apple growers may wish to grow it. They simply graft the desirable apple (though found in the woods) on understocks and thus perpetuate the identical apple indefinitely. It is exactly the same as if the apple were deliberately bred and raised in a nursery for the production of new varieties.

As long as an apple is produced sexually and not simply grafted from the tissue of one tree, it will be different from other apples. It may be less desirable than its parents, or equally desirable, or far more desirable. If it is outstandingly different and better, it will probably be noticed and propagated by grafting from then on out. An outstanding apple may be discovered in a breeder's nursery, or a woods, or a pasture, or an amateur's back yard, since any apple from seed will vary from its parents and may be better, just as it may be worse.

Another souce of new apples is the sporting of some existing variety. On one tree of 'Delicious' apples you may find that all the apples are the usual color, shape, texture, flavor, and so forth, except on one twig you may discover an apple somewhat different from all the others. It may have a slightly different color or shape, or the flesh may have a slightly different aroma or texture. If you think it's a nice change, you can graft tissue from that variant twig to an understock and wind up with apples just like the variation you discovered on the one particular twig. Again, sex has been bypassed; there has merely been a change in the original tissue.

When two parents are used to produce offspring, the progeny will vary from both. Some plants, especially wild plants, have existed for so long that variation is only very slight. (Some animals, too. If you breed a Jersey cow and bull, you will get a Jersey calf nearly identical with its parents.) Thus, if you sow dandelion seeds, you will find the new dandelions much like their parents. Same with regal lilies and many other plants.

If, however, the plants have been produced through hybridization, using quite different parents, you will get wide variations in the offspring. Regal lilies produce regal lilies just like themselves, with very little variation, because (I speak only of the wild plants) no new outside lines of genes have been introduced into the parentage. Tall bearded irises, however, may vary enormously, because a number of quite different species of irises have been bred together in the past, and today's progeny may acquire genes not from just one wild species (like the regal lily) but from a number of species, all quite different, with quite different genes to pass along. The more mixed-up the parentage is, the wider the variety you may expect in the offspring. The closer the breeding has been (in the wild or in cultivation, it makes no difference, as long as new genes are kept out of the line through not using new parents of different genetic makeup), the less variation you will find.

Except for occasional and rare instances of sports, all new varieties of apples or people or anything else come from sexual blending of two different parents; hence the mongrel nature of all humans and of most garden flowers. Sex is, however, somewhat more complicated than it seems on the surface. Many have noticed this.

❖ In Mr. Jefferson's Garden

This weekend I'll be in Charlottesville, Virginia, at Thomas Jefferson's garden, Monticello, God willing and the creek don't rise, and it seems to me surprising that I first prowled about the place some fifty years ago and have been there probably 150 times. The first year I saw it there were double hyacinths, old and small bulbs, and the wild lady tulip, *Tulipa clusiana,* both of which were descendants of the ones Jefferson planted, I was told.

Now the grounds are in far better shape than they were then and the great thousand-foot-long vegetable garden has been restored.

The orchard has been replanted with as many of the varieties Jefferson grew as can be found. Of course, the Taliaferro apple still eludes Peter Hatch, director of grounds and gardens, despite heroic efforts to locate it. None of the Taliaferros have come up with it — a pity, as Jefferson thought it superior for cider.

It's easy, especially for southerners of the pre-Elvis era, to fix on Jefferson as the outstanding American, along with Franklin and Washington, but as I was taught great skepticism at school, I try not to go overboard.

Now I take with some caution Jefferson's various enthusiasms. When we say Jefferson greatly liked such and such a plant, we are often relying on a single mention in his letters or memoranda, and what every gardener knows (and not every scholar does) is that one is forever saying, "'Whopper' is the best tomato I have tried," to be followed later by "This year 'Whopper' has been a severe disappointment, but 'Red Brandywine', probably the best tomato I have ever tried . . ."

Jefferson thought highly of the 'White Marseilles' fig and praised it for its hardiness, but as I recall he got it from his neighbor, General Cocke, who had to give it extraordinary protection in winter. At Monticello, however, it is one of the two best figs, the other being 'Brown Turkey', which does so well in Washington and in the cooler parts of the South.

I share Jefferson's disappointment that Lewis and Clark never were able (despite serious urging) to find a mammoth for him in their expedition to the West, and with him I share the gardener's common frustration in not getting other people to do useful things. His poor daughter had enough to say grace over without continuing admonitions to do this, do that, maintain records and note when the first blooms appeared on everything.

He once wrote to his sister that "I now enclose some seed which Mr. Hawkins sent me, the name of which I have forgotten, but I dare say it is worth attention." I have often dared say the same thing and gotten unsatisfactory answers (as Jefferson did) to later questioning on what ever happened to Mr. Hawkins's seeds.

I try to stay out of the house at Monticello, though it is useful for its evidence that Jefferson was mad as a hatter in some respects, despite the orthodoxy that he was our finest colonial architect. Anybody who sticks little windows in an entablature is zany, and that dome, which cost plenty, is devoted to a virtually worthless room, reached by stairs so narrow as to be unworthy of Vermont, and an outrage in Virginia.

When his beautiful rotunda burned at his university, a distinguished firm reconstructed the interior with an uninterrupted view from floor to top of dome, but now it has been restored to Jefferson's odd notion of making it two floors, thus wasting the dome on both. The dome room is a very uneasy room to sit in, and except for Jefferson it would be called ill-proportioned.

Furthermore, if the great man's frailties are not apparent enough, there is this in a letter to his overseer: "Next, to secure wool enough, the negroes' dogs must all be killed. Do not spare a single one."

The design of the garden itself is ridiculous in the sense that great labor is needed to produce extremely little effect. On the other hand, no other president (not even Washington) ever devoted so much thought, ingenuity, and effort to a garden. That in itself atones for almost everything.

Fortunately, there is now the Thomas Jefferson Center for Historic Plants (Monticello, P.O. Box 316, Charlottesville, VA 22902), which sells, along with T-shirts and stuff, seeds of plants grown by Jefferson, maybe grown by Jefferson, or that Jefferson probably would have liked. At $1.50 a packet, they are as follows: love-lies-bleeding, native columbine, European columbine, red orach, blackberry lily, cleome, larkspur, sweet william, hyacinth bean, globe amaranth, strawflower, heliotrope, standing cypress (*Ipomopsis rubra*), and 'Tennis Ball' lettuce; rose campion, mallow, four-o'clock, nicotiana, love-in-a-mist, opium poppy, black-eyed Susan, scabiosa, sesame, African marigold, French marigold, black hollyhock, double columbine, butterfly weed, New England aster, bachelor's button, English daisy, Canterbury bell, fringed pink, purple coneflower, foxglove, dame's violet, candytuft, cypress vine, perennial pea, English lavender, cardinal flower, honesty, Maltese cross, sensitive plant, corn poppy, annual phlox, white eggplant, nasturtium, and Johnny jump-up.

The garden includes far more than the serpentine walk with flower beds in the lawn. The grove is being restored, and the old trees, including a few planted by Jefferson, now receive careful attention. An original larch was once hacked on with the idea of removing it as it was thought dead, and admittedly larches look bad in the winter. Such a thing is unheard of now, however (fortunately, Jefferson's larch survived).

The view is nothing less than noble. Jefferson went to enormous expense to level the site for his house, and to this day the wide prospects justify all the trouble he took. I have seen it at all seasons, in sunshine, clouds, and thunderstorms, and always the views were superb.

Nowhere else do you feel so strongly Jefferson's bouncing optimism, his lively fascination with novelty, his devotion to "practical" gadgets, and his passion for plants. He grew (but did not necessarily eat) tomatoes in the eighteenth century; he bought from nurseries; he exchanged seeds and plants with gardeners in France and England. His occasional extravagances in architecture were not bad for an amateur, and of course no other grouping of college buildings surpasses that of the University of Virginia. His record with dogs is clouded at best. No man is perfect.

❖ Glorious Flocks of April Phlox

One of the prettiest flowers of April is the wild blue phlox. Along with the Virginia bluebell, it is one of the handsomest and showiest of American wildflowers. You can see great drifts of the phlox along the canal at Great Falls, and indeed anywhere else in damp forested land in much of eastern America.

There are several variations of this beautiful creature, *Phlox divaricata,* including 'Fuller's White', and the mere fact that all three of mine died the first summer does not diminish my admiration of it. These phlox are about a foot high at blooming time, bearing clusters of flowers at the tips of the new growth, and they are so abundant that if a piece of ground is planted solid with them, a mounded carpet of lavender blue will result and the foliage will be hard to see. They are especially desirable, I think, at the edge of azalea plantings, where they spread out from seed.

Quite different is the Virginia bluebell (*Mertensia virginica*), which is not as showy as the phlox but even more beautiful as an individual plant. In early spring it sends up sharp cones of furled leaves, and if the weather is mild the flowers appear as if by magic within a few days. They are hanging clusters of straight bells, a blending of rose and lavender blue. It too is a flawless flower for the kind of shady places many gardeners have beneath dogwoods, mahonias, nandinas, hollies, azaleas, and so forth.

Both the bluebells and the phlox die away with hot weather, to remain invisible till the next spring. I have never succeeded with the bluebells, because when the first ones happened to perish, I did not persist. Stupid of me, as no spring flower is more desirable.

❖ *Letting Nature Take Its Course*

All the spraying and fertilizing in the world will not keep hybrid tea roses (and many others) from being killed to the ground or killed outright if a hot spring is followed abruptly by a spell of nights in the twenties. My own experience over many years is that gardening has certain sorrows built into its nature, though it is rare indeed that in fifty years I have lost anything to insects. It's true I do not produce edible peaches or worm-free apples. Too bad.

Also I have had tomato hornworms, bean beetles, occasional scale on camellias, leaf miners in the box bushes, and, in brief, my share of grassypillars and caterhoppers. But they have never amounted to a serious problem. I scrubbed the camellia stems with a stout scrub brush, and once with brown laundry soap, hoping the alkali would not kill the bushes. Worked just fine.

The box bushes I mulch once a year with rotted horse manure.

I water them in droughts. I saw out heavy branches from oak and maple when I think the shade is getting too dense. The box looks fine.

The hornworms, easily detected when the gardener notices only skeletal ribs left on his tomato plants, are picked off by hand. The bean beetles eat a few leaves, but the bean plants are pulled out and composted as soon as the short bean harvest (I speak of bush green beans) is done.

Iris borers, one of the few truly serious insect pests I ever encountered, can make it impossible to grow that most beautiful of all flowers. A mulch of wood chips helps, some say. I tried various things, and nothing helped. I stopped growing irises.

On roses, black spot is harmful and results, in hot, damp months, in early dropping of the leaves. It can weaken roses to the point of death. It is absurd to spray roses. I give them manure, plenty of water, and what I think is reasonable attention. If they succumb to black spot, they can die and good riddance.

Even so, I have had at least my share of magnificent roses. The great grief in roses that I have experienced is not leaf miners, viruses, fungi, chafers, aphids, and the other woes you hear a good bit about — they do not seriously interrupt my delight. What is grievous is for the "perfectly hardy" climber 'Madame Gregoire Staechelin' to be killed to the ground by topsy-turvy spring weather. Compared with that, no bug or fungus is a problem at all. And to prevent that, no spray does the trick.

To go a step further, consider the laurels of the eastern mountains, the sequoias of the West, the cypresses of the bayous off the Mississippi — nobody sprays or fertilizes those plants, but they are unsurpassed in beauty. Shouldn't you ask how such supreme beauty and vigor are possible without anybody running about with poisons? Or take those occasional true disasters, by which we lost the American chestnut and the American elm. How does it happen that despite all the commotion we lost those trees, and the arsenal of poisons did nothing to prevent it?

Take the azaleas of the middle South. They grow like weeds all over the place, and most of them are never touched with anything except weather. They could not be better. Someday, I suspect, disease will overtake them. Do you really think that when that time comes, spraying will save them? Our native dogwood is now threatened with a terrible leaf disease that becomes fatal. If by spraying we could stop it, maybe spraying would be a good idea. I doubt that anything will stop it, and I suggest praying that the anthracnose will become less virulent.

Since we have dazzling examples of plants that cannot be improved on, despite natural hazards and despite the absence of sprays, and since we also have dazzling examples of plants that die everywhere, in spite of heroic chemical efforts, I conclude that sprays are rarely the answer to anything, at least in the home garden. I am cautious when speaking of agriculture. If I grew oranges or apples and noticed that the fruit was full of bugs, and noticed that American customers (for some odd reason) preferred fruit and vegetables without worms crawling about, I suspect I would spray, if I found that spraying produced unblemished produce. But I cannot for the life of me see why anybody with a city lot would even dream of spraying poisons all over the place, when it is obvious that nothing is gained by it. Sometimes I have seen gardens in which great trust is placed in various sprays, and I wonder what the gardeners think they have accomplished. In particular I have often noticed quite ratty little lawns on which quantities of poison have been sprayed or dumped, and for what?

You would think gardeners, of all people, would hesitate to fling poisons all over the place. I have heard of gardeners who actually spray against aphids. In the fifty or so years that I've grown roses, grapes, and other plants of which aphids are fond, I have never sprayed them (except, rarely, with water, which dislodges and unfortunately kills them) and have yet to detect any damage from aphids. The same is true of Japanese beetles, cicadas, webworms, and other alleged horrors. The alarm that some gardeners feel about bugs derives from illusions of their brains rather than from damage done by bugs. One of the few (somewhat evil) pleasures I take in the misfortunes of other people is smiling at their bug problems and watching them spray all over the place and noticing that their problems continue for all their sprays.

❖ *Discovering Bulbs*

When I was a small lad, I discovered one day early in March a grassy slope full of low-to-the-ground flowers, little shining cups of varnished gold and lavender and purple and white. Not having had all delight in nature knocked out of me, as I was so young, I promptly picked hundreds of these miraculous flowers and reported that the grass was all in beautiful bloom.

My mother was horrified and said they were crocuses and our neighbors had planted them all. But I said not at all, the whole grassy bank was in bloom. My mother said that was because they had planted hundreds of crocus corms in the grass. The neighbors were generous and amused, and that began my fondness for crocuses.

Later, as a young man, I was visiting some friends in Mississippi in September. There was an orchard of pecan trees that I had seen in the spring full of daffodils but had never seen in late summer. Beneath the trees was a solid sea of Guernsey lilies (as we called them), or *Lycoris radiata.* Never before had I seen such a display, and never since.

These flowers are both waxy and diamond-dusted, consisting of sunburst clusters of rich pink spreading trumpets atop foot-high stems. No flower is more elegant, and none is more surprising when seen in masses, blooming without leaves. Leaves come later in the fall, then die down in late spring.

Soon after, I received a couple of huge sacks of bulbs, more than five hundred of them, and planted them beneath the pecan of my own garden, where they bloomed but never did so well as in the Mississippi Delta country. I often think of those bulbs when I see them listed now for two dollars apiece. I never see any bulbous flowers without a flood of memories from those heady excitements decades ago, when I first discovered their beauty, whether crocuses or Guernsey lilies or crinums or others.

One year I planted a clump of the lavender wild Asian lily *Lilium lankongense,* which was relatively rare, and for several years it produced forty-inch stems loaded with flowers against the curious gray-rose-purple leaves of *Rosa rubrifolia.* Like so many lilies, it petered out after a few years, and even when it was in perfection it was not one of those flowers you could see a block away. Still, when I think of the most wonderful things that ever were in the garden, I often think of it.

Another year I found a great seedpod on the hybrid garden lily strain called 'Imperial Silver' and scattered the seeds on the heavily shaded west side of the house between two window wells. To my astonishment they grew, and now they still produce six-foot stalks of white gold-banded lilies on the first of July. They look like the wild *Lilium auratum* but are in fact hybrids. It is not often that a garden variety of some plant has the virtues of easy cultivation and robust health but also the fragile elegance of the wild ancestor.

Still another revelation of the beauty of bulbs came to me as a teenager when I saw a woodland garden, a bit on the swampy side, covered with thousands of old white-trumpet daffodils. We called them goosenecks. There were a number of slightly distinct kinds of these trumpets, most of them with nodding flowers, and I doubt anybody today could ever straighten out their names. Now they are rare. None was very white — they were all off-white — but you could not see them without thinking you had never seen a display of daffodils with quite that kind of beauty.

One of the wild tulips of the Near East is the so-called lady tulip, *Tulipa clusiana,* with almond-shaped flowers with petals alternating off-white and rose on foot-high stems. It is surprisingly permanent in gardens, lasting perhaps forever and certainly for years and years. A friend of mine planted a half-dozen bulbs near a little trench she dug to keep water away from the bulbs of *Lilium henryi.* Within a few years the lady tulip had seeded itself the length of the trench, where water had carried the seeds. I have some of these tulips struggling for life beneath the encroaching branches of viburnums, and although only a few of them are still blooming, they are a great sight (to my mind) every year.

I think the point of all this is that every gardener should start early in his hobby to explore bulbs. Even a handful of a variety, or even just one, is worthwhile.

❖ How the Garden Grows and Grows

A gardening friend of mine has quite lost her mind — not that it distresses her much — and no longer makes an effort to conceal her madness.

I estimate her garden to be twenty by twenty-two feet, and she started out all right a few years ago by paving the center with brick and acquiring a little table and four chairs, with a rose, a lilac, a camellia, a few lilies, a peony, a grape, and so on around the edges. Everyone thought she had done well. But of course it didn't last. At first she dissimulated about things, and was much given to saying, "Oh, I think you have seen the Japanese anemones, they've always been here." She said things of this sort when she had broken down and been tempted beyond her strength by a catalogue or garden center.

She was very bad about garden centers; we all noticed that from the beginning. She would go on some stated mission of acquiring a sack of peat moss, but would surreptitiously (entering stealthily at night, I suspect) bring home several flats of snapdragons and the Lord only knows what else. It got to the point where things were planted on top of each other, so of course many of them did not flourish greatly, and this gave her an excuse to yank them out. "I cannot think why the platycodons did not perform this year," she would say, pretending to be puzzled about why they were no longer there and (suddenly) ten lily bulbs were.

But as time passed, she dropped all pretense. That much, at least, was a step in the right direction, no doubt.

It all came to a head when she converted a basement room (in which an unfortunate maid had once lived, it was said, though even in the old days there were laws against open cruelty, surely). This room has one small window, so she painted the whole thing white and installed enough special lights to illuminate the Capitol, and got someone to build a batch of stages on which she could set as many pots and flats of dirt as could be managed.

She no longer hid her packets of seed. They sat there in great rows. She had two hundred packets of seed at once — eggplant, tomatoes, thunbergias, snapdragons, zinnias, and endless other things.

"Do you think you have room for eggplants?" her saner friends would say — before it finally dawned on them that she knew she was mad, and did not wish to be sane.

"I've got some big pots for them," she would say in November. Sure enough, in February the eggplants would produce some tumescent objects which she said were eggplants, and which she proposed to eat, until somebody told her (for no good reason except that the eggplants looked loathsome) that if she ate them, they'd kill her, since they were obviously poisonous. She persisted and recently set great pots of eggplants on the brick pavement of the garden.

She whacked back the climbing roses to skeletons, sawed down the camellia and two young magnolias, ordered great quantities of asparagus, strawberries, and half-barrels, in which she said everything would fit beautifully. A fig, a plum, and a peach were supposed to live in barrels. As for the strawberries and blueberries, she said she was going to take up the bricks and build ziggurats where the table used to be, and on the little terraces, she said, the strawberries and much else would grow to beat the band.

She said it was silly to have all that space (about twelve feet square) just for people to lounge about drinking coffee and eating apricots. The only reason there are any bricks at all (the tiny paved area still remains) is that she could not figure how to take them up herself, and none of her friends would have any part in the project.

Once, in rather bitter jest, I suppose, someone offered her some little sequoia trees in pots. She accepted, but I never saw them planted out.

There is a vast space of wall, about twenty-eight inches wide, beyond the French windows, in which she planted a trumpet vine, a quite vigorous grape, and several clematis, and when they did not grow as rapidly as she thought they should, she filled in with blue lobelias and I think heucheras, along with petunias, alyssum, and whatever else the garden centers happened to be selling. Unfortunately, a very fine musk rose flourished and has reached well into her bedroom windows on the second floor, and an admirable pink honeysuckle has defied all law and reason and settled in lavishly on an iron railing she installed for it several years ago. Rammed up against the iron spindles are perhaps two dozen sorts of perennials, some of which (including the white campanulas) are trying to spread, while others gallantly hold on as long as breath holds out.

Where the produce of two hundred packs of seed, growing madly in the basement, is supposed to be planted in this garden, nobody knows.

This is an extreme case, of course, of the affliction common to almost all gardeners, and I mention it to make everybody feel much better. Most of us, after all, merely have to wander about the garden holding a new rosebush, wondering if it could not perhaps be tucked in between the hollyhock and the peony, since there is a good ten inches there, and beyond doubt the hollyhock can be tied up a little and pulled to the left. We do not, most of us, wonder where to plant an additional thousand seedlings raised in the basement in a twenty-foot garden already jammed beyond hope.

My friend, as I say, does not seem to suffer much. She is tremendously busy throughout the year, and has mastered the fine art of the scalpel, opening little slits here and there for one more plant, and she has become expert at last rites for the dying. On the whole, she is happier than she was before this madness set in. We who like her, however, are in some distress about where it will all end. Still, as her friends tend to comfort one another when her name comes up, she's in better shape than if she took up raising cattle — a thing that mercifully has not yet occurred to her.

MAY

IT's HUMAN NATURE, or at least a gardener's nature (which is not quite the same thing), to want to live at least one and preferably two climatic zones warmer than where he gardens. Thus, in Washington the gardener wishes he could grow the flora of New Orleans or at least Savannah. Such a gardener is forever trying to find hardy oleanders and Confederate jasmines. In Boston, though, they are not even thinking about oleanders or gardenias, but as someone recently wrote me from there, "What I would give if we were warm enough for evergreen hollies." There are gardeners in the far upper Midwest whose dreams are simply to be able to grow the rambler rose 'American Pillar'.

I spent a little time on a paradise island once, where the air was full of butterflies as big as saucers and the trees were hung with glossy vines laden with scarlet waxy flowers. It was there that I woke up one morning with a scorpion sitting on my chest. I had an excellent view of him until he stung, at which time I rose up with greater speed than usual, and this has colored my view of tropical paradises. The pain was no greater than that of a wasp sting, but an egg-size lump swelled immediately over my sternum; it subsided in forty-five minutes, and I had no aftereffects beyond new insights into the folly of envying those in warm climates.

As Eudora Welty once wrote in her fiction (a country school-teacher's exhortation to her pupils as a tornado approached),

"We're in the best place right here." That could be the wise gardener's motto. Wherever one gardens is the best place right here.

❖ *Staying in the Pink*

Pinks and carnations — the *Dianthus* tribe in general — dream of sunny crystal dry air on the face of a limestone crag, rooting about in rotted stone and a bit of leaf mold. The last place on earth they wish to grow is a muggy lowland garden on acid soil with old oaks casting some shade and with fat azaleas rummaging about in damp peat. Pinks are ill suited, in other words, to acid woodland gardens, and they do not regard us well even if we saw down a few trees and let in the sun.

But often in town gardens I see half-barrels set here and there along a terrace or a walk, and often these vessels are planted with marigolds or geraniums for nonstop summer color, and that is fine. If, however, you have had it up to here with their bright sunny faces, you might try pinks in the tubs. A spadeful of ground limestone and enough gravel or sand to make the soil light can be added to the barrel, along with some fully rotted leaves — the grainy black kind you sometimes see at the edge of city alleys.

Occasionally gardeners who know no better have excellent success growing annual carnations from seed. More experienced gardeners, who do not expect success, usually fail. And I do not think it worth anybody's time and trouble to attempt the usual greenhouse carnations. But there never was a gardener, surely, who did not melt a little at the very thought of the clove-scented pinks that you used to see everywhere in small city gardens, but that you rarely see now.

Dianthus plumarius, the pink that most gardeners remember from the old days (if indeed they remember anything), comes in white, off-white, tints of pink, and tones of red — usually white or light pink. The petals are commonly fringed or pinked along the edge, and the flowers have an astonishing perfume. "Clove" is as good as any other word to describe their perfume, but it is sweet as well as spicy, and the flowers on ten-inch stems are fine for cutting.

The plants form creeping mats of impressive gray-green leaves, not really gray, but gray enough to stand out among other greens. No plant serves better along the edge of a paved walk to give that substantial, well-tended, Old World look. If the soil is too rich, the mats spread out at a very satisfying rate, but then fungoid ills appear in sweltering summers and the gardener is chastened. He learns not to plump up the pinks too much with fertilizers. Gritty soil with leaf mold, not fat soil with stable manure, is what pinks revel in. Or survive in. They are doing us a favor even to grow here. They are easy enough to increase from cuttings, but the gardener does well not to get too satisfied too soon, and must resist the temptation to hurry them along with high culture. They respond well at first, then collapse.

Sometimes in small gardens you see a little retaining wall of brick or (and it need not always look awful) cinder block. Usually there is nothing very interesting hanging over the edge. If the soil is made light, as I have suggested, the clove pinks flourish, rooting down by the cool inside face of the wall and flopping over the edge. There they rest their leaves against the dry face of the wall, or hang out in the air itself, so no moisture stays at the base of their curving stems, even in wet weather. From time to time (if the plants get leggy) they are trimmed back, so they do not wander too far from home — that is, the stems do not get long and bare.

One of the glories of the past was the laced pink, a double flower usually white, with each petal banded or laced in deep red. And then for many years you never saw laced pinks. In our own day they are back again, thanks partly to the intensive breeding work of the firm of Allwood in England. There are also nowadays good strains of border carnations and other garden pinks, all of them superior to the variety available when I was young.

The thing to keep in mind with all forms of *Dianthus,* whether dwarf or alpine or clove or carnation or laced or anything else, is that they do not like shade, dampness, heavily manured soil, or peat. Light, a bit hungry (not starved, of course), and open to the sun: that's the recipe for pinks. Needless to say, you never mulch them.

Pinks are a very nice plant to illustrate a point about hardiness: they are perfectly hardy on light dry soils and perish wonderfully in heavy wet soils. Some gardeners suppose, therefore, that pinks and carnations cannot take much cold. It's not that. But they cannot take much (or any) soggy clay.

❖ Gone But Not Forgotten

Sometimes people complain that such-and-such a flower fades quickly, and people new to the natural world (having been weaned on aluminum) are almost always startled to learn that peonies, irises, and lilies, for example, bloom only once a year. And the first time they discover the sad and gaudy life span of these flowers they are shocked. Often I meet people who roar up and demand to know why their favorite flower only lasted three days, and what do I intend to do about it?

Well, nothing. If you don't like the way flowers do, nobody makes you grow them. You can always go in the house and play with your computer, as I point out, and this is undoubtedly what a lot of people were born for.

One well-known peony, 'Red Charm', is a great favorite of gardeners, since it is like a somewhat squeezed globe, exploding with hundreds of shredded red petals that open red and stay red, not wavering off toward purple (not that there's anything wrong with reds that hanker after purple), and it blooms a few days before the early regular peonies such as 'Festiva Maxima' and 'Monsieur Jules Elie'. On a fine Saturday in May, my 'Red Charm' opened the first of its flowers. On Sunday it opened seven more. On Wednesday all eight blooms shattered, and that was that till next year. Thus we see, we mathematicians, that the plant was in glory for four days.

Irises are somewhat more generous in their stay, though the individual flower lasts only two days. There are (or should be) plenty of them on the stalk, opening in succession. As a rule, you may allow two weeks for the stalk to develop and two weeks for the clump to be in bloom. For as long as I can remember I have read about some variety in which the flowers "lasted in perfection five days" or five months "under the blazing sun of Kansas" or Louisiana or Maryland. These are simply lies. I have grown two or three thousand varieties of iris in my time, including a lot of those with "incredible substance," and can say that I never knew one that looked good for more than two days. The third day, if it's cloudy and cool, the flower still sits there looking a bit tubercular, no great ornament that I can see. Which is why you pick the fading (a euphemism for dead iris flowers, which writhe themselves into a soggy mess) blooms off, lest they ruin the effect of the flowers ready to open.

In both peonies and irises you can easily obtain varieties that bloom early, midseason, and late, so the season may last several weeks, but when I grew five hundred kinds of iris in my former garden, I noticed that the great blooming season lasted two weeks, with stragglers fore and aft. Fourteen days of delirium, I confess. The flowers were glorious at 5:30 in the morning and at 11:30 at night (by flashlight or floodlight) and all hours between.

Then they are gone. It does not do at all to say, *Well, we'll look at them next week,* because next week is always too late. When peonies or irises or lilies bloom, you stop and look at them. The dentist will be there next week, the office will be there next week, and if people can take off time for funerals, babies, plague, and conventions, they can take off enough time to get properly saturated with the iris or the rose.

One year I took off two weeks during the peak of my irises, and for some odd reason the weather was flawless and the irises were having one of those exceptional years and I sat there and strolled there morning to night for two weeks. There were two thousand stalks of flowers, with about seven flowers on a stalk, and not one of them opened that I did not see in full head-on focus.

Now I have no irises. I must raise beds for them before I try them again. I never regretted the day-after-day saturation in the irises that great year. I visited hardly any other iris nuts that year, and I got my fill.

It is curious to me that so many gardeners occupy their leisure making things neat and tidy. It is one thing to trot past a fine bush of, say, 'Mrs. Anthony Waterer' laden with attar-scented blooms, and another thing to settle down and gaze at it for an hour. What is the point of growing a rose in the first place if you just admire it in passing?

It is like dogs. They are a sufficient headache and expense that there is no earthly point in having them if they're not all over the place at all hours, though here is one tip — certain short-legged hounds and certain terriers are unable to leap up on the bed if you keep adding mattresses and if the bed is an old one that almost requires a ladder to get into. Setters, however, and Dalmatians and springers and boxers and Danes, can get up on any bed a human can manage. Sometimes a pup can be started off on a rocking chair and will sleep there or on the bathroom tiles (depending on season) the rest of his life, but in general it is simpler to get a bigger bed.

We must not wander. The chief flowers, like dogs, are too much bother unless the grower lives with them on a high plane of intimacy. Then they are rewarding enough, and never mind how brief the season is. I cannot imagine any sane person sitting there gazing at marigolds day after day. That is why only beautiful flowers are worth growing.

The idea is to grow at least a handful of the great flowers and then drop what has to be dropped when they bloom. Please do not inform me of what I know all too well: that a regular job interferes in the most disgusting way with a garden. A good bit can be done, however, by declining every human contact that can possibly be declined during the iris season, for example. For some bizarre reason, people who have behaved themselves perfectly well all winter start having suppers and brunches and God knows what else in May. If you think ahead, and do not mind being ostracized by the human race, these grim events may be largely bypassed.

❖ Agave, the Can-Do Plant

I should say a word for the agave, or century plant, as it is some-times called. It is native to our West and to Mexico and Central America, and while one or two varieties are doubtfully hardy here, the great one is far too tender even to try outdoors in the winter. That is *Agave americana.* I have the kind with yellowish stripes on the great sword leaves, which are spiny down the sides.

The first one I had (it was pitched out in the trash by somebody years ago) flourished mightily and soon had pups, which I grew along in separate pots. They too have had pups, so I have three big ones, three or four feet wide, and a number of smaller ones. They come indoors the end of October and go out again in April.

With scissors I cut off the spine at the end of each leaf, as it is as firm and sharp as a hypodermic needle. My house is small, and if you sit in certain chairs in the living and dining rooms, you slide in cautiously to avoid bloodshed from the side spines, which are sharp enough to do damage but not sharp enough to put your eye out.

In Madagascar I got seeds of another agave which is more squat — only the size of a bushel basket — with silvery white stripes. It is an American plant, and one is pleased to collect seeds of our own native flora off the coast of Africa.

Eventually, agaves get as large as a Volkswagen, but only after breaking a good many pots. Many plants sicken and die when they get too big for the pot, but not agaves. They are can-do plants, and their roots simply crack and split open even a heavy twelve-inch clay pot.

They are called century plants because people said they bloomed once per century. Wrong. They bloom when they reach a certain size and vigor, maybe twenty years, maybe less. Then, like many desert sword-leaf plants (furcraeas, dasylirions, and yuccas among them), the plant dies after flowering but leaves offsets, which in turn grow to blooming size.

In moving these large plants indoors and out, one should prudently place a blanket between oneself and the plant in one's arms. I have never done it and always regret it. It is also wise to have the earth dry as dust, to reduce the weight. It is also wise to remove all pots hanging on kitchen walls or any other movables along the route.

Somebody once offered to take the agaves off my hands, thinking I considered them a nuisance. Well, of course they are. So are dogs, but people don't come up offering to rid you of your dogs. Agaves unfortunately become dumb, fiercely armed pets after a few years. I give each large agave perhaps a pint of water every two months in the house, and let the rains of heaven fall on them as they may during warm months outdoors.

❖ The Lilacs That Bloom in the Spring

For some years a person in the family has been making noises about lilacs. I grew up on the Tennessee-Mississippi border, a country in which lilacs were thought as exotic as spruces or hemlocks or rhododendrons or allamandas or papayas. My mother, who was a Yankee, planted three lilacs, but after fifty years they were only four to five feet high, and no sooner did the main stems reach that height than they died, to be replaced by suckers. I suspect the variety was 'Madame Morel'. In any case, when the pitiful creatures put out a few flowers in April, people used to come to see them.

Lilacs, of course, are much happier in northern states than southern, but they grow reasonably well as far south as Washington or in comparable climates. When I was in school in Piedmont, Virginia, the common lilac (*Syringa vulgaris*) did well at the side of the fraternity house where I lived, reaching ten feet or so.

With lilacs, as with every other favorite flower, the breeders have been hard at work since the 1870s, and there are now about two thousand named varieties, each of which is (according to the man who raised it) glorious. In 1900 the great gardener Gertrude Jekyll observed of an old variety of lilac, the white 'Marie LeGraye', that it was fully beautiful, that it had reached the height of beauty and was content to stay there. The same might be said of the ordinary purple or lilac kind, which is perfumed to perfection. Decades ago, great connoisseurs such as E. H. Wilson pointed out that the garden varieties of lilac had reached a kind of pinnacle, and we need not expect to see any advances from further breeding.

But there have been great advances, at least in some directions. We have new colors (nearer blue, and vaguely primrose yellow, and purple with white edges to the petals), and the size of the clusters and of the individual florets has been vastly increased. All these things are obvious advances, but whether the final result is a more lovable, more beautiful plant than the common purple is something each gardener must decide. I know my heart leapt a little when I saw that a nursery of our region, Carroll Gardens of Westminster, Maryland, was offering 'Agincourt Beauty', a massive purple single-flower said to hang in clusters like grapes. It was raised twenty years ago but has been rare in commerce.

There are also great advances in very early and very late lilacs, which extend the blooming season. Among the "new" sorts (remembering that it takes decades for a new lilac to get on the general market) is the early reddish purple 'Pocahontas' and the quite late reddish purple 'Miss Canada'. I have no personal experience of these, but if I had more than my small city lot I'd try a dozen or so for starters.

Lilacs should be planted at least eight feet apart, preferably ten feet, and this means that six feet is the absolute minimum. The ones I am ordering are only a foot tall, raised from cuttings. That is, they are on their own roots, and are not grafted on either privet or the common lilac, a practice that sometimes brings trouble later on from unwanted suckers. It will be at least three years before they bloom much.

Some years ago I planted the white 'Maud Notcutt', a great large single-flower, and after several years it bloomed superbly. Then it died, for no reason I could tell, though I suspect it simply got too dry in a drought one summer. Lilacs will not abide wet feet, but they are not desert plants either, and I should have had sense enough to notice Maud's thirst.

Besides that, I suspect the old common purple and common white are tougher than the fancy newer sorts. With plants as with people, we take beautiful old friends too much for granted, and cannot believe anything will ever happen to them. But the point is that many shrubs, including lilacs, are best planted in the fall in moderate climes, though in the far north it is better to plant them in spring. South of Washington, Richmond, Birmingham, and Memphis, lilacs are chancy indeed, but north of those cities, all the way to the North Pole, I suppose, they are a joy of full-blown spring. They make up, a little, for the lack of crape myrtles and oleanders in arctic-type places.

❖ Chip Off the Old Bush

I am kept busy propagating a rather common and unexciting shrub, *Kerria japonica,* for people who (as the late Margery Fish used to say) are bent on chiseling off a bit. I say "common and unexciting" because I have had it for years, and gardeners think if they have it in their garden, it can't be very select. And yet I well recall decades ago when I first saw this bright canary-yellow creature — golden quarters spangled the length of bright lime-green stems — in a Mississippi garden. I did not cease from whatever negotiations were necessary, and perhaps some chicanery, but that was long ago. I got it.

The kerria, a member of the rose family but without thorns, and much given to making an arching shrub four to eight feet tall, comes from China and Japan and was introduced in 1834. The first plants received in Europe were full double-form, the flowers like shaggy small yellow carnations or chrysanthemums along the stems. This is the old Jew's mallow. It is a festive, showy bush, which everybody used to grow in my boyhood neighborhood, and it was therefore rather despised.

But the one I am talking about now has single flowers, just five petals. It is my impression that it takes more shade than the double, and that it blooms off and on through the year a little more freely. I grow mine beneath the branches of a pin oak, back of azaleas. The sun rarely strikes it, but the oak branches are high, so there is plenty of light.

The reason the kerria is where it is, against the south or entrance front of the house, is simply that I could not think of many good plants that would survive in dry shade, and besides, I wanted the green stems to be there in winter. Indeed, they are just as cheerful on a January day as I expected they would be.

I did think, briefly, of the Kurume azaleas, which clot up in mid-April like a giant's scrambled eggs in pink, white, scarlet, and magenta. No fear, I said, since the kerria always bloomed in the old garden with the irises, when the azaleas were past. But up here, in a different exposure, the kerria blooms not with the irises but with the azaleas. From the sidewalk, if you gaze past the seething azaleas and expect to find a soothing sight like a gray shrub, you are surprised to see instead a nice mass of Day-Glo yellow with the kerria. It is a lovely yellow, but it knows nothing of modesty. If you've got it, flaunt it. It clashes with peculiar vibrancy against scarlet and magenta. One notable year it was assisted by the intense electric-violet flowers of a clematis, 'Etoile Violette', which did little to subdue the riot.

This all shows, among other things, that it does no good to recall the precise average flowering dates of shrubs when you move from one garden to another. A slight difference in soil texture, in exposure, in the minienvironment, can make a difference of two weeks, and while that does not seem worth bothering about, it can mean that all of a sudden the flaming canary begins to sing with the scrambled eggs, so to speak.

The effect does not strike everybody as it does me, and as I say, a certain number of people line up in April applying for babies. An old kerria usually can be pulled apart, since it suckers a bit;

otherwise, cuttings are grown from semimature wood. It grows fairly rapidly. A knee-high bush reaches six feet or so in a year or two. If mine had a more favorable site, it would bloom off and on through the summer.

❖ Garden Pests Don't Bug Me

Bugs, I know, are a problem for many gardeners, and sometimes I am surprised that they never bother me, but the truth is I do not spray for anything.

I think there is a case for poisonous sprays in commercial agriculture. I think there are trade-offs in life, and one of them may be the acceptance of a few pounds of poison in the gizzard in exchange for a food system that (no matter how annoyed one gets with it sometimes) at least provides string beans in every grocery store. Sooner or later, obviously, we are going to have to have a better method of insect control than spraying poisons. But that is a very involved subject, which is not really answered by fury that our farms have as much poison as topsoil on them.

One thing I am certain of: the home gardener — at least this home gardener — need not have and should not have any truck with sprays. The first thing I have noticed along the years, spray-wise, is that sprays do not do the job. Period. Sorry, because I know the faith people put in them. No spray has ever done the job for me. Maybe if I had had better machinery the spray would have worked.

A friend of mine grows grapes seriously. He fainted with joy when benomyl came along, the answer to his prayer regarding that terrible rot that garden grapes get. It was only later that he discovered that if you spray more than twice a year with benomyl, you get cluster rot. One year I sprayed my own grapes. I might as well not have bothered. They were as full of fungus as always.

I yield to few in my distaste for wormy apples (and worse than them, peaches), and my wife refuses to carve around the worms.

I, however, eat my apples with gusto, carving out the worms. (My tree, by the way, was supposed to be a particular crab apple but turned out to be mislabeled, as plants increasingly are in the American nursery trade, and proved to be a regular apple of quite acceptable quality. One learns to roll with the punches.) The true choice, in my experience, is ruined fruit or poisons, and since we deal lavishly with Mr. Magruder and the other grocers, we do not worry much about our vegetables or fruits, and ours are allowed to be as wormy as they please.

We come now to bugs. Bugs have never bothered me nearly as much as rats, say, which are wall-to-wall in this capital because there is no interest in controlling them in the sewers or other rat-breeding places. Bugs have also bothered me far less than fungi and blights generally. If the only thing the matter with a plant is bugs, I perk up wonderfully and consider the battle won.

I do not have Japanese beetles, and must therefore be forgiven for not caring much about them. In the winter we feed every starling between Savannah and Bangor, but we stop in the summer. The poor creatures eat the beetles. I have never believed they like them. One makes do. Once chemical fumes from paint chased the birds away for several days and we had zillions of beetles. When the fumes passed, so did the beetles.

I spoke of trade-offs. I do not grow anything that has to be sprayed. Any rose that can't make it without sprays is a wretched weakling, and if anybody wants to coddle the thing, fine, but I don't. Why should I, or any other sane man, be expected to expose my hound to poisons in the garden? She eats blueberries in season, she commonly sniffs everything, she buries bones, she eats grass; I am responsible for her, and she is not going to eat poison as long as I am around.

As you approach middle age, however, you learn how little you know, and a great modesty sets in, or at least it has done so with me. I do not think I know everything or even anything much. I am not interested in persuading the world at large to my way of thinking. I do not spray bugs, to return to the opening point, and I am not going to spray bugs, and I am in no way heartbroken for gardeners who do spray bugs with no beneficial results. Spray if you please. There are plenty of rich chemical corporation folk who can answer any question you may have about sprays. They, after all, are the ones getting rich off you.

❖ The Beauties of the Black Locust

This week I was walking home from the subway with my brain in neutral, as usual, when suddenly I saw a large old specimen of the black locust tree. I was astounded. Of course, all my life I have been around locust trees and of course always admired them as possibly the most beautiful of American trees, but I suppose I hadn't thought of them lately. Coming on this one unexpectedly, just looking up and seeing it, stirred me. It was in full bloom, its lower branches hanging almost vertically.

Everybody has his own notions of what smells wonderful and what does not. I think the scent of wisteria and locust (which is much like wisteria) is irresistible. Other people cannot stand that fragrance. My mother deplored the smell of the night jasmine and tuberoses and didn't like magnolias much either. My wife cannot detect the smell of the sweet olive, one of the most intense of floral scents, and of course many people (including Thomas Jefferson) do not like the smell of boxwood.

Sometimes the smell from the locust flowers perfumes the air, but not often. When conditions are just right, and there are a lot of locust trees, and the sun has just gone down, and the air is damp, a whole countryside will be perfumed. But usually you have to go right up to the flowers and sniff.

Coming to this tree suddenly, I was transported to the Virginia countryside that I drove through early in May years ago on the way to my wedding. As everyone knows, a perfume that is come on suddenly and without anticipation has the power to evoke not only old memories but also a particular place and a precise instant. This past winter I smelled a croup kettle for the first time in half a century, I guess, and was surprised at how it took me back to my childhood of such kettles and mustard plasters and hot olive oil squirted through my nose (a treatment then regarded as superb therapy for something or other).

The locust, to get back to it, has several drawbacks as a garden tree. Its brittle branches come down in storms, and often it perishes before reaching great stature. Old locusts often go hollow in the trunk with a huge hole to the outside. Sometimes black snakes live in the hole; sometimes wild bees do. I prefer the black snakes, as some of those black bees are far less gentle than the Italian bees and more likely to sting. All the same, I have never been stung by what we used to call German black bees (which may or may not be the correct name) and have been stung often enough by the gentle Italians. A moral there, probably. Whereas the black snakes never bother anybody and of course should never be killed.

But the locust tree, with or without ornamental fauna inside it, has feathery or ferny leaflets and a most beautiful crown of branches, often arching and sometimes almost weeping. Even when the skeleton of the tree is rigid and gaunt, as it sometimes is in old trees, the delicacy of the leaves makes it graceful. The billowing trees seen in the pictures of the French Romantics are unidentifiable because they never grew on earth, but the locust comes closest to giving the effect of strength and airiness.

Sometimes tree experts, as they are called, say terrible things about the locust, or call it a weed tree. I imagine one such expert chose the city-planted trees of my block, which are almost the only trees I have ever seen that are positively ugly. They are some rare kind of maple, some variation on the Norway, that manages to have no beauty of flower, bark, summer foliage, fall coloration, or winter skeleton. And they die over a number of years, getting uglier by the season. The one nearest my house has a nice hole in it that the woodpeckers work on from time to time, and I believe the city will finally cut the wretched thing down about the time the hole is big enough for some woodpecker to live in, which might have been one redeeming aspect of the tree.

Locusts (to turn from ugliness to beauty) grow quickly and in pretty dense stands, so it is (or was in past years) easy to collect fence-post–size young locusts very easily. The wood is said to be resistant to rot. When I was a tad and commented on the great locusts precisely outlining some fields, an old man told me the green fence posts had sprouted years before. A tree authority, however, later told me that is not possible. I imagine it is not only possible but was a common thing, since not many farmers would go around planting locusts at the edge of fields.

❖ *Keeping Envy Out of Your Eden*

It is not important for a garden to be beautiful. It is extremely important for the gardener to think it a fair substitute for Eden.

I recall a garden I used to see this time of year in which the specialty was irises and roses — there was nothing else, so it was dull much of the year. Furthermore, the roses were pruned to two inches above the graft every winter and therefore were not fine large bushes, and the irises were all outmoded and superseded varieties. But the gardener, a professor, was enchanted with it, and as the years went by I began to understand better what he saw in it. Finally, I thought it beautiful too.

This week, in my own garden, I have been rather content and do not envy anybody. Out the kitchen door I first come to a seven-foot plant of the purplish red rose 'Roseraie de l'Haÿ' and then a six-foot bush of 'Mrs. Anthony Waterer', followed by a large shrub of 'Hansa'. These are all in tones of red and purple, then a tall columnar yew. Back of these roses, peering around the side of the yew, is an eight-foot shrub of the rose 'Sarah Van Fleet'.

Just at 'Hansa' there is an arch with a young plant of the rambler 'Seagull' to the right, rising from a little thicket of the old Siberian iris 'Perry's Blue' (there are vastly better Siberians now, so don't go looking for it). On the left, growing on wires on the arch (if wires are black they are invisible) and tangling a bit with the purplish rose, is a plant of the wild-looking smallish clematis 'Venosa Violacea', which is purple with a white center or white with a purple edge.

You go up a step and encounter an old red hybrid perpetual of unknown name, possibly 'General Jacqueminot'; it certainly smells like it. Here you have a fine patch of hosta leaves that the slugs for some reason have ignored this year.

There are other arches with roses too young to need mentioning, as they do not yet count in the picture, but one of them is blooming with the pink 'Blairii No. 2', a Bourbon rose of 1845 that an old gardener (I have read) used to call "Old Bleary Eye." It has a fine and strong scent, and its large full pink blooms fade at the edge so they seem to have a white rim.

The yellow rugosa rose 'Agnes' comes next, with only the last few flowers remaining, as it is the first of all to bloom, with its leaves that remind me of crinkly parsley, and a smell both sweet and with a bitter undertone, no doubt inherited from its parent, the Persian *Rosa foetida* (stinking rose — a somewhat rude name not justified at all). Along the right side of this walk are occasional bushes of the red 'Dr. Huey' that I do not value and keep chopping down, but they persist in sending up a few long branches, and in bloom their very deep coloring is attractive.

I also have a couple of grapes that used to be allowed to make garlands along iron-chain catenaries, but I took against them and butchered them down to standards, like little trees on four-foot trunks. They are there simply to provide foliage, and require continual pinching and snipping through the summer to keep them from turning into great vines again.

Young plants of the white rose 'Moonlight' are in bloom, along with the purple rambler 'Violette', but these are still too small to show up much, and the same is true of 'Mutabilis', an old five-petaled China bush rose that I hope to persuade to grow eight feet and thus cover an arch. It opens orange-buff and dies off a raw carmine and is showy in a large plant in full bloom, suggesting great butterflies. There is also a pillar rose, the reddish 'Gladiator', that I do not esteem but do not feel like grubbing out, and I see that the first bloom of a purple clematis, 'Lord Nevill', is open, though it is not yet large enough to smother the rose.

At last, on the left, comes a great favorite, 'Jaune Desprez'. It is powerfully perfumed of musk, and was an 1830 effort at producing a yellow Noisette rose (its parents are supposed to be the common

China daily rose and the yellow China tea rose, bred along for a couple of generations). The result is a rose about three inches wide, in clusters, of which five or seven are open at the same time. They are a rather definite pink as they open, but then become shot with apricot, buff, and orange, winding up an amazing blend, rich but soft and not assertive. Naturally I have it in a place that will never accommodate its full growth — it wants to romp about for fifteen feet, and I have it tied to a wooden post seven feet high. But of course it has no intention of pretending to be a pillar rose, and has shot out stems ten feet here and ten feet there, invading a peach tree and generally making a most lovely nuisance of itself.

On the fence is the long-suffering (twice she has had fence people putting in new posts in her middle) 'Madame Gregoire Staechelin', which is the handsomest of all pink climbing roses — one great burst of ruffled pink two-toned flowers lasting a couple of weeks, then nothing till next year. Invading her from the north is the wild-looking rambler 'Polyantha Grandiflora', which has beautiful shiny leaves and massive clusters of orange-scented white blooms not much larger than wild blackberries. Not many would want it.

In the pool are small pink and yellow water lilies, and here and there are fragrant pink cluster roses, five-petaled and no larger than a nickel, that I raised from seed. I call this rose 'Ginny', though it is hardly possible that its parents are 'Madame Gregoire' and 'Dortmund', the two I crossed. For one thing, it is a musk, with the styles fused in a column; the Lord only knows what its parentage is. Anyway, it has a musk fragrance and it reblooms a time or two during the summer — it is not worth notice, except I like it because I raised it. It is supposed to bloom (my view, not the rose's) with the blue clematis 'Perle d'Azur', which has made a great tangled mass of far-flung stems. The clematis begins as the rose is going out, but usually I have the two together for about three days.

It is all rather jungly, and I spend my life pulling out bindweed — if I did not, it would overrun every plant I have mentioned. For this week, at least, I see none of its disgusting twining stems on any of my babies.

It is agreeable to waddle about in one's own paradise, knowing that thousands of others have better gardens with better thises and thats, and better grown too, and no weeds at all. To know this and grin as complacently as a terrier who just got into the deviled eggs, and to reflect that there is no garden in England or France I envy, and not one I'd swap for mine: this is the aim of gardening — not to make us complacent idiots, exactly, but to make us content and calm for a time, with sufficient energy (even after wars with bindweed) to feel an awestruck thanks to God that such happiness can exist. For a few days, of course.

JUNE

THERE ARE SURPRISES that keep the gardener amazed through the years. Today as I was admiring my small purple clematis, 'Etoile Violette', I was astonished to see two great cecropia moths mating as they clung for dear life to its wiry stems. The cecropia is the largest moth of the eastern states, and if you hold one, it will cover the palm of your hand with its outstretched wings. They are fairly gorgeous in brown, red, purple, with a band along the wing edges of buff yellow, and some large spots like eyes; the spots are translucent and present an eerie effect if you see light shining through them.

Earlier in the day one of the moths had freed itself from its cocoon, which I had been watching for some weeks in the house, sprinkling the beast every week or so with a little water and hoping it would emerge from its case of leathery leaves just as well indoors as out. It did. After it had exercised a bit, and tried its furry red legs until they gained some strength, I set it on a wire outside, in a place I hoped would be safe from birds and other dragons. The moth climbed leisurely upward until it reached the tangle of purple flowers, then stopped. It showed no signs of working its wings in preparation for flight.

Within a few hours another cecropia arrived. The one I freed was a female, and the visitor was a guess what, and they were observed mating over a period of twelve hours. They arranged themselves so only their bodies touched; their wings did not, and when they felt like it, both moths raised and lowered their wings leisurely, all four of them fully visible.

This sort of thing enlivens the gardener's week.

❖ *Tea Roses: The Secrets of Success*

My handful of tea roses has not been worth growing, I could say with some justice and some feeling, but then, this is their first year. They arrived late in February and I potted them in two-gallon plastic pots and kept them under fluorescent lights, then lugged them in and out of doors until April, when they were planted in their permanent positions. If I did it again, I'd ask for the plants to arrive in November or early December. I'd plant them outside immediately. Or if they came in February I'd plant them out then, even if a few leaves had sprouted. My experience over the years is that plants are safer outdoors, never mind the weather, than they are indoors under my care.

All the dozen or so tea roses are on their own roots. That is, they were raised from cuttings. Some of the young plants were only four inches high. Three of the plants are doing well. 'G. Nabbonand' is an ivory-flushed soft pink, 'Blummenschmidt' is a yellow that fades to white, and 'Beauté Inconstante' is a carmine that can vary surprisingly. I have hopes that the rest will come on strongly next year. Tea roses are tender to cold, but many of them should be hardy in Zone 7, or as far north as Philadelphia or the warmer parts of New England, along Long Island Sound or in sheltered spots on Cape Cod.

This may be the place to say that hybrid teas, which are descendants of tea roses, are supposed to be hardier, yet they frequently die outright in spring freezes. Hybrid teas are often injured or killed in winter also, if they have been weakened by losing their leaves from black spot the summer before. You might think that rose societies would plant a couple hundred hybrid teas together and see how they fared. This would be a more valuable activity as far as the ordinary gardener is concerned than the production of rose shows and lectures on which chemicals to use against bugs and blotches.

There is nothing wrong with hybrid tea roses if they are well perfumed and resistant to black spot (though very few, if any, have these virtues), and there is nothing wrong, or at least nothing utterly evil, in raising scentless roses that require weekly spraying and that can be sheltered and shielded, patted and pampered, until at last an enormous flower can be entered in a rose show. Without rose shows, and without roses that have never been outside an intensive care unit, society would suffer. Many people who are now safely occupied with the care of roses would be loose on the streets.

All the same, I have no intention of futzing about with sprays every week. Parts of the nozzle always get lost or the line gets clogged or the pressure is wrong. To say nothing of the chemicals themselves. Surely we get enough of them in the air, in food, and in drink. We hardly need to fetch in more for the garden.

China roses also resist black spot, and while I have seen a diseased leaf here and there on such China roses as 'Old Blush', 'Madame Laurette Messimy', and 'Mutabilis', it is nothing that requires spraying. And my tea roses are clean as a preacher, cleaner than some.

I should think up some scheme to keep wind off the roses in winter. It's not a question of heat — it's as cold at the bottom of a wall as in the open garden — but you escape the wind-chill factor. A Delaware grower of tea roses once told me that the secret of success with tea roses in Delaware was protection from the wind, not from cold. In any case, if tea roses are killed to the ground by cold, they usually or often (not always) come right back from below ground in the spring when they are on their own roots.

This is not to say that normal gardeners should pitch out hybrid teas and floribundas in favor of teas, Chinas, and Noisettes simply to have black-spot–free plants, for I know many gardeners would be disappointed with them. All the teas, Chinas, and Noisettes have relatively small flowers, and most of them are not strongly colored. When they are "yellow," it is ivory yellow and it usually fades. When they are "red," they are far from stoplight intensity. Furthermore, the Chinas are sadly deficient in scent, ranking well below hybrid teas in that respect. Besides, I am aware that lovers of the tea roses are not normal, and as a group probably do not read *People* or *USA Today*. Lovers of the tea rose are not superior; we merely require superior roses.

There is such a thing in the breeding of wild plants (and all garden roses are of course derived from wild roses) as going just so far and no further in increasing the size, concentrating the color, or emphasizing some other attribute. And then, when the best balance of beauty and health has been reached, you stop. With roses, that balance was reached in the tea roses. They are not good roses for zero-temperature winters, but where winters rarely reach zero, they are worth a try. Even if you have to get small plants, even if you have to persuade your heavy clay loam to lean toward a sandy loam, even if you have to worry about wind in the winter, even if —

You don't have to worry about black spot.

❖ *The Right Bedfellows for Roses*

Often in a small garden in town there is not much sun for flowers, and often the best spot is given to a bed of roses. But this means not much of anything else, and the question arises of what can be planted under the roses or around the edge of the bed to get more variety than roses offer. Rose fanatics, needless to say, easily persuade themselves that this plant, the rose, has a wider range of color and form than any other plant, which is nonsense. They even go so far as to imagine that the bush itself is handsome, though the average rosebush is as nearly ugly as anything in the floral kingdom.

Sane gardeners long ago decided the rose is worth putting up with, but they never deluded themselves that a bed of roses (on, say, July 27) is any great ornament to the garden or to the human spirit. So they started planting other things beneath and around the rosebushes. Some gardeners, besotted beyond redemption by the perfume of the rose, hold that no leaf or root or even shadow may be allowed within a stone's throw of the precious plant, but as I say, the sane gardener with very little space for gardening is not of that opinion, and some great gardeners have stuck in all manner of small plants with the roses.

The trouble is that the roses are much easier to manage if the soil about them is bare or heavily mulched. You cannot dump five inches of horse manure (to encourage the roses) on top of the bed if you have planted many little oddments among the roses. And it may as well be admitted that weed control in a rose bed is far easier if no other little treasures share the space with the Queen of Flowers. And if spraying is to be done, it is a far easier and less perilous task if the ground is not alive with dozens of plants that do not much like chemicals.

The great gardener William Robinson of Gravetye worked it out. He said a mulch of manure was "unnecessary" and aesthetically displeasing anyway. He said you should dig three feet deep, put in a few cartfuls of manure before planting the roses, and forget manure thereafter. Thus (he went on) the surface of the bed would be free for violas and "any little plants to spare." While this advice still makes rose nuts faint, it worked well for Robinson and has worked well for many other gardeners.

You have to use common sense. If the rosebushes are jammed in sixteen inches apart (and three or four feet is more sensible in this climate if you expect the bushes to grow to full size), then of course there is not going to be room between them to plant anything else.

Often in a bed the rows of roses are three feet apart, and I have had happy experiences planting daffodils down the middle. At the edges of the bed, many bulbs may find a home, to bloom before the roses come into heavy leaf to shade them too much. Snowflakes and snowdrops, fritillaries of several kinds, many sorts of tulips, hyacinths, blue starflowers, grape hyacinths, crocuses, and squills may be used. If you are slightly mad — and many town gardeners are driven to it by the lack of space — you could even have some of the smaller crinums, such as 'Carolina Beauty'. I have used large white trumpet lilies, which do not take up much space, though their stems after blooming are not very ornamental, poking up among the roses. Still, you do the best you can and make do.

Many small or smallish plants may be fitted in about the edges of the bed. Really small things like Johnny-jump-ups, which happen to be very tough, can actually be grown beneath the bushes, right up to the stem. Such small violas as 'Bowles' Black' are not showy but still very interesting and can be stuck in all kinds of crannies, though with me they never were permanent and had to be sown anew every year. Various sedums can often be obliged to grow beneath the roses if the shade is not too heavy.

But getting back to the edges of the bed, rather than the part of the bed right under the bushes themselves: a lot can be managed. Not everything, but a lot. It may be that instead of a rose bed in the center of the garden, there are some big shrub roses along the side and not much else. Well, many hostas are useful for planting in front of them, to keep down weeds entirely. Equally weed-inhibiting are several epimediums, and such a planting saves the gardener from having to crawl among the thorny shrubs to get weeds out.

Suppose a few flowers better than hostas are desired. Few things are as dandy as pinks, especially varieties of *Dianthus plumarius,* though I have never grown pinks at all well. They like gritty limestone soil and do not care much for my heavy clay loam, high humidity, and acid ground. Still, many gardeners simply add some sand and succeed with them, and their foliage is as attractive as their flowers.

Other quite sensible candidates for the rose bed are soapworts, especially *Saponaria ocymoides,* and I would allow in a favorite plant of mine, the double bouncing bet, *Saponaria officinalis,* though most gardeners would think it too coarse or weedy. Also many alliums, perennial geraniums, foxgloves (where their tall spikes have space to display themselves), lamb's-ears, bergenias, catmint, and other mints. Uncommon and pretty long-blooming perennials from South Africa are *Diascia elegans* and *D. cordata,* rarely offered except by California nurseries.

Some artemisias are good, with their gray leaves, though others are too tall and weedy. The lady's-mantle, *Alchemilla mollis,* is flawless, and so is rue, an old herb said to be useful in flavoring cheese. As one who has often nibbled rue, I cannot imagine it would be edible, but its small, almost blue leaves are as elegant as anything in the garden. So is the gray lavender cotton, *Santolina chamaecyparissus.* Various thymes are pretty and low, and if taller herbs are appropriate, there are always lavender, rosemary, and caryopteris.

Coming down to earth again, you have the utterly ground-hugging ajuga, or bugleweed, and you can get it in a purple-bronze –leaf form too. Equally purple and equally useful with roses are coral bells, or *Heuchera* 'Palace Purple', and somewhat similar are the foamflowers, or tiarellas.

Small veronicas are a good source of blue; so is the sun-loving, nonclimbing *Convolvulus sabaticus,* with flowers of sky blue, pretty with the Mexican fleabane, *Erigeron karvinskianus*; and what's wrong with sweet alyssum? More robust but still manageable are snapdragons (not the giant ones that reach four feet, mind you) and evening primroses and nasturtiums. Two small wild irises are useful: *I. cristata,* with blue or white flowers, only four inches high, from our own woodlands; and the foot-high blue or white *I. tectorum,* from China.

Many poppies, such as Shirley poppies, are fragile enough to fit in with roses, though the great opium and Oriental poppies may be thought too competitive. At a corner of the bed you might allow yourself a mullein, such as *Verbascum bombyciferum,* which does make rather large gray-white fuzzy rosettes on the ground (a minimum of two feet in diameter) but is marvelous for very thin gray spikes six feet or more in height, with small yellow flowers.

The rose campion, with rich magenta flowers and gray-white foliage, is to my mind as beautiful as a plant gets, but more delicate taste may prefer the variety with white flowers. A workhorse flower and handsome enough too is the fourteen-inch-high *Vinca major,* and the white ones with red eyes are cool-looking in summer heat. Verbenas in various colors are old favorites, though the gorgeous scarlet ones may overpower the roses, so lavender or blush may be preferred.

Surely this is enough for a start. If you carpet your rose beds with some of these dandy plants, however, don't let any of your rose-fanatic friends in the garden.

❖ I Try Not to Do Stupid Things

Every gardener knows that sometimes a plant refuses to grow, even when well planted and cared for in a seemingly perfect spot. On an arch I have a plant of the 'Late Dutch' honeysuckle on one side and thought it would be good to have our native wild scarlet honeysuckle on the other. The best red honeysuckle for a garden is the hybrid called *Lonicera heckrottii,* which is rose outside and vaguely yellow inside. It is fragrant after sundown, though not as fragrant as I would like. It blooms freely throughout the growing season. I did not plant it on my arch, partly because I have grown it elsewhere. Often we pass over nearly faultless plants for something that to us is a bit less common.

Hardly anybody grows our native wisterias, as they are far less showy than the Chinese. The Oriental wisterias exceed our natives in size, color, and perfume. For all that, I have a young white native wisteria that has grown three or four feet up a stake I set beside it. The time will soon come when I must decide how to manage it. Naturally, I planted it where I do not want a twenty-foot mound, but in the way of gardeners I say it will take several years for the plant to show its stuff, and in the meantime maybe something will work out.

I try not to do stupid things like planting a wisteria where there is not space for it, but this one is rare. I have never seen it anywhere except the Henry Botanical Foundation at Philadelphia, and although it is inferior to Chinese and Japanese kinds in showiness, it is still a splendid sight in bloom.

I have spent most of my life, I often think, whacking back the beautiful fleece vine, *Polygonum aubertii,* which grows atop a sort of open wooden screen or clairvoyee that has three arches cut in it. The idea is for the vine to luxuriate along the top, hanging down here and there, but I am supposed to see right through the arches. The vine takes only three weeks to send its high growths right to the ground, completely blocking out the eight-foot arches. In theory all I need to do is use the hedge shears on it occasionally to keep it from making a solid wall of green, but in practice it takes longer to do these things than one thinks. If I had any sense, I'd dig up the vine and replace it with clematis or honeysuckles or some of those roses with pliable long stems. But nowhere in the book of life does it say that a gardener is supposed to have any sense.

❖ Foliage for Nooks and Crannies

It's a question not just of a plant's beauty but also of its performance where you are growing it. Nothing is handsomer, in a two- or three-foot-tall way, than the blue grass *Helictotrichon*. I gave it a place of honor at the side of the main fish pool and for several years it was splendid, but then it went back — the shade increased just enough to discourage it. On one side the clump of *Hemerocallis citrina* waxed great and on the other side some Japanese anemones started flourishing, and the competition was resented by the blue grass. It is now gone.

Back by the garage I had another ornamental grass, the striped *Miscanthus sinensis* 'Variegatus', which rose to ten feet with its longitudinally white-marked leaves. One spring I dug it up and moved the main clump four feet back of its original site, against a garage wall. It has not really flourished since. It now grows to six feet and no longer flops on a path (the reason for moving it), but the base of the garage wall is drier than its original spot and the grass resents this.

It is important to remember when you plant something against a wall that the site is probably drier than you think. Extra watering, especially the first year, may be in order. And even when the plant is fully established, it may miss the wetter conditions of the open border and, like the striped grass, restrain itself. Of course, this may be all to the good.

You might wonder what to do when a favorite plant weakens or dies. You can replace it, obviously, but in the case of my blue grass there was no point in that, since it failed through competition from other plants near it and from a slight increase in shade. I shall do nothing but let the daylily and anemone fight for the space.

On another side of the pool there is a strip three feet wide and twelve feet long running against the raised side of the pool. There are some wild native swamp irises in a clump, and for a while there were some foxgloves and bunch primroses. They all got tired — they need renewing by seed or division every year or two. It was an ideal site for the yellow moneywort, but the moneywort did not know it and refused to grow. Some eau-de-cologne mint wandered over from its home twenty feet away, and some wild buttercups with their varnished yellow flowers have appeared — a lovely weed, except that after blooming it dies away and the ground is bare in the summer.

What could be grown in such a space, dampish and half shady, between brick pavement and the concrete wall of the pool? Well, if I moved the wild irises (*Iris versicolor* from a local swamp) out and dug in a barrowful of leaf mold and some peat moss and let it all settle down nicely, I could grow *Kirengeshoma palmata*. This is a perennial posing as a small shrub, growing three feet or so, with leaves like a Norway maple's and hanging yellow bell or trumpet flowers in October. I have never seen a photograph of it that would make anybody desire it. And yet I have never heard of any gardener who, seeing it in the flesh, did not want it. It's not the leaves and it's not the flowers — it's the way the plant is put together with such refinement and freshness.

Well, it could replace the wild irises. Then there is a raised brick step that should be kept clear of plants, though sometimes cymbidiums in their pots are stood there for the summer over my dead body. Beyond, the narrow planting strip continues. I shall certainly keep the clump of merrybells (*Uvularia grandiflora*), one of the prettiest of our woodland plants. It shoots up in the spring with foot-high stems decked with leaves like a Solomon's seal and a set of hanging pale-yellow bell flowers at the top. It blooms in April, then dies down. It will not stand competition from other plants jammed up against it.

All the same, I am considering several plants for this strip. The virulently poisonous veratrums are all desirable, including our native *V. viride*. They boast pleated, broadly lance-shaped leaves in spring, and possibly no other garden plant rivals them in beauty then. Unfortunately, slugs like them even better than hosta leaves, and the veratrums can soon look wearier and wearier. When fully established after a few years they send up a flower stalk to four or five feet, packed with tiny flowers that are insignificant, but because of the masses of them along branched stalks they are conspicuous. Especially desirable is *V. nigrum,* with flowers that look almost black. The plant is extremely hard to find, and you have to weigh its slow growth and often ratty appearance in summer against its singular beauty of leaf in spring.

Some of the smallest astilbes would also do in this spot, especially *A. chinensis* 'Pumila', which reaches two feet in height, with feathery magenta plumes of flower in summer for some weeks. The color will not suit those who dislike magenta, but the foliage is divided like a coarse fern. If you wanted to be reckless, you could try the taller *A. tacquetii* 'Superba', which reaches five feet, with great feathery magenta plumes. I once noticed it in a Maryland suburban garden blooming with daylilies and coveted it. I have heard this plant called *Spirea superba.* For general purposes, for most gardeners, probably the commoner *Lythrum virgatum* 'Morden Pink' will serve as well to provide the small blast of magenta desired (by me, at least) with daylilies.

The plant formerly known as megasea and now bergenia is the one with cabbagelike evergreen leaves and (sometimes) magenta flowers of no great consequence in the spring. You grow it for the foliage. It is especially handsome against stone, and since it sits right on the ground like a cabbage, you want to give it a forward position. I used to grow the esteemed variety called 'Ballawley Hybrid', which loathed the dry shady spot near a box bush that I chose for it, having seen it doing nicely in England in such a site. Here I think it can stand a bit richer living and more water.

The chief point is that there is never any shortage of wonderful plants to try, even if a favorite plant in the garden dies. There will never be time or space enough to explore the riches of garden plants.

❖ *Daylilies by the Bouquetful*

Often I wonder how gardeners fared before the great surge of modern daylilies, as these are a mainstay of the summer garden. Most varieties last three weeks in bloom; that is, a well-grown clump with many flowering stems will show flowers for that long. And there are early and late kinds, so that the season is a good two months or even longer if very early and very late kinds are chosen. Daylily flowers range in size from one and a half to eight inches, on stems one to six feet high.

Still, it is a mistake to think the daylily will take care of itself like a weed, as the wild *Hemerocallis fulva* does. That is the burnt-orange kind you see along alleys and at abandoned sites, where it persists along with chicory or dandelions. The garden daylilies will not stand such weed competition. They are disease-free and insect-free, for all practical purposes, but they are not made of iron. They require sane treatment, and they flourish with good treatment.

Once a breeder of daylilies gave me a single fan of a new variety, and I planted it in a washtub-size hole in which I had mixed several spadesful of peat moss and some leaf mold. I watered it during dry spells. By the third year I was astonished at the number of bloom stalks and at the almost tropical appearance of the clump. But the same plant, if set in raw clay, would grow only slowly and would flower only sparingly.

If daylilies are planted in a border, as if they were roses or tomatoes, the gardener will soon see how magnificently they flower.

In Washington the height of the bloom season is the first week of July, as a rule, and I count on them from late May or early June into September.

At the National Arboretum there used to be a huge clump of the 1947 red — near scarlet — called 'Lochinvar', which nobody grows nowadays. It was stunning. Many old daylilies, now superseded by later and usually better varieties, can nevertheless make a great show in the garden when allowed to grow into ten-year-old clumps.

Another thing: many daylilies that never won important awards from the American Hemerocallis Society are beautiful. Such relatively unnoticed kinds as 'Abstract Art', 'Rubens', 'Swiss Strawberry', 'American Craftsman', and dozens of others are excellent. This does not mean that award winners are no good. They are in many cases superb. The Dykes Medal winner of 1974, 'Winning Ways', remains as beautiful a light yellow as it was the year it rightly won the highest daylily award, though it is a back number in gardens where the newest varieties are sought.

The beginner with daylilies should visit local gardens featuring these flowers and jot down the names of varieties that seem most beautiful. Then consult a price list, and buy only the cheapest. That is the way to begin. New varieties from breeders, which in many cases are surprisingly similar to inexpensive older sorts, often cost from $35 to more than $100 for a small division. It is absurd for the gardener with a moderate budget to buy them. Within a few years most of them will be out of commerce, and the few that win a place in catalogues once their novelty has worn off will be cheap indeed. Often daylilies can be bought from a local hobbyist, and there are dozens of specialist nurseries that ship nationwide.

Once I got a phone call from a true daylily fanatic, Steve Webber, who must grow one thousand or maybe two thousand varieties at his nursery outside Washington. He wanted 'Gusto', an old (early and good) bright red. I wondered why, as he had dozens of reds considered much better. But of course he knew, as all gardeners soon learn, that every variety has a singular charm not quite duplicated by any other. He still grows some of the very earliest introductions as well as current novelties, and I was more than pleased when he published *Daylily Encyclopedia,* a soft-cover, 168-page book with notes on culture and time of bloom and a modest annotated list of "one thousand grand daylilies and a few others." It may be ordered ($13.95 plus postage) from Capability's Books (phone 800-247-8154) or Webber Gardens, 9180 Main St., Damascus, MD 20872.

One final thing. While daylilies will not grow in a swamp, they grow unusually well in places that are well drained but never dry out. I had a clump of the yellow 'Sunblest' just below a stone that marked a ten-inch drop in the land, and it bloomed three times a year. I moved the clump to a good but less damp spot, and it blooms only once a year. Sometimes we gardeners are too clever by half and cannot let well alone.

❖ *Small Gardens: The Big Picture*

Most gardeners just start digging holes and stuffing things in (such as the fastest-growing maples and poplars they can find) and are perfectly happy for about three years. Then it dawns on them that the garden does not excite them much, and this revelation usually occurs about the first time they see pictures of a fine garden — constructed on other principles. "I could have that," they say, correctly. So here are a few things to know about designing a small (quarter-acre or less, and usually much less) garden.

First, keep the center open. This is not a rule and you will not necessarily go to the bad place if you break it, but when you do clutter up the center of the garden, be aware of what you are doing and be willing to live with it.

Do not think in terms of small details. Your average gardener — and I am an authority on what the average gardener thinks, since I am he — begins by worrying about crocuses. *Let's see,* he says, *where will I put the crocuses, and which are the best colors, and —*

No. The crocuses will take care of themselves; you will have no problem fitting them in once you know what the garden is to be, and what its bones are, so to speak. But if you start with details and just keep going till there isn't any space left, you will not have the happiest result possible.

Start by drawing the garden on a piece of paper — not the crocuses, but a map of the land. There is such a thing as measuring it and finding it is thirty feet wide and eighty-one feet long. Get graph paper and allow one square per foot (or whatever scale suits you best). Show the ugly concrete walk, as it exists. Show the garage or the garbage-can stand and all the lousy Norway maples and everything else that is too large to ignore and that already exists. Don't worry about the walk. There will be time later to widen it, or crack it up and put it elsewhere, or whatever you have in mind. First show it on the map. Then do a similar map showing what you would like if nothing existed. Show it without the wretched maple, for example.

It is just here that some gardeners falter and say gee, they don't know what they'd like, exactly. Which brings us back to the first point, keeping the center open. Let it be a lawn or (especially in tiny gardens) a pavement of cut stone or brick or concrete or whatever, and confine the plants to the edge of the property. Sometimes a lily pool will do well in the center, if the space is large enough, but usually it is a mistake to fill up the center with flowers.

Around the edges, where there is a fence or wall, you put your main plants, not necessarily your favorite ones. You may love peonies above all else, for example, but when you make the green walls of your garden you cannot use peonies. You use small hollies, yews, pink locusts, maybe a sassafras, maybe some large shrub roses — whatever you like. The idea is to have enough bulk of plants to enclose the land, but not so many that you feel you're in an airtight box. You want (probably — there is plenty of room here for your personal notions) enough winter green to look cheerful through the dismal months but not enough yews and hollies and so on that you think you're at a memorial of some sort.

If you have kids who need play space, allow for this from the beginning. If you have dogs, allow for them. Needless to say, I never knew of a gardener with dogs who actually did this. You do the garden and let the dogs out and wonder why they bed down on the sprouting irises or (in my case) gnaw the thorny rosebushes. So you should work it out.

In a small garden, one walk is usually enough. Do not be afraid to make it six feet wide, if that looks right. Whether it looks right can be found by sticking stakes along the proposed route, or garden hoses, and then looking at it for a few days. Walks are usually too narrow. Four feet is about the minimum for wheelbarrows, humans, and other irksome necessities.

Having planted (in imagination) the perimeter with shrubs, and having left the center open for a lawn or pool or sitting place, decide where your other passions fit. Peonies, crocuses. Maybe in a large bed along and in front of the shrubs; maybe in a long, wide border; maybe in front of the garage (decently clothed with climbers and exalted by an arbor with a bench).

Just here the center may collapse. Often that is the best place for the roses or peonies or whatever it is you are keen on. Then use part of the center for them, keeping your larger things still along the perimeter.

Do not be afraid to try things out, preferably in your mind and preferably with the aid of temporary sticks and poles moved around until you get the effect you like. For example, although you are admonished to keep the center open, do not hesitate to try temporary poles to see how you'd like a summerhouse, maybe overlooking a pool in the center. Or see how it would work to cut the center up with a hedge or columns or posts with vines on them. Or a small copse of thorns and aralias and andromedas and azaleas.

If you wind up planting things in the center (which, you recall, we were going to leave for lawn or quiet sober pavement), then consider a swath through the middle of the copse, or the beds, to keep the view open and uncluttered all the way to the end of the garden. This is usually a garage or an alley gate, but much can be done to improve its impact.

Often if the garden is relatively long and narrow, it can give a happier effect if it is broken up by screens crossing it, or hedges, or grade changes with two steps. You do not do more than give the illusion of a barrier; you do not want the cross-hedges or screen to coop you up in a tiny space. But something you can see through or see over will often give a sense of spaciousness that will surprise you, so do not hesitate to experiment.

There are two big things. Try never to do anything too grand. Avoid hints of pretentiousness, such as bronze urns in front of a modest wooden garage. Question yourself at every point about whether you are being silly. This is hard to do. Every single inch may be planned to a fare-thee-well, and the garden may be complex beyond the dreams of a computer, but it should not look fussy. Avoid too many accents. If you use a piece of sculpture or a small pool or a magnificent Oriental maple (it's a base canard that I dislike maples — just big ones in small gardens), then let it speak for itself and don't hem it in with a dozen other eye-catchers.

You cannot have everything. A bog garden should not adjoin a desert garden, and a paved and tiled courtyard garden cannot also be a wild stretch of sand barren. Things should not contradict each other in the garden, and ingenuity or fertile imagination should be reined in sufficiently to avoid a restless and asinine clutter.

Avoid wiggles of line, avoid walks that do not go directly to their destination (if they have no destination, then have no walk to begin with), and avoid making things too small. If you have a lot of wonderful old jugs, you do not necessarily have to set them all over the garden. Trade them in for one big jug and set it on a serious-looking plinth and make it the focal point, and give up forever all the other little jugs. You get the point.

✦ *The Grand and Noble Magnolia*

The magnolia of the South, *M. grandiflora,* is a tree that many southerners have mixed feelings about, and certainly I do. No tree makes a house gloomier, though I have a somewhat depraved friend from Valdosta who has planted these great evergreen trees all about her house and is happy now that they are getting large enough to defy any light of heaven. In England, where gardeners are likely to do unreasonable things, this magnolia is a favorite for training flat against a house wall. The labor of whacking it back over the decades is, of course, incalculable.

The "correct" way to grow this magnolia is to plant it in soil heavily laced with peat moss, then give it plenty of water as a young tree. It grows with astonishing speed when well treated. The lower branches are left alone; indeed, the whole plant is left strictly alone, so that within twenty years you have branches touching the ground. Inside them you find a thick duff of leathery leaves, dead birds, and other things, but at least from the outside the tree presents a noble appearance.

In bloom it is not very showy, as the enormous white suede-finished flowers are sprinkled here and there like raisins in a muffin. The two-day-old flowers turn brown, the petals (usually about nine) fall off, and attractive five-inch velvety cones form, with cells for individual scarlet seeds. These hang out on slender threads before dropping. I am not sure which birds eat them — probably mockingbirds, which eat everything, including the sourest crab apples.

At my place I noticed a young magnolia perhaps twelve years ago, evidently from a seed dropped by a bird or other beast. It had only two leaves, then four, and I certainly did not want the great magnolia in my small garden but of course did nothing about it. In time, I thought, it would provide plenty of fine leaves for bringing into the house — the leaves look good in an old silver wine cooler. The tree is now maybe twenty-five feet high and has bloomed well for several years. In our happy climate of warm summers, all magnolias begin to flower while still bushes, though in cooler places gardeners allow twenty-five years for them to start.

Although I do not love this magnolia for my own garden and would much prefer to see it at a distance on somebody else's property, I do admire the individual flowers. On June 9 I cut one that was fourteen inches in diameter. In measuring, you lay a steel tape measure across the flower, not flattening the cupped petals out (which is cheating) but just measuring the diameter as the flower naturally reposes. Two days later I cut another one, which measured thirteen inches. Usually the magnolia flowers are ten to twelve inches across, so these were noticeably larger than usual.

There are several, perhaps many, named varieties of this species, some said to be hardier than others, and some larger or smaller than average. My bird-planted tree is as good as any, and I might as well admit that a fourteen-inch flower is impressive.

The fragrance of this magnolia is both obvious and overrated. It is powerful enough to scent an ordinary room if the windows are closed, and is agreeable enough, with an undertone of turpentine and an overlay of lemon. It is not at all sweet in the way night jasmine, tuberoses, gardenias, or regal lilies are. And certainly there is none of that even more beautiful scent of pinks, lilacs, alba roses, or lilies of the valley.

As many persons of the North have infiltrated the American South and are cutting magnolias for the first time, a word about the blossoms' behavior as cut flowers may be useful. First, you cut them in bud, but not too early. The buds begin as fat cones in a furry covering, then turn into rather narrow, tall white cones. Sometimes when cut at that stage they will open the next morning.

If you cut them when fully open, it is hard not to damage the petals. If you cut them in globular bud Sunday evening when the sun is going down, they will open Monday and be beautiful until Tuesday night. On Wednesday they will be solid brown. On Tuesday they will shed their large stamens, about a handful of them, all over the table or floor. That is why southern women always put them on stone tables or at least large tables, so the stamens can be gathered easily. If they fall on a carpet, they do no harm that I know of but are a nuisance to clean up.

Some excellent people are color-blind. Once I was summoned urgently to see a magnolia with shell-pink flowers. They turned out to be simply brown and aging blooms, but the proud owner of the tree saw them as rich, pure pink.

Like water lilies and buttercups, magnolias evolved long before most other flowering plants. I am not sure whether dinosaurs nibbled or smelled them, but at least they bloomed in full glory before any ancestor that could be called human.

Formerly, before people learned they could frame paintings of solid yellow, or stripes or spatters, all southern art shows included paintings of this magnolia. It was thought all the best people had such watercolors somewhere about the house. Fewer such magnolia portraits are produced now, I believe.

The common name of this magnolia is said to be "bull bay," and I have often wondered about it. A bull bay would simply be a bay of large or coarse aspect, much as a horse chestnut is a coarse echo of the chestnut. The thing is, I never once heard the magnolia called a bull bay, not in more than half a century of listening. I wonder if "bull bay" is an invention of literary Yankees.

JULY

A BRIEF and anguished note: it was wrong ever to boast of having rid the garden of bindweed. I deeply regret having boasted in this way, and have been severely punished by a sudden flourishing of bindweed from roots that have been grubbed up the past ten years.

It is not generally known, and botanists do not believe, that bindweed sprouts not from little fragments of root (as the books say) but from earth that once held those roots. It is possible that bindweed and nut grass are the only two forms of life that come into existence spontaneously, without seed or root or anything else.

Generally it is believed that life on earth began with single-celled organisms and things like algae. My own view, which will probably become gospel once more research in paleobotany has been conducted, is that bindweed and nut grass came first. (The latter, fortunately, is not serious as far north as Washington.) And will last longest.

There are people who have seen bindweed at six o'clock on a soft August morning, decked with its small white morning-glory blossoms and swelling green seedpods, and who think it beautiful. Of course it is beautiful. So are coral snakes and cancer cells under a microscope. I don't see what beauty has to do with it. Country people rightly call bindweed "devil's guts," and never mind the beauty.

It was formerly the custom when grain began to be harvested on August 1 to have a "harvest lord" who organized labor in the fields. He had various duties and prerogatives, as a queen of the May does. You could spot him in the fields because he alone wore a wreath of bindweed on his hat.

And here ends my effort to be civil about bindweed. I honestly did think I had eradicated it from the garden, but all is vanity and vexation of spirit and it seems to me that I might as well never have bothered. There are confirmed cases of gardeners' moving away merely to escape the bindweed.

❖ A Home for Fish and Flowers

A fish pool with water lilies gives the gardener greater returns for less labor than anything else, but like some other things you can think of, there's more pleasure in doing it right than wrong. Here are some things to keep in mind.

The pool should always be in full sun. It usually isn't, and usually you can make do, but keep firmly in mind that water lilies like full sun from the time it rises till the time it sets.

The pool should be twenty-four inches deep. Not sixteen. Not twenty. It would be nice if it were thirty or thirty-six or forty-two inches deep, but you need a permit for anything over twenty-four, so I settle for that.

The pool should always be larger than you think is right. Ten by twelve feet is a good size, since it is small enough to be manageable for the handy home fellow to construct and large enough to offer some scope for action.

Sometimes the gardener looks at a new concrete pool and thinks it ugly, looking into the water and seeing the raw concrete sides. If you wish you may paint the interior black, following the instructions on the can of special aquatic paint (do not use ordinary house paint). It is an exercise in folly, however, since the sides of the pool will soon look black even if the gardener does nothing whatever. Painting the inside of garden pools is good for paint companies, nothing more.

The water of the pool should look like a dark crystal. It should not be murky and disgusting. On the other hand, it should not be perfectly clear. Some gardeners install filter systems to keep the water absolutely clear. I do not use such a thing myself and would not have one if it were free and somebody came out to install it. The few I have seen in operation have not worked, and nothing has thrived. Also, there is nothing uglier in the garden than crystal water with filter systems clearly visible. These gewgaws are fine if one happens to have a purity fetish, but they are not necessary or desirable.

The pool should have "seaweed" in it — I mean oxygenating grasses that live beneath the water. The common ditch grass, or Babbington's curse, or elodea, does quite well. You can buy it from a fish store (aquarium dealer).

In late April the water of the lily pool may turn greenish or the color of turbid coffee. By this time the water lily pads will have reached the surface, though they will still be small. It is best to do absolutely nothing. Within a few days (maybe weeks?) the pads will become large enough to shade the water and hence to shade out the small organisms that make water green. I have never put any chemicals in my pools in any garden and do not intend to.

The fewer pipes in a pool, the better. I have none. Once a year I drain my pools by siphoning the water out with a garden hose. I start the hose, go back in a few hours, and it's done. I do not understand what drainpipes in pools are for. The place where the pipe passes through the concrete is a common source of leaks. Pipes are said to keep pools from overflowing. How odd. My pools never overflow, and if they did, what would be the harm? A pool needs to be drained no more than once a year or once every two years. Then it can be scrubbed with a broom and filled up again.

Pools look best when full to the brim. Some like a water level two inches beneath the pool rim. Why? I keep mine so full that another cup would make them run over. But then, I do not like sparseness. Fill yours to whatever level you think looks best, and let it go at that. But try it full, and see if you don't like the effect better.

In this damp capital, it is virtually unheard of to have to top up the pool with water. Water evaporates, but in Washington we get more than enough daily rain to fill it up again. If the level should fall an inch or so below your notion of perfection, run the garden hose in for a few minutes and all will be well. It is *wrong* to keep flushing out the pool or running a lot of water into it.

There is an odd passion for covering the floor of the pool with dirt, in which the water lilies are planted. This is indeed a natural sort of thing to do, and water lilies flourish and fish love it. But the first time you drop the car keys into such a pool you will comprehend why it is not recommended to cover the floor with mud. No, keep the floor absolutely bare, and set the water lilies in individual tubs of earth. It is then much easier to clean the pool when the time comes, and you can keep the water lilies under control better. I confess the fish are happier with a mud bottom, which they love to root about in, often muddying the water. If you have plenty of slave labor, as from sons not yet seventeen years of age (after which they are useless, generally), you may have a mud bottom; otherwise, stick to tubs.

How many water lilies you grow depends on the area and the vigor of the plants. In a ten-by-twelve-foot pool I have three quite vigorous hardy pink water lilies, each growing in a half-barrel, plus one or two miniature water lilies. Obviously, the same plants, if grown in buckets instead of half-barrels, would make smaller plants and would cover less of the surface with leaves. The smaller the vessel of earth (within reason), the more water lilies the pool will hold. But I like all plants to grow to their limits, as a rule, so I must content myself with fewer plants.

Ducks and water birds generally eat fish. It is what God tells them to do. Raccoons also eat fish and gnaw on water lilies, as the devil instructs them. Turtles eat fish, but a couple of smallish native painted turtles will not do much damage in a garden pool. Also toads, which do no damage at all, are splendid, though they are only in the pool in the spring, when they breed. They have coal-black tadpoles. As they grow legs, they hop out of the pool and fend for themselves on land. Do not keep dumping them back in the pool.

You do not need anything like as many fish in the pool as the pool will maintain. A ten-by-twelve-foot pool will suit 120 goldfish six inches long. Such a number is absurd. Twenty to forty such fish will give the impression that the pool is positively alive with them.

Golden orfe have never liked me. They grow quickly, and their tubular torpedo outlines, swimming rapidly at the surface, are wonderful. They die out. They do not like hot summers. If you try them, put in at least a dozen at once; they like to swim with their kind in a little shoal. But I suggest common goldfish.

Cheap goldfish are as good as costly ones, often better. I bought mine from an aquarium house that sells "feed fish." They are about two inches long. Within a year, if you put twenty of them in a roomy pool, they will be five or six inches long. Even their first year, the year they are babies, they will spawn and have gangs of fry. The books say they will not, but they will.

Common goldfish are best. In our beautiful climate they turn a gorgeous red. But the black moors, the fantails, the comets, the shubunkins, all do well outdoors. The fancier sorts, such as celestials, should not be entrusted to such a rough-and-ready environment as the outdoor pool.

Dragonflies are glorious. They lay eggs in the water, and these hatch into miniature dragons that eat tiny fish. The dragonflies should not, in my opinion, ever be destroyed, despite their diet.

❖ A Water Lily's Lust for Life

I have an old white enamel pan four inches deep and the size of a large book that I am forever growing something in, and at the moment it holds an infant water lily.

Such brains as I have seem to leak out about the middle of April, which is when I start thinking of Projects, none of them very ambitious, but most of them foolish, if judged by strict constructionists. This year I got a packet of water lily seeds and sowed them in May in the enamel pan. Nothing happened indoors, and as I left for England early in June I set the pan outdoors, on the rim of the fish pool. The pan has two inches of dirt and two inches of water, and when I left there was no sign of a sprout.

When I returned there was only one tiny water lily, the whole plant no larger than a penny. You had to look closely to be sure it really was a plant and not a fragment of leaf that had blown in.

There were rainstorms and crows and probably coons and certainly the terrier and the hound trotting about the pool rim. And there must have been days when the water was all evaporated. So I expected nothing at all, and really I should have fifty plants instead of just one, if the seeds had been properly cared for.

But there it is. In recent weeks it has grown a good bit, and it now covers a surface of perhaps sixty square inches. Now I must lift it and set it in a four-inch pot of good tenacious rich clay. Somehow I shall devise a way to set the pot in the pool so four inches of water covers it, and then (if all goes well) I shall move it once more, into a plastic pail, and set it back in the pool with about ten inches of water over it. It may very well bloom by late August or September. Then it will come into the house for the winter (about November 11) and go back in the pool the end of next May.

There is not much sense in growing water lilies from seed. There are dozens of kinds of great beauty already on the market, and my little seedling is almost certainly not going to be as handsome as most of those I already grow. But it has lovely olive-green leaves with blotches and streaks of bronze, and tiny as it is, it has that lust for life that is such an attractive feature of all water lilies. It will probably be a semidouble pale lavender with about twelve petals — you notice that I have already got it blooming in my head.

This past week I got an old pottery pitcher and cut fifteen water lilies to put in it for a buddy who has been going round and round with doctors. There were some big yellow ones ('Charlene Strawn') and a couple of shell-pink ones shaded carmine on the outer petals

('Pink Opal'), and then the rest were blues or lavenders or purples (the wild *Nymphaea colorata,* 'Pennsylvania', 'Blue Star', 'Mrs. Martin Randig', and 'August Koch').

This year I do not have the wild blue *N. gigantea,* probably the most beautiful of all water lilies, because of some mishap or other over the winter, when I stored the dormant tubers in a cookie tin in damp sand. But I do have the rose-colored 'Mrs. C. W. Ward', which somehow got into the same tub as 'Pennsylvania', though I have no recollection of planting her there. I suspect she is from a tuber that was sort of half rotten, which I threw into the pool to float loose until I thought of something, and instead of floating she sank down in the whiskey barrel holding the blue water lily. Anyhow, there she is, and looking very smart, thank you.

I do not like water lilies in a vase very much, unless there is some good reason for cutting them to give to somebody who doesn't grow them. They are much handsomer just rising out of the water of a fish pool. It doesn't take many of these flowers to make a great impression on the gardener. The only thing I hold against them is that they are not open early in the morning, which is the best time to poke about the garden in hot weather. If they were only open at 6:00 A.M. it would be well, but most of them are not open till about 9:00 (which of course is 8:00 A.M., real time). 'Mrs. Ward' is always the first by a good hour or so, then 'Pennsylvania', and then the others. The miniature yellow 'Helvola' doesn't open till nearly lunchtime, and they all close well before sundown.

Still, there are blazing hot weekends. The thing to do is make some onion sandwiches, preferably with Walla Walla onions if you can get them, or maybe Vidalias, or just plain onions in a pinch, and get them very cold in the icebox. Cut them in half and seize two and dash out about noon, munching rapidly to prevent heatstroke. You can then view the water lilies for two or three minutes by the clock, then dash back into the house. This can be repeated a number of times on Saturdays and Sundays while the onion supply lasts. It is not the most leisurely way to view your water lilies, but perhaps the most exciting way. Such a pleasure is totally unknown in all the great gardens of Britain.

❖ *A Word about Petunias*

I often wonder why gardeners shy away from petunias, the single best annual for sunny places. Of course, any plant that grows like a weed yet does not take over the garden and that revels in real heat is likely to be looked down on, a phenomenon I attribute to Yankees.

It's true that the marigold is ubiquitous, though it loves heat like the petunia, and I have no explanation for its popularity, since it has no color range, no perfume, and no grace of habit. It's just one of those things.

The best petunias are the semiwild ones that spring up as seedlings, in a neat color range from off-white through lavender and off-rose. Often they are strongly scented at night. Usually their foliage is sublimely healthy if rather ordinary-looking, and the plants have an obliging way of flopping down or creeping up according to site. There is one chain-link fence I often visit in the summer just to see the wild petunias gaining on it as the hot weeks pass.

I suppose there are petunia fanciers, but if so, they are not as conspicuous as the connoisseurs of other flowers. Certainly the petunia comes in enough colors, shapes, and habits to deserve specialist interest. Some people admire the globular doubles. Fifty years ago I first encountered these, raised in my town by an excellent leathery lady who was also the only one around who grew lavender really well. She loved to say the petunia seeds cost more than gold — a great deal more, since gold was about $30 an ounce.

There are huge ruffled petunias in a full range of colors, and petunias that stand up modestly and decline to sprawl. Other petunias are born to stand on balconies and lean over in case anybody is serenading. Red and yellow are two relatively recent colors in petunias, and among the most sweetly scented are some of the dark blues, which really look blue. And the pure whites are very good for gardeners who wonder if the best people do not always go for white.

These are annuals that can be plopped in even in hot weather, and very satisfactory they are for sticking in where daffodils grow, covering the ground nicely with flowers until November.

❖ Plants That Need Wet Nursing

There was a faucet out the back door in a pleasant square bit of land, fifty feet on the side, where the hounds spent the day, and as the faucet was always being used for buckets of water, I wondered what plant might take advantage of the dampness. I tried a ginger lily, *Hedychium coronarium,* and it flourished, though the spot got only half a day of sun. It bloomed heavily every summer for some years. This ginger lily has highly perfumed white flowers, somewhat like small canna blooms, along the stem, which reaches three or four feet.

This year, not having had ginger lilies for years now, I planted one, and it is making slight progress. I grow it in a whiskey barrel in full sun, and fear I do not water it enough. How curious gardeners are; they grow a plant to perfection, then after a few years grow it again. But instead of giving it the same conditions in which it flourished, they grow it in utterly different ways (dry soil in a barrel instead of damp soil beneath a faucet) and whine that it is not doing very well.

This ginger lily, by the way, is hardy in Connecticut along Long Island Sound if given wall protection and shelter from gales. It dies down in winter, when the root should be heavily mulched, but it grows anew in the spring and blooms beginning in July or August.

Another lover of damp soil or shallow water is papyrus, the elegant Egyptian aquatic from which paper was made and from which the word *paper* derives. It is better if grown in heavy, rich soil with three to six inches of water over it, but will grow in saturated soil, as beneath a faucet, provided the spot is sunny. The ordinary papyrus of the Nile reaches seven feet or so in much of America, and even greater heights in tropical places. For many gardeners, the dwarf papyrus, which grows to perhaps three feet, is easier to manage than the tall form.

For a long time I did not know how to keep papyrus over winter, as one hesitates to carry over a plant so tall and vigorous in the average house, which lacks not only space but also strong light. I used to bring the tub of papyrus indoors, but it always wound up in the basement, where there was little light and where I was neglectful in watering it, so it was always dead by the end of April, when it should have been set out in the pool again.

But now I know that if the old papyrus stems with elegant green tufts at the top are allowed to mature and die naturally, they fall over into the water, and little plants root at the tips. If these are potted in a six-inch plastic vessel (the kind you keep leftovers in, in the icebox) with about four inches of dirt in the bottom and three inches of water over the dirt, they will survive the winter nicely. The plastic container is set in an east-facing or south-facing window. There is only one problem: it is easy for the water to evaporate in so small a vessel, and if this happens more than twice, the papyrus will die. In other words, you have to keep an eye on it and not let it dry out. But this is much easier than trying to bring a large plant through the winter.

Less thirsty than papyrus but still a lover of damp earth is ligularia, and the commonest form of it is one called 'Desdemona'. The plant has leaves the size of salad plates borne on stems a foot high or so, and they are oily, glossy green flushed with purple-bronze. Flowers are produced in hot weather on stems up to waist high, and these are intense saturated yellow, like vitamin-full daisies. Some people cut off the blooms as being of neon brilliance, but they are handsome if you like intense hues, as I do.

Other good plants for damp spots are the various rodgersias, which I keep meaning to grow and never get round to, though I admire them greatly. These have leaves divided like a hand with fingers, a foot or more in width. Some of them are bronze, others green, and the flowers are not important.

I love the butterburs (*Petasites japonicus* 'Gigantea' is the one I think I have), with leaves that in rich damp soil are more than two feet in diameter. In summer heat, these great leaves wilt during the day but revive as the sun sinks. They are coarse, and few gardeners, I think, would like them. In the Orient people sometimes pull the leaves off and use them as umbrellas in downpours, discarding them after dry shelter is reached. Monet, who painted his water garden so often, grew butterburs at the end of the Japanese bridge sometimes shown in his pictures. These plants like damp soil but do not grow in water, I think.

The only trouble with all water-loving plants is that with rich soil and full sun they are not the only plants that flourish; weeds do too. It is important (as I am here to swear) to keep coarse weeds and such creepers as bindweed and Virginia creeper away from your damp-loving plants; otherwise, they will take over and smother your treasures.

❖ *Madame Galen*

The most spectacular summer-flowering vine in Washington and in much of temperate America is a hybrid trumpet vine called 'Madame Galen'. Its parents are the wild American and Chinese trumpet vines. The Chinese parent of the Madame is *Campsis grandiflora,* which is hardy at least in Zone 7, but which is not so handsome as the hardier Madame.

Recently I saw this vine growing over a small wooden arch at the sidewalk entrance to a front yard, and while it was pretty, it is as vigorous as a wisteria and requires a massive framework to support it, or else a high masonry wall to which it clings by rootlets, like ivy. In July my plant, which grows up a west-facing brick wall, is about four feet wide and eighteen feet tall. It hangs out from the wall three feet. It had thirty-eight clusters of flowers open at once early in July, each cluster the size of a small or medium-size cantaloupe. Trumpets about four or five inches long and one to two inches wide at the throat make up each cluster, and there may be twenty of them, with perhaps ten open at once and the others coming along later. The color is soft orange hinting at apricot, a strikingly rich color with a flush of red on the outside. The foliage is emerald green, and the leaves are divided into handsomely cut leaflets.

I want my plant to turn the corner and grow on the north wall, and for some years I have bent some of its long growths and fixed them in place. For a season they will stay there and I think *Ha,* but the next year the part on the north wall is dead, while on the west wall the growth is vigorous.

This may be the place to say that this trumpet vine (and all others) will grow up the wall to reach any house roof and will get under tiles or shingles and lift them up. You simply keep your eye on it and prune it back before it takes the roof off. "Prune it back" is not altogether easy when the vine is at the roof line, as I well know, and one solution is to cut the vine back to about nine feet from the ground in the winter. It will still reach the roof in a matter of several weeks, but it does not tear the tiles off if you keep after it every winter.

It grows exactly as our native trumpet vine (*Campsis radicans*) does but does not produce as many suckers. Even so, the Madame is capable of drooping a stem or two into a basement window well, traversing it and coming up to root in earth on the other side of the well, then growing up the wall. So you have two enormous plants. But it is certainly easier to control than our native wildling, which is such an ornament to farm fences but which can send up babies all over a small city garden.

The trumpet vine has no perfume, but then it has no fungus or bug ailments either, and hardly any plant equals it for attracting hummingbirds. Their nests are like half a golf ball, almost impossible to see even if you know where they are, but one year we had three infant hummingbirds sitting on a trumpet vine twig for several days before they gained enough strength to take off permanently. They sat in a row like tiny owls.

Ants are fond of trumpet vines, and you may wish to dislodge them if you cut the flowers for the house. You simply submerge the flowers in a bucket of water. The ants float off, then you empty the bucket on the ground; no need to kill the ants, which do no harm to anybody or anything, but some people prefer for them to stay outside.

'Madame Galen', when treated well, blooms fairly steadily from the end of June to October, usually reaching a peak about July 15 in Washington.

❖ For Dragonflies, a Place to Rest Their Wings

Dragonflies do not like to land on water or hover a quarter-inch above it, nor do they like water lily pads that float on the surface. They like reeds; they like to perch as eagles.

We have a circular steel tank eighty inches across that had to be moved a hundred feet, for the simple reason that it was too far back for us to keep up with the things going on in it. What a heroic effort. The tank was lined outside with cement and tiles, and these had to be removed. The water had to be got out — I have never seen the pool drainpipe I could trust, and I will not have one. The gunk on the pool bottom clogged the siphon hose, so bailing was necessary. And moving the monster without damaging too many plants was tricky; I fear several daylilies will never come back.

So much for dark nights of the soul. Within days, in its new site near the kitchen door, the pool had a look of settled age. It sits atop the earth, but the crinum and other hefty plants already conceal its naked sides.

In the pool life races ahead. Three tubs of dwarf water lilies are blooming their heads off, and some further tubs of water lilies from seed are a daily pleasure as they grow in strength. The goldfish are much at home after a ten-day sulk; they now swim in two schools and sample the waterweed.

One morning I saw a blue dragonfly sitting on a lily pad. That evening it was floating in the water, dead. I fished it out, as often insects seem drowned but revive nicely if dried off, but this one had perished. Promptly I found a thin bamboo stake and stuck it in a tub of water lilies, and since then no dragonfly has drowned. Almost any minute of the day you will find one of these elegant insects perched on the stake.

The lesson to be learned today, therefore, is to provide either reeds or a stake for your dragonflies. They do not bite or sting people, a thing I mention in case you are a city ignoramus and thought they did. They are nothing but good and fair, a sufficient reason for summer to exist.

❖ The Lessons Never Learned

Sometimes we planted irises in November and about half of them bloomed the next May, but the proper time for planting is July through September. In the South we used to lay the rhizomes from dealers on the floor in some out-of-the-way room (when houses were big enough to have out-of-the-way rooms) until late August, then plant them out. If planted in July they sometimes rotted, if the weather was both very hot and very wet.

Where I am now, the ordinary tall bearded irises are not a success. The combination of not quite enough direct sun, a heavy clay loam, and iris borers has wrecked — killed — my several attempts at growing them. But of course a gardener never really learns. The other day someone kindly offered me some irises planted about twenty-five years ago, and for unfathomable reasons I took eight of them, with no idea what the varieties are, and planted them at the edge of some young tea roses — there seems so much room there.

In fact, I know better than to do this. The irises, if they grow at all, will require intense individual weeding. There is nothing like a clump of irises to attract wiry grass from ten counties around. It gets in among the rhizomes, the tops of which are right at ground level, and is for all practical purposes impossible to get out. Fortunately, irises should be lifted and divided every three years, and the grass can be got out then. But having the irises at the edge of the tea roses will make weeding the roses difficult.

I know the further temptation: in October the irises will occupy no space worth speaking of, and the old leaf fans will be trimmed back, and the new fans of leaves will be only an inch high and will stay that size all winter. So why (the gardener demands to know) should there not be a fringe of violas or pansies just outside the irises, which are just outside the roses? Planted in October, the small pansy plants will have "plenty of room there," and many of them will bloom off and on through the winter. How nice.

In March everything will start getting out of hand. Chickweed and other nuisances that have bided their time during January will suddenly be all over the place. The pansies will quadruple in size. The tiny iris fans that were an inch high will start flourishing to their full height of two feet. The roses will leaf out, and a few vicious weeds will come through the mulch around them.

The gardener on his knees will begin to cope.

The gardener learns (or at least perceives) that roses are far easier to take care of if the gardener can get right in among them, which means no irises and certainly no irises edged with pansies. Irises also are easily managed with a broken-off butcher knife for the weeds, provided they are in a bed by themselves. But if you have to do balancing acts to get among them, or find there is no room to maneuver (the flourishing pansies on one side and the rapidly growing thorny roses on the other), it is almost impossible to keep them in good shape.

But that is nothing compared with what happens the first summer, after the irises and pansies are finished blooming. Then in rich garden soils billions of things start to grow, beginning with bindweed and coarse vicious grasses brought in with the horse manure. The weather turns hot, there are days of one hundred degrees, and no gardener is going to be out in those irises then. What he does is admire his tomatoes and cucumbers and beans, or else sit by the fish pool and admire the water lilies and angel trumpets. He will say he has to get the dead leaves off the water lilies or dip out some fish, which are increasing their numbers too rapidly. The hours will pass, agreeably enough, and the Bermuda grass will begin to work its way through the irises. After Labor Day, struck with chagrin, the gardener will attack the irises as best he can, but he doesn't want to pull up any iris roots to get the grass out, lest he disturb the plants and they fail to bloom next spring.

You can always spot a wise and experienced gardener. He does not jam things in. He knows that the roses have plenty of space in August, and he knows that they will need every inch of it within the next two years. He does not plant "just eight little clumps as a token" of irises or anything else. He does not squeeze in a few dozen pansies four inches from the row of irises. He knows that the irises will bulge out like a series of bushel baskets, and he knows that every pansy will turn into a twelve-inch globe. So he does not get started on the course that will lead to frantic adjustments. He has, alas, more sense than I.

❖ *The Perfect Order of a Bulb Garden*

I know the gardener is not on fire for crocuses at the height of summer's heat, but this truly is the time to order those spring-flowering bulbs that you plant in the fall.

In my youth, when school was out, I would often go swimming and come back in midafternoon, and for several days I'd flop on the bed studying bulb catalogues. Eh, it was good to be a no-account wastrel teenager. I could never make a suitable list of bulbs to buy, as the first cut always vastly exceeded my money. I still regret the breeder tulip 'Jesse', which always got dropped at the last, so I have never grown it, though I suppose I could afford it now.

The occupant of the small garden will want the following bulbs, maybe not all the first or second year, but eventually. The thing is to make a beginning, then add as the years go by.

You will want crocuses, and if you order your bulbs in July (though it is still legal to dawdle and get them at a garden center in September) from a catalogue, you can begin with the beautiful October-blooming light lavender-blue *Crocus speciosus*. Once I ordered all the fall-blooming crocuses I could find, but none of the others was quite as pretty or quite as reliable or anything like quite as cheap as *C. speciosus*. Plant as soon as you can get the corms, in August or September, and you will have these flowers with brilliant orange stamens in October. Needless to say, plant them where you will see them every day, especially if you get only a handful. No point having them if they're lost far out in a garden border where everything else is winding down for fall. These crocuses are good in front of azaleas beneath oaks.

Other crocuses bloom in spring, or February-March, which gardeners in Zone 7 consider spring. In a manner of speaking. Particularly reliable are the varieties of *C. chrysanthus,* which range from white through light blue to buff and chrome, with good sound names like 'Lady Killer'. They are all small, half the size of the somewhat later-blooming Dutch crocuses.

Some gardeners are snobs and love only wild crocuses, but I have learned to love the big fat Dutch crocuses also. They often start flowering only a week later than the *chrysanthus* varieties, and the first one is usually 'Yellow Mammoth'. It is full rich yellow verging on orange, and in Zone 7, at least, you can have it with rich purple giant crocuses and solid white ones and whites with blue feathering.

Before the shrubs crowded them out I grew big purple and yellow crocuses on a bank by the sidewalk, well within toddler range. And said toddlers invariably picked the purples and cared little for the yellows. Odd, but then people are.

Another spring-flowering bulb worth attention is the grape hyacinth, or *Muscari*. Ages ago I bought six little bulbs of *Muscari tubergenianum* and then got going on this pretty family. There must be at least eight kinds of grape hyacinths readily available. Somewhat similar is the flower that used to be called *Muscari azureum,* which now undoubtedly has a different name. I used to pay two dollars per hundred for it, but I see nothing like it listed for that price now. It has little down-pointing tightly packed florets of sky blue. All of these are well worth growing, even if only by the half-dozen. Ruskin once wrote of their "cells of bossed and beaded blue," which is well put.

Hyacinths are heavy grand flowers with one of the sweetest of all scents. There are many new kinds now, and an odd thing is that they are relatively less costly than they used to be. Blue, white, and pink are the standard colors, though now you can get them in red, yellow, and purple. Sometimes the bulbs persist for fifteen or twenty years, producing smaller flowers that are even prettier and more graceful than the heavy spikes produced by new bulbs.

One of my hyacinths, a purple, set two stems full of seedpods, but they contained only aborted seeds, a kind of false pregnancy. There was a family dalmatian that used to have false pregnancies, then without warning in late middle age produced twelve splendid pups. So I shall keep tabs on the hyacinth.

With bulbs we have hardly begun. Daffodils, including small wild ones as well as the great bouncing beauties of the show bench, and tulips, including many wild ones and endless garden varieties with enormous flowers in a fabulous color range, to say nothing of lilies (of which much must be said) and squills and anemones and chionodoxas and snowdrops and snowflakes and fritillaries and trout lilies — these and more are all planted in the fall and may be ordered from catalogues now for fall delivery. Don't forget alliums. Don't forget triteleias. Don't forget any of these flawlessly condensed wonders that unfold, like those Japanese paper flowers in water, every spring.

AUGUST

I HAD AN AUNT who once had a marvelous garden but who wound up in a flat on California Street during the war, and I asked if that wasn't pretty hard to accept.

"Not at all," she said. "I thought it would be terrible not to have my garden, but to my surprise, I don't mind it in the least. The thing is, when I had my garden I almost wore every plant out just looking at it intimately, all through the year. If you have to give up your garden, it's easy — when you have to let it go — if you've really put yourself into it all those years. It's much harder if you haven't really loved and enjoyed it when you had it."

My aunt fetched up at the last in another beautiful garden off the Carolina coast, with two-hundred-year-old live oaks and indigo buntings all over the place and sweeps of marsh grass on the horizon and old camellia trees. So it all worked out.

But I think she was right about not grieving over it if you really got everything out of it during your tenure. Proust used to say that the things we bitterly regret are the things we never let our hearts long for.

❖ *A Bulb I Can't Resist*

I never met a crinum I didn't like, though I know these handsome bulbous creatures with tall stems crowned by lilylike flowers are not hardy much north of Washington. Still, many of them will stand occasional freezes to zero. Once in Memphis the temperature dropped to twelve below zero and I feared for the crinums, just sitting out there unprotected, without even a mulch or a nearby wall for shelter, but they bloomed as well as ever the following summer.

Some of us have rather a peasant strain in gardening. I do. I cannot easily resist plants with enormous leaves or huge bulbs — so much material there. Crinum bulbs may weigh twenty pounds, though the ones I grow have bulbs the size of oranges or perhaps small grapefruits. You plant them in spring or summer, and it may as well be said that it often takes them several years to start blooming. This is the third summer for three of my crinums that have yet to flower, but once the plant clumps up a bit from offsets, there is no stopping it.

Many years ago I read that the pink 'Cecil Houdyshel' was outstanding, and I bought it. It grew for many years in my former garden, and now I have it again. You should know that digging up crinums is very like digging up the concrete foundation of a garage; that is, get somebody else to do it if possible. For me it has never been possible, so I leave crinums alone forever and ever. The lesson here is to think quite a time before you plant the bulb, as the chances are that it will be there the rest of your life.

Crinum leaves tend to be long and floppy. The white 'Carolina Beauty', a free-blooming small white with clusters of fragrant trumpets on eighteen-inch stems, good for cutting, has neat leaves that stand up, and they are narrow. But most other crinums can soon occupy a circle five feet in diameter. The leaves may flop flat on the ground. If they are near a path, the gardener will trip over them twenty times a summer, and if well back in a garden border, the leaves will lounge happily over any plant within hollering distance, and the gardener will wonder what ever happened to those phlox or irises or whatever it was that used to be there.

Once in Canterbury I saw a traffic circle planted solid with *Crinum* × *powellii,* a good rich pink with stems about waist high. Kent is pretty cold and sunless, by standards of continental America, and I was surprised at how well the plants bloomed. I decided they did not need full sun here in Washington, and I now know they will take some shade. Not like a camellia, no, but they will grow on the east side of a house where they get no afternoon sun, and they will grow in the open garden in competition with grapes and rambling roses, as long as the sun falls on the crinums maybe five or six hours a day. They are not plants for woodlands.

They are grand plants for big wooden tubs or barrels that are stored in garages or sheds over winter; thus gardeners north of Philadelphia should be able to manage them. Do not ask me how you move barrels of heavy soil in and out, with or without crinums. Obviously, wheeled contraptions and inclined planes are involved, and hearty sons if you have them.

Crinum latifolium I no longer grow, though perhaps I should. It's the old milk-and-wine lily of my childhood. It produces great fleshy seed clusters, bulbils the size of radishes, and these grow to blooming size in a couple of years. I often saw the white flowers, somewhat drooping, the central rib stained deep madder, in fat clumps in old parts of southern towns, and the sight of them (they bloom off and on from May to October when they feel like it) used to reassure me that winter was a long way off.

Most crinums are fragrant, though I do not much like the smell. It suggests thin sugar syrup to me, though I notice specialist growers of crinums keep insisting that it is the headiest perfume in the world. It is nothing like the tuberose or night jasmine or gardenia, so don't count on it too much. Still, it gives the nose something to do.

A yearly mulch of rotted manure along with long slow drafts from the hose every two or three weeks in summer will inspire the crinum to grow more heavily. Though once they start performing, there is little incentive to prod them into even lusher growth.

❖ Beauty or Black-Eyed Susans

Sometimes the gardener misses those rich effects he has seen in great and famous gardens and hopes to capture them at home by planting more and more bright flowers. It's true that the more flowers you try, the more you see the richness of the world of plants, but it may be disappointing when the mere plenitude of things in bloom does not accomplish the richness that was hoped for. I shall give an example of richness.

There is a large box bush, and in front of it is a fat clump, three feet across, of the plain white Japanese anemone (*Anemone japonica*), and at the base of the anemone and box is a wide drift of the fall crocus, *Crocus speciosus*. To one side is a violet aster with small leaves and flowers no larger than a thumbnail, and this is reflected in a small fish pool with common and gorgeous red goldfish and a plant of the water lily 'Yellow Pygmy', which bleaches to cream color in the sun.

There are two critical elements, the big box bush (the most important) and the quality of the few flowers. To show by example, this effect of great richness and elegance would not be achieved if instead of box you used forsythia (which is equally green), and instead of the anemone you planted black-eyed Susans, and instead of the blue-lavender crocus you used the smallest marigolds. That might be pleasant enough, and the colors would be fine together, but the effect would suggest a farm roadside — and that, too, is good — and you would never achieve the elegance of the first example.

Some might argue that no plant is beautiful or ugly in itself, but all depends on how it is used. Those who think so are wrong. It's true that all plants are beautiful in their particular way, and of course it's unarguable that all plants are more beautiful or less beautiful depending on what is around them. Without wishing to enter a metaphysical debate, I will simply say that the first arrangement of garden plants will strike almost anybody as more beautiful than the arrangement of forsythia, black-eyed Susans, and marigolds. That is so even though the second arrangement is flawless in itself.

There is no ultimate reason, to put it another way, that a rose is more beautiful than a goldenrod, but then we are not ultimate creatures and gardens are not ultimate expressions. As a relative matter and a practical matter (and to save the gardener a lot of time and disappointment), you can take it as a fact that some plants are going to seem far more beautiful than others in a garden.

What is the difference — and you're on your own to decide — between two short random lists of plants that I will give, and why are those of the first list so much more admired than those of the second (keeping in mind that those in the first list can be unimpressive when used in silly ways and those of the second can be highly impressive when used to show them at their best)? First consider irises, daffodils, lilies, roses, pinks, larkspurs, pansies, violas, verbenas, trout lilies, crocuses, water lilies, anemones, squills, tulips, hyacinths, ivy, figs, azaleas, hollies, honeysuckles, tuberoses, lobelias, and sweet peas. Next consider perennial mallows, black-eyed Susans, goldenrod, marigolds, trumpet vines, dahlias, kolkwitzias, altheas, poinsettias, passionflowers, night jasmines, bananas, privets, zinnias, tithonias, sunflowers, daisies, and gloxinias.

In the second group there are plants no gardener would be without; certainly I yield to nobody in my fondness for trumpet vines, night jasmines, and zinnias. But all of them lack the inherent beauty of plants in the first group. A dahlia can be gorgeous, but it is never going to be an iris, and that's that.

Some plants of the second group may be far better in some parts of some gardens than plants of the first group — a bed of tuberoses may not be nearly as effective or give as much pleasure to the gardener as a bed of daisies. All the same, larkspurs are more beautiful than marigolds, though both are common and easy to grow.

I think any gardener should give much thought to what are the most beautiful flowers and should concentrate on them. In practice, I have had to expend more effort on bananas and night jasmines than on trout lilies, ivy, or honeysuckles. The mere fact that many less beautiful or less elegant plants are worth even more bother than many plants superior to them in beauty does not prove anything about beauty.

I have had dogs of exceptional beauty, and from animal shelters I have had dogs so odd-looking that people laughed to see them, and my present mongrel is as close to my heart as dogs far handsomer. Same with plants. But with dogs as with people, physical beauty is relatively unimportant, while in plants for the garden, physical beauty is a much greater consideration.

Take it as unarguable (and of course it can be argued forever) that box with white anemones and violet crocuses is more beautiful than forsythias fronted with black-eyed Susans. Further, take it as unarguable that black-eyed Susans are not worth growing. Unless, of course, they remind you of something disreputable that happened one summer when you were seventeen. Which, I am sure, is why people grow them. Can't think of any other reason.

❖ Tomatoes of Good Breeding

There's some confusion among gardeners about old varieties of flowers and vegetables, and even more confusion about hybrids.

Take flowers that are planted from seed — things like sweet peas, zinnias, verbenas — or vegetables like cucumbers, tomatoes, beans, and so on. Suppose you want to grow a variety of zinnia, say, from the eighteenth century. Well, the only way any such variety has been preserved is by saving seed, planting it, saving seed, planting it, and so on for a couple of centuries. What are the chances that over those centuries the flower has changed enormously? Suppose you wanted the ancient variety called 'Red Empress' (to make up a name for a mythical variety), and suppose gardeners had faithfully saved seed each year from that variety. You still would have no idea whether your 'Red Empress' was anything like the one of 1790.

Who knows how many bees over the years brought foreign pollen to that variety, so that gradually its original characteristics were swamped by new genes? Or suppose that special care was taken to keep bees away, and the variety was self-pollinated over the years, and you were fairly sure that no new genetic qualities had entered the strain. Even so, it might now be very different from the original. Somebody had to decide which flowers to save seed from. Would he save seed from the smallest flowers, or would he save seed from the largest and brightest flowers? A hundred generations of seed from the "best" blooms would result in a flower quite different from the one grown in 1790.

Or take a tomato. I grow one called 'Brandywine', which is supposed to be more than one hundred years old. My plants are more than eight feet tall now and they bear heavily and the fruit is possibly better than any other tomato, or at least the equal of any other tomato, though the plant is not supposed to be resistant to any disease. Well, mine have no disease. They don't even have hornworms or flea beetles or aphids. The fruit is almost globular, thinskinned, superbly flavored, large, juicy, loyal, courteous, kind. It is in shape and glory an utterly modern ideal tomato this year with me, and I suspect it is altogether different from the original variety of that name. I suspect that careful selection over the years has made it far finer than the first 'Brandywine'. If, indeed, there ever was an old variety of that name. The one now going by that name is superb, and that's enough for me.

But take a quite different tomato, a modern hybrid like 'Better Boy'. I find it excellent, though it would do you no good to save its seeds (as you might do with 'Brandywine'), for the hybrids like 'Better Boy' have to be raised anew each year from two quite different parents. It is only the particular combination of those two (unknown to me) varieties that results in seeds that will produce 'Better Boy', and most of them will be inferior.

It's a fact of vegetable life that sometimes when two fully distinct varieties are crossed — that is, when the pollen from one variety is dusted on the pistil of the other variety — you will get seed that produces a plant of uncommon vigor, with qualities more desirable than are found in either parent. Heterosis, or "hybrid vigor," can in some cases give superior fruit with wonderful resistance to disease. But that assortment of wonderful qualities is found only in the first-generation cross of those two varieties, and unless you cross them every year you will not get 'Better Boy'. The labor of hand-pollinating by the commercial seed grower every year, using only the two parents known to produce 'Better Boy', is a major reason that hybrid seed costs more than seed of varieties that can be kept going indefinitely through self-pollination, without the seed producer's doing anything at all.

At my place this year the nonhybrid 'Brandywine' is better than 'Better Boy', but it might be a different story in another garden in another region. And suppose some tomato disease were introduced to my garden. Then all my 'Brandywines' might die in a matter of a few days, while all the 'Better Boys' would resist the disease and keep on producing excellent tomatoes.

Nothing in vegetable life is fully perfect. You may trade some small edge, some little excellence, for resistance to disease, resistance to early cold, resistance to heat (some tomatoes are more finicky than others when it comes to setting fruit on ninety-degree days). 'Better Boy' is probably a perfect example of a plant in which very little (if anything at all) in the way of excellence has been traded for a lot of new virtues in disease resistance. But then, 'Better Boy' was meant for home gardens. It was not offered as a market variety.

Suppose you make your living truck farming, however. You might agree that 'Brandywine' is a superb tomato, but it does you no good if it dies of various tomato diseases. And it does you no good if its delicate, thin skin breaks when you try to put it in boxes and truck it to market. It does you no good if it has to be picked fully ripe to display its superior qualities, whereas you, the farmer, have to pick your tomatoes green and let them color over the days they spend in shipment and storage.

What you want, as a trucker, is a tomato with a thick skin and meaty exterior walls that resist the bruises of handling and shipping. You want a variety that colors blood red even when picked utterly green. You want a tomato that will sit there without rotting for days on end. And when you find such a variety, you won't quibble too much if its flavor and texture are not up to 'Brandywine' or 'Better Boy'.

I personally will not eat pale, mealy tomatoes in restaurants. I scoop them out of salads and ask the waiter who the hell he thinks will eat such a tomato. I have to admit, though, that some commercial varieties, while by no means the equal of the best dead-ripe home garden varieties, are good enough to eat in a small way. They do not necessarily or always ruin a salad or a sandwich.

There is no such thing yet as a tomato that can be shipped about the country, trucked to supermarkets, dumped in bins, and allowed to sit around for some days that will also have the flavor of the best tomatoes. Housewives learned long ago that spaghetti sauce is much better made with good canned tomatoes than with inferior fresh ones at the store. Yet at the height of summer, at some groceries, if you're lucky, you can get quite good tomatoes, or at least good enough to prevent rioting in the streets.

The cost of raising superb-quality tomatoes in the home garden can be considerable, if you have to buy or make tall cages for them to grow in and have to protect the fruit with nets or wire mesh. If you go to that trouble and expense (and in most years you have to water them heavily once a week, and you have to have rich soil in full sun, which means you have to cut down on roses, irises, and other plants that also demand the best spots in the garden), you are foolish to grow varieties bred for truck farmers. You could grow, for the same trouble, varieties unobtainable at groceries and vastly better.

It's very like having a pet animal. You could, I suppose, try to catch a fox or a possum or any other common animal of the neighborhood and try to make a pet of it. But the bother and expense are such that you do better to get a good dog to begin with, or even, if you're not up to a dog, a cat.

❖ *Cleome for Summer Heat*

An excellent, lovely American weed is the cleome or spider flower, which will grace our alleys and gardens steadily until frost. It has unusual (if limited) merits. It grows like a weed, which is one reason it is one, and it never flourishes so well as when the mercury rises, the skies steam, and the nights swelter.

Furthermore, it yields to few flowers in elegance. Usually there are four or five stems — fitted with little spines, by the way, so be respectful of it — each crowned with a blooming cluster of pale magenta and white, or salmon pink and white, or solid white, depending on variety. These clusters are the size of an orange or small melon, depending on how well the gardener grows his weeds. They are composed of long tubular flowers, suggestive of honeysuckle, and they have a slight scent. As the flowers fall (they are neat in death, which is always a consideration), pods longer and slenderer than string beans form, and these eventually split lengthwise to release the seeds that will sprout next spring where they fall, but only after the weather has got distinctly warm.

A single well-grown cleome plant (given full sun and good rich earth such as you would choose for corn, tomatoes, or roses) will reach six feet in height and will branch out the same width. If starved, the cleome will still prove its determination to bloom, though it may reach only a foot in height.

❖ Birds and a Few Beasts

We are up to our ears with birds in the garden, most of them welcome, and after fifteen years of not venturing inside our fence, the crows have concluded it's now safe. I liked them better when they sat on neighbors' roofs and just looked.

Both mockingbirds and catbirds can be seen at almost any minute of the day, and cardinals dependably show up early and late in the day. Carolina wrens chatter rebukes almost anyplace I walk, as they have young in nests, and an American goldfinch of brilliant canary with black wings has turned up, along with nuthatches, tufted titmice, purple finches, and all those less distinctive birds I call sparrows — incorrectly, in many cases.

Street pigeons have mercifully vanished, through no action on my part, and sea gulls do not come closer than four blocks away. They would make short work of the goldfish in the tanks, no doubt, so I hope they never discover them.

Hummingbirds are to be seen almost every day, though not in the numbers I'd like, and I've seen them investigating the late-blooming daylilies and roses as well as their more usual buddleias, trumpet vines, and monardas.

The squirrels built a summer nest in the crotch of an old maple and then abandoned it, as I could have told them they would. It was about twenty feet off the ground, but there were no leafy branches near it, just the massive bare wood of the trunk and main limbs. So after all that work they moved far up in the maple, maybe forty or fifty feet, and now seem satisfied. We hope this year to keep them from moving into the attic in December.

Earlier in the summer we were sorry to see a number of Japanese beetles in the garden, as we never see them at all as a rule, but they did no damage and have now disappeared. We have no starlings this summer, which is quite unusual, and thus far only one blue jay — the last three years we have had none, though formerly they were as thick as mockingbirds. I miss the big flickers and pileated woodpeckers that used to visit us, but several smaller woodpeckers have favored us with daily visits ever since we put out suet feeders.

What with viburnums, mulberries, plenty of grapes, and other oddments in the neighborhood, the birds seem to be eating pretty well. They like the combination of open space and thick hedgerow-type growth, and they like the constant supply of water provided by the main fish pool, which I try to keep brimming.

Among dragonflies we have the usual heavy representation of the bright blue ones and occasional massive bronze ones, and a few damselflies, also blue. We have no lizards or toads, which I greatly miss, and more than anything I wish we had some of those black skinks with yellow stripes and metallic blue tails. If there is anyplace to buy some, I'd like to know it. I have ideal conditions for them — plenty of sun-warmed masonry, billions of leafy twigs, and undisturbed compost in which the young could grow. The young are much larger than the adults and look very different.

❖ A Single Sunflower

Sunflower seeds please a lot of birds, notably cardinals, and we use 150 pounds a year in the bird feeders; therefore, like everybody else who carries on in this way, we have plenty of sunflower plants sprouting in the spring. They are weedy, of course, with their big fuzzy scratchy leaves, and do very little to enhance marble pavilions (if you happen to have such a thing), but at my place, where they are by no means the only weeds, sunflowers are handsome enough. Usually I weed them out in May, but this year I left one, which began to bloom in July. I feel better every time I look at it.

The sunflower is an American flower. It would do quite well, as far as I am concerned, as the national flower, and while we think of it when we think of Kansas and similar outposts of the empire, still it flourishes virtually everywhere, provided it receives sun and heat.

There is no sweet scent to the sunflower. I always associate them with the scent of June bugs, which clustered thick on the plants I first knew. There was a railroad a few blocks from our house, to which we kids were forbidden to go, since there was a hot-tamale shop down there that (my Aunt Frances Bodley said) sold tamales positively fatal if eaten, unless one were Spanish or something. Besides, she said (and we had no idea how she knew), it was an utter den of utter iniquity and you would not believe the things that went on there. Years later, with the boldness of a teenager, I surreptitiously went to the place and was terribly disappointed that the iniquity was pretty moderate, and consisted largely of paying for the tamales, which were excellent and not fatal thus far, and I am no longer a teenager.

Anyway, the train tracks were lined with sunflowers that I remember as being 165 feet tall. Perhaps they were not quite that; a little boy on a daring errand of viewing the prohibited sunflowers by the prohibited train track near the prohibited tamale shack is not the most reliable of reporters. Many a summer morning, however, I viewed them, with the tamale stand on the horizon, and therefore comprehended early on the paradox that high beauty and evil may coexist.

Near us was a place called Ashlar Hall which I suppose startled people who were not expecting a Norman castle on the Tennessee-Mississippi border. The chatelaine was remarkable, partly for jack-knives off the diving board at the age of eighty and partly for a night-blooming cereus that required four men to lift when it came indoors in winter, and that on some nights had sixty-three blooms open at once. But the great thing was that right in front of a massive limestone column was a single sunflower every year. It probably would not have been the choice of the architect, but we all admired it greatly in the fall, when little birds hung on, pecking out the seeds.

One year I grew some fancy sunflowers that were double, the size of melons, the flowers with petals like a shredded carnation. They came in both the usual yellow and red. As with so many novelties, they seemed rather on the marvelous or gee-whiz side, but they lacked the style of the plain railroad-track sunflower, and I never wished to grow them again.

But even aside from the sunflower's role in memory, it is a glorious, robust, dignified, I-am-what-I-am sort of flower. Wherever there is full sun, and a gardener not too delicate and not too fancy, it should be found.

❖ Uprooted by Nature's Plans

You'll be astonished to hear that sometimes carefully thought-out garden projects fizzle, and when they do the gardener has two common choices. He can curse God and die, as suggested in the Book of Job, or he can dig it all up and start again with another wonderful scheme.

Several years ago I thought the herbaceous clematis, commonly known as *Clematis davidiana,* would be just the thing to shoot up in the spring and wrap around a little circular water basin four feet across. The clematis has big deep-green leaves somewhat like the paws of the grizzly bear, and in late summer clusters of blue flowers fragrant and shaped a bit like hyacinths.

In furtherance of this plan I planted it to the north of the basin, and after a couple of years it did indeed wreathe about, except it was not fragrant and the blue was almost white. Also it refused to stop at three or four feet but went off to one side, threatening a six-foot clump of lilies.

After this great scheme got started I built the doghouse. The truth is that like your average gardener, I am terminally devoted to building small structures that are beyond my competence. Somebody threw out a pagoda-looking copper shelter that had hung over a front door. I looked at it for several days in the alley while walking the terrier, and despite pleas from housemates I could stand it no longer and lugged it home. It sat for two years very much in the way of all until I erected four posts sheathed with copper (another gift of American wastefulness) and put the pagoda roof on top, over a bronze lion from Bangkok. The back of the doghouse (as we call this beautiful structure) is filled with a heavy ironwork grille, another scrap item, and in front of the lion is the small circular pool. On top is a weathercock, a carp that had been installed elsewhere and was obscured by surrounding foliage. It looks fine. Or so I think.

But now the shrubby nonclimbing clematis has decided to climb and is up into the weathercock, where, if you look closely, you can see a pallid fringe of blossom. All this planning, and thanks to the clematis it is not good. So the clematis will be dug up and stuck somewhere else; it does not deserve a prominent place, and don't ask me why it climbs, which is quite against the rules.

Going up one of the posts is a potato vine, *Solanum jasminoides,* which has shiny small oval pointed leaves and clusters of inch-wide snow-white saucer flowers with bright yellow centers. It has no scent, but otherwise is a glorious thing to have. It grows to about ten feet the first summer if you plant it out in May from a small potted plant. It looks nothing like the potatoes you grow in a vege-

table patch but is an aristocrat. It is said by some to be hardy in
Zone 7, but I doubt it. I shall bring it indoors for the winter until
it develops a kind of trunk, then leave it out to see what happens.
And I will make cuttings in pots so that when it dies in January (as
I expect), I'll have replacements.

Replacing the clematis on an opposite post will be the hyacinth
bean, I think. It is a coarse annual vine with tropical-looking leaves
that suggest an overfed beet, and foot-long spikes of purple pea
flowers from July till fall. It is neither rare nor difficult and is probably too gross to associate with the elegant bronze lion, but I am
good and tired of that pale fringe of nothing on the clematis. Away
with it.

Actually, the hyacinth bean is one of those flowers that do not
grow very well in many or most parts of the world but that grow
to perfection in Washington. I see it sometimes on those little
waist-high iron railings on Capitol Hill, and it is wonderful on a
white wooden fence around a vegetable plot. As I see it now in my
mind's eye, it will be dandy growing in shades of purple up to the
green copper roof opposite the solanum, which (in my present vision) will be a cloud of white flowers also reaching the roof on the
other side.

You plant the hyacinth bean from fat seeds started indoors in
late March and set out in May. Apart from being fine for my copper doghouse and various low fences, it is splendid, in an overly
lush way, when grown in a half-barrel in full sun. It also flourishes
in half-sun, as on an east or west side of a building, but likes the
sun to hit it hard for at least half the day.

In another year or two I may write a little note about the grand
failure of the solanum-and-hyacinth-bean project, just as now I
complain of the clematis. Already I have wavered about the potato-
and-bean business I have just described. I am tempted by a moonflower on one side and that subtropical morning-glory from Brazil
that used to be called *Ipomoea learii* on the other. Both of them,
especially the moonflower (which formerly was a *Calonyction* and
is now an *Ipomoea,* but will probably be something else next year,
thanks to pesky botanists who have nothing better to do than paw

through crumbling herbarium sheets and change the names of well-loved flowers) — both of them exceed the eight- to ten-foot height I require. My moonflowers usually exceed twenty feet by September.

But then, garden plants can be made to adapt. And why not, the rest of us do.

SEPTEMBER

THE TIGER SWALLOWTAILS have been busy, two or three at a time, in the flowers of *Buddleia* 'Ile de France', and a number of medium-size reddish butterflies have been sailing about without landing. I don't know them well enough to identify them in flight. And recently a cloud of silver-spotted skippers, twenty-five of them, were working over the perennial pea that grows on a bank. Usually I see them only singly or in quite small groups. Although we grow parsley, a favored plant of the black swallowtails, we have had none this year, though recently at the National Arboretum I saw several pipevine swallowtails (which I have never seen in my garden) in garden-variety verbena flowers.

No gardener dislikes butterflies, probably, and most of us are moderately enthusiastic about them. It's an agreeable thought that by planting at least a handful of the favorite plants of various butterflies we can help them in some small way. The mere fact that black swallowtails feed on one's carrots and parsley in larval stages does not ensure that the adult butterflies will hang about one's garden, of course. God gave them means to take off.

Still, if everybody grew a few butterfly plants, there would undoubtedly be more butterflies in town. Now we are talking of building a fourteen-lane highway around the city, and almost within a stone's throw of my place the small shops and modest offices have been demolished and tall buildings now replace them. All such nonsense is bad for butterflies, and sometimes I marvel that there are any left.

❖ Felicitous Flowers for Early Fall

One of the most obliging of all garden plants, and maybe the best perennial for the early fall garden, is the Japanese anemone. Once you have it, you have it. There is no question of replacing it every few years. It spreads moderately but is not invasive, and so far as I have seen it is not bothered by mildew, viruses, or bugs.

From a tuft of basal leaves it sends up flower stalks three or four feet high, with many buds that open over a period of several weeks. The individual flowers are about the size of silver dollars, either white or rose pink, with conspicuous yellow stamens at the center. There are also semidouble forms. I like the plain single white ones best, but the rose-colored ones are equally tough.

To my dismay, the hound chose a pink Japanese anemone to gain purchase for her hind paws while drinking out of a raised pool this summer. I had fenced off her usual standing place to protect a new tree peony, leaving several feet between it and the anemone. The hound, instead of using that space, moved a bit farther to stand on the anemone, a thing I discovered after an absence of several weeks. Even so, the poor pink anemone is blooming, its stems almost horizontal. I mention this to suggest the resistance of the plant to various outrages.

One year, wishing to treat this plant well, I gave it a mulch of manure and never let it get dry through the summer. Its stems were about five feet high that year, but they leaned about more than usual. I resolved not to treat it so well after that. Ordinarily, if it is not coddled, its stems are strong enough not to need staking. Of course, one good late-summer storm of near hurricane force will knock the stems over, so it really is better to set out slender stakes in August, not that I ever do.

In the bishop's garden of Washington Cathedral (Episcopal), I have often admired the white anemone blooming amid fat old clumps of box, one of the happiest associations imaginable. The anemone also looks good in back of late-flowering hostas. But the hostas are too dense for the anemones to compete with, so they should be separated by three feet or so. When they bloom together (their bloom overlaps, though the hostas finish before the anemones), the two kinds of flowers almost touch. One year they both bloomed right together with a background of water sprinkled with blue and pink water lilies.

At Dumbarton Oaks in Georgetown, there is a narrow border of white anemones against a masonry wall. When I first noticed this one year in the spring, I thought, *Now that is a mistake, because the anemones will lean toward the light and flop all over the walkway.* But in the fall the anemones stood straight up, the result of careful tying in of the stems. It is not really that much work to tie them back to the wall, and the result is well worth it, but of course it is one more task for the gardener. If you had a whole bed of these anemones you would have flowers from mid-August to mid-October, but you should not expect so long a display from any single plant.

Another splendid creature for late summer and fall is the creeping plumbago (*Ceratostigma plumbaginoides*), which bears electric blue flowers the size of a nickel from late summer till mid-November. It is used with fine effect in the bishop's garden, and looks good between the old box bushes and the pavements.

It will grow in heavy dry shade — it will grow in dry places if it's watered, and you may say, *Well, if you have to water it, why say it grows in dry shade?* In fact, most flowers will not grow in dry shade no matter how much you water.

I have a scrap of this plant on a dry bank beneath a large pin oak, and what rain gets through is seized by the rather large azaleas that struggle along. (They do not really struggle so much, as I never let them get dry and have to water them off and on through the summer, while other azaleas of the same type that are not on the bank but on a flat space do not get watered at all.) Anyhow, the little plumbago, which is utterly overwhelmed by the azaleas and the various other oddments, still manages to bloom. You will see its gentian-blue flowers sparsely scattered about where it has found a tiny patch of light here and there.

The plumbago is happy in full sun but will bear as much shade as a lily of the valley. The more sun, the more beautiful its leaves in the fall, when they turn rich tones of crimson. But however obliging this plant is, it does not smother weeds. Do not plant it expecting it to form a weed-proof carpet. The only plant I have grown that really does not allow weeds to come through (and that is handsome enough to use in a garden) is the little tribe of epimediums, or barrenworts.

If I had a patch of land beneath old oaks and maples and did not want grass (which is a royal pain in shade and dry places), I would consider patches of the plumbago, barrenwort, lungwort, purple bugleweed, and periwinkle, making each patch eight feet wide, say, and let them fight it out. Beneath that cover I would plant such bulbs as might have a chance of coming up through it in the spring.

❖ On Oddments and Changelings

For years I have loved those creepy-crawly succulents with flowers like quilled portulacas. You see them growing in sand or rocks at many coastal villages. The group as a whole is called *Mesembryanthemum,* but there are a number of genera with flowers quite similar but varying in details of seed capsule and so forth. From the Scilly Isles I brought home seeds but never could make them grow, and I have tried cuttings with no success either (though they all grow "readily" from cuttings). Many or most of them are subtropical, so even if I had succeeded in getting a plant, it would not have survived more than one summer.

And then I bumped into the *Delosperma,* which is said to be hardy in Zone 7, or even Zone 6. Washington is Zone 7, Philadelphia is Zone 6. It has flowers of deep rich magenta-purple. Its leaves are much fatter than portulaca leaves, but the plant has the same habit, right on the ground, the flowers borne only an inch or two above the earth. I can hardly wait for winter, to see if this dandy creature really is hardy. It is one of those innumerable flowers that the landscape professionals never heard of and would not look at twice, as it makes no great statement. It is merely a festive frippery of a plant, and one that would give pleasure to a gardener with a blazing-hot balcony, for example. Or to me, who grows it in a copper boiler with a semi-shocking pink verbena and a few other thises and thats. To see it, I have to make a special trip, brush aside the tall unknown artemisia (which I am assured by the giver, a botanical expert, is excessively rare), and peer down into the copper. In full bloom it is below the rim, so you understand it is not very showy in the general scheme of things.

Not only are there endless minor flowers like this one that every gardener should explore, within reason, but there are also startling surprises to be had with common plants. Several years ago I noticed that a tiny black locust had sprouted in a clump of nandinas, and of course did nothing. But I thought about it off and on for two or three years, then realized it would have to be either cut out or transplanted.

I find it hard to cut down young trees, though I am hell on wheels when it comes to big maples and wild cherries. I have twenty-year-old oaks not yet twenty inches high, as I whack them down every year. I can't bring myself just to kill them, and I certainly have no space for any more oaks. Not even the blue-green evergreen *Quercus glauca* that has salmon-colored new leaves — an oak I used to grow and now miss in a sad way, but there simply is no space for it here. I commend this particular little oak to all who love oaks. You do not believe it's hardy, but I grew it through below-zero winters, and usually it's the size of a medium dogwood.

But not to wander, after I moved the baby locust tree back near the alley, it grew steadily along. And then, without warning, it began blooming this August. August? And not with locust flowers at all, but more like a goldenrain tree.

The point is, I have known our native black locust, possibly our most beautiful native tree, for nigh on a century. As I've mentioned, I have known fields bordered with locusts that sprouted from fence posts (locusts make superb fence posts). To have your locust change into something else is unsettling, as if your sweet old hound suddenly turned into a rabbit or a tiger one day. Now I have to paw through books to see what the nonlocust is. I should know, but I don't.

No doubt I should keep a sharp eye on the big oak and big maple in front of the house in case they suddenly turn into poplars. Or zinnias.

❖ Divide and Multiply

Where I live, almost any woody plant can be planted in the garden now, though for magnolias, sour gums (which nobody ever plants), dogwoods, and red oaks, I'd wait till spring. But for viburnums, hollies, camellias, azaleas, nandinas, clematis, box, hawthorns, and virtually everything else, fall is a grand time. There will be two months for them to settle in before real winter. The ground is easy to work, there are not going to be hot, dry winds, there is not going to be a drought, and all the hazards of spring will be avoided.

This is also a fine time to investigate any friends who have cows or horses, since manure is endlessly valuable in the garden. Some people say, *What about weed seeds?* As I could not possibly have more weeds than at present, this is no terror to me. You may have to wait till January to get manure from the country, when the barns start filling up. I never mind the straw mixed with it, considering that straw is as admirable as manure. Many books speak of cow manure, but horse manure is not to be sniffed at, being even better on heavy clay soils.

In my experience, September is the best month for planting daffodils, though most gardeners get them in late in October. They can be planted up till Thanksgiving, and in a pinch up till Christmas. I have planted them in February. None of which changes my view that September is best. But you know how gardeners are — a day late and a dollar short — so I try not to scold.

It strikes me that garden tools have got rather expensive. I have a bad habit of leaving them outdoors, leaning against the garage. They should go inside. The wood gets weak if they stand out in the weather, and one fine day the handle snaps. Theoretically, it takes only a minute to paint a bit of scarlet on the handle, for easy retrieval in case you leave them in some lush growth somewhere. Neat gardeners never leave anything anywhere, but I have located many a trowel over the years by spotting the little flash of scarlet.

Every year without fail a certain number of shrubs send forth a few flowers in the fall. Many azaleas, rhododendrons, magnolias, viburnums, thorns, quinces, pears, and other things may be found blooming now, very halfheartedly on one or two twigs. Some gardeners seem never to have noticed this and call excitedly, wondering what to do and hoping this will not ruin the spring display. There is, needless to say, nothing one can do, except maybe enjoy the unseasonal flowers. I do not notice any difference in the spring performance.

Many gardeners like to tidy up now and divide perennials, which (they reason) are perfectly hardy to cold, so why not divide and replant them now? And indeed this is the perfect time to divide and replant peonies. An astonishing number of people do not want to divide peonies. But after they have been there for some years they should be cut apart into sections of root with five eyes, and if you are in a panic to see a lot of flowers quickly, you can even plant two such sections in a large planting site. Otherwise, five eyes, and simply wait three years for the new clump to form.

It is better not to divide irises than to do it this late. Sometimes they do all right if divided as late as November, but often they resent the cold or something and do not bloom the first year. So divide them at the end of July as you are supposed to do.

Some perennials abhor fall division, notably Shasta daisies and many phloxes. They are extremely easy in the spring, after new growth starts, and with me they have a wretched habit of dying over the winter if divided now. There are some other perennials that look so thick and lush in the fall — Siberian and Japanese irises are prime offenders — that you cannot imagine their dying if you pry them apart in October. The result of this usually is that they look fine all winter and die totally in March. So leave them alone now. I am saving you work by the paragraph.

❖ No Dallying with Dahlias

Now we come to the great season for the dahlia, which is a plant utterly easy to grow provided its few requirements are fully met, and which is not worth growing otherwise. I've grown them both ways, superbly and slothfully, and I can say superbly is better.

With dahlias now at their peak, the gardener should take a sharp look at his space. He should reflect on his improvident ways and resolve to do better. Specifically, he should lay out a little space for next year's dahlias, remembering that they require six hours of sun a day, and while small plants obviously require less space, the big dahlias should be thirty inches apart in the row, and the rows three feet apart. In short, dahlias require the best spot in the garden, just as roses, irises, and a good many other things do.

September and October are excellent times to dig a sunny patch for the dahlia tubers to be set in next spring. If feasible, dig the dahlia patch to a depth of two feet. Dahlias like a good friable loam, and plenty of leaf mold or other humus as well as fully rotted horse manure can well be dug in this fall.

The National Capital Dahlia Society, Inc., recommends planting the dahlia tubers five inches deep from mid-May through June. You may, of course, plant them sooner, but nothing much is gained, and there is a substantial hazard that the roots will rot in cold, damp ground. Besides, most dahlia lovers do not want them to bloom before the end of June. A dahlia that is in full flower early in July is not going to keep producing good flowers in September, which is when most gardeners want dahlias most.

In the spring (sometimes as early as February, and always by

April) the dormant roots begin to send out tender sprouts, which are, by the way, brittle and easily broken off. This is true whether you store the roots (the society recommends vermiculite in a sealed container, if you are storing your own over winter in a cool, preferably forty-degree room) or buy new ones from dealers.

Some gardeners like to pot up these roots and grow them in the house until mid-May, and if this is done properly, the plants will be sturdy indeed and a foot high while still indoors. This system, which I have tried, has two drawbacks. First, it is a lot of trouble to keep the potted plants from becoming drawn and thin in response to the relatively dim light of even a sunny window. Second, the potted dahlias, once liberated in the bed outdoors, are in heavy bloom by early July and have pretty much run their course by September.

The society recommends planting the tubers directly outdoors, covered with five inches of soil, once the soil has warmed to sixty degrees. Put the stake in just before the dahlia is planted, not after the new shoots have emerged from the ground.

Some gardeners like to grow dahlias from cuttings an inch and a half or two inches long. These root easily and quickly in sand and are then planted in soil in small pots, and shifted to larger ones until ready for the outdoor garden. But the society recommends planting the main tuber just as received from a specialist or just as you get it in a plastic bag in a garden center or hardware store.

For the first six weeks after planting, the dahlia bed should be lightly cultivated, just enough to keep weeds from gaining a foothold. The first or second good dry day after a rain, it is helpful to scratch the soil to keep a crust from forming. By August the roots will have begun to grow strongly upward as well as downward, so don't cultivate after early August or (some gardeners believe) mid-July. Mulching is practiced by many, perhaps almost all, dahlia growers. Apply the mulch once the young plants are ten inches high.

Usually there is enough rain to keep the young plants growing steadily. If there is a drought, soak the dahlias once a week with the equivalent of an inch of rainwater. If there are restrictions on water, a good three-inch mulch and soil with plenty of humus in it will prove their worth. Once flowering begins, the dahlias should be watered slowly and deeply once a week.

The Dahlia Society recommends letting only one stem grow from the tuber. This results in the largest possible bloom. Gardeners not fully intent on the largest conceivable bloom may leave four stems, and of course they will have many more flowers but need not expect to win so many prizes.

Disbudding makes perfect sense, unless the dahlia is being grown for garden color and is not intended for cut blooms. If the blooms are to be cut, for a show or for the house, it is pointless to leave the side flower buds, as these will never open once the terminal bloom opens and is cut. But for garden color, the side buds may as well remain, as in due time they will flower (simply cut out the terminal bud once that flower has faded).

Even for garden decoration, a reasonable amount of disbudding is good. When the young plant has developed three good sets of leaves, pinch off the top growing point. New shoots will appear. Keep the two new shoots nearest the main stalk and pinch out the others. As the plant grows it will produce flower buds, usually a central one and two side ones. Pinch out the two side ones as soon as they are large enough to be dealt with, smaller than peas.

In the first week of July, the society suggests, each plant should be given a handful of 5-10-10 chemical fertilizer, lightly scratched in and watered. The fertilizer should not come closer to the stem than six inches. As the flower buds appear, apply a dressing of three parts bone meal (three or four pounds per hundred square feet), one part phosphate (0-40-0), and one part potash (0-0-60). Do not give any further fertilizer, and make sure the plants have ample water, not light squirtings from the hose that merely dampen the surface.

Cut the flowers early or late in the day, not while the sun is on them and they are limp. Put them directly into cool water, and keep the water cool. Keep the blooms separated, otherwise petals will snag on neighboring blooms and be torn. Support the stems of really huge dahlias after cutting them so the weight of the bloom does not make the stem break.

Dahlias are allowed to keep blooming long after September, until a real freeze blackens the leaves. Then cut them to within two inches of the ground and dig them up. Use a spade and cut a circle about ten inches from the stem, and with some care lift the tubers. Keep them cold or cool but away from freezing; let the dug-up clump dry naturally for a couple of days, then carefully cut individual tubers from it. Each tuber must get part of the old stem, as that is where new growth will begin in the spring. A tuber without part of the old stem is worthless and should be discarded, as it will never produce a plant.

Dahlias like a soil less acid than most garden soils here. It is thought that a pH reading of 6.8 suits them best. If you think lime is necessary, use ground stone (not finely ground powder) and apply it in the fall.

❖ In Some Gardens, Only the Shadow Grows

There are too many trees in Washington gardens, probably because Americans are brainwashed in elementary school with the notion that trees are sacred. They are not. Trees are, obviously, glorious creatures in their place, but then so are tigers, and we do not insist that every garden have six tigers in it.

In small gardens, trees make it impossible to grow almost everything from roses to zinnias, and this may be the place to bash once again the absurd notion that shady gardens can be a blaze of color. That notion is a favorite of the more simple-minded gardening articles in careless magazines. When you get to the brass tacks of the piece, you find that this shady garden blazing with color is in fact not shady. Usually there is a crab apple tree to one side or in the foreground of the picture, to suggest trees and shade; but the garden is essentially sunny, and that is why they have all those flowers there.

Sometimes through fate, quite grim fate, a garden is irremediably shady. This often happens in congested places like Georgetown, or in slums in general, and the gardener must make the best of it, giving thanks that he has any outdoor space at all. Such gardens can, of course, be beautiful. But the limitations are severe.

In a twenty-by-twenty-five-foot shady garden, the obvious thing to do is pray to the god of architecture, and he will often save you. Cardinal attention in such a garden must go to the walls or fence, to the open space at the center, which should be paved as handsomely as means permit, and to one dominating feature (not a dozen), such as a fish pool, a wall fountain, or a piece of sculpture of the highest quality (at least in the eyes of the gardener). Then, in what amounts to a shady outdoor room, there can be such architectural (but quite inexpensive) items as an arbor, a handsome bench set between pillars or posts on which shade-enduring vines grow, and arches covered with vines of elegant foliage such as the akebia. Grapevines also endure surprisingly dense shade, though they do not fruit well — but usually well enough to provide excitement for the mockingbirds. There can be tubs or urns (fiberglass specimens are lightweight, durable, relatively inexpensive, and an excellent choice). You can grow only shade-enduring plants in them, but if you sink pots of flowers, they will provide color for some days before you have to replace them.

The pool, by the way, will not get enough sun for water lilies in heavily shaded small gardens, but a clump of water hyacinths will usually do nicely. In any case, common red goldfish alone will provide endless interest. If the gardener does not find goldfish endlessly interesting, he should learn to do so.

All of which is very well, but the gardener in such a site should forget lilies, roses, irises, peonies, and plan on achieving beauty by less flamboyant means, with hellebores, hostas, ivies (sadly neglected, by the way), and even tropical foliage plants that must be brought in for the winter. Still, all the usual houseplants, like tropical ficus, schefflera, bananas, small feather palms, and dracaenas, can produce striking (sometimes too striking?) effects in the shady courtyard all summer.

Perhaps, in gardens as small as twenty by twenty-five feet, it could be argued that gardening is so limited in scope that it makes no difference whether it's in heavy shade. But I have mentioned some of the obvious possibilities of such a garden to keep those who have nothing better from falling into despair.

In larger gardens, maybe fifty by a hundred feet, the gardener often goes mad and confuses his eighth of an acre with the great outdoors. For some reason, which may have to do with tree worship among our ancestors, he is likely to plant a few trees. He should not.

I yield to nobody in my love of oaks, beeches, sycamores, sophoras, ginkgoes, and other noble trees of great size, but they are not easily managed on small lots. I grew up in a garden that boasted a pecan tree nearly a hundred feet high, planted from a seed, but we finally concluded that in the fifty feet surrounding it (even though the pecan does not make dense shade) the best thing was to mass drifts of daffodils for spring, a few hundred Guernsey lilies for fall, and let it go at that.

If a tree is needed, then, the two best choices are the common dogwood, *Cornus florida,* and the Washington thorn, *Crataegus phaenopyrum.* Both are beautiful throughout the year. Other sensible choices are the Sargent crab, which is usually a good-sized shrub rather than a tree, witch hazels, persimmons, sourwoods, shadblows, or our wild red cedar. The star magnolia, which rarely surpasses sixteen feet, is another admirable ornament, and the smaller hollies are fine.

It is usually a mistake to plant a batch of fruit trees, though in size they do well when on dwarfing stocks. I find it hard to live without a peach tree (in the city squirrels and rats will get all the fruit if the gardener does not take heroic measures) and an apple of some kind. But the gardener must recognize that such trees are not particularly handsome apart from their flowers and fruit, while the dogwood and thorn are ever-handsome.

If you must have an oak or one of those wretched Norway maples, at least plant it in the center of the garden and build the garden around it, thus sparing neighbors as much as possible from the effects of folly.

❖ *The Common Splendor of Barberry*

A plant that almost always separates gardening snobs from gardeners is the Japanese barberry, *Berberis thunbergii,* an aristocrat commoner than dirt. This is the densely twiggy four-foot-high barberry
often used for hedges. Its sharp spines discourage dogs and mail
carriers (both of whom are much given to arranging thorough-
fares through small treasures), and the shrub is handsome all year,
though not evergreen. Its little leaves, half an inch or so long and
nicely oval, are good steady green and somewhat leathery or firm,
turning in the fall to orange-crimson and scarlet — a display not
sufficiently exclaimed over by garden writers, if I may say so, who
commonly tend to be snobs themselves.

Amid the blaze of this barberry are hundreds of small scarlet
oval berries that hang on even after the leaves drop around Thanksgiving time, and often last until April. Birds don't eat them, much,
and often young plants can be found near old bushes. Even when
bare of leaves, the dark black-red stems are so dense that the shrub
looks good in winter, and it is fine when iced with snow.

When it arrived from Japan in 1874, its beauty was instantly ap-
plauded, even before gardeners discovered that it will grow in dry,
barren, hostile ground with no fertilizer, no spraying, no care. As
a result, it was soon to be seen in all manner of dismal places,
holding on for dear life on bleak, cold, windy December days in
Pittsburgh and Chicago.

Like the tree of heaven, the ailanthus, which grows along railroad tracks in the industrial Northeast and in New York slums, the
barberry flourishes in graceless places, and because of this it is
neglected or even despised by many. Gardeners seem to feel that
if they plant the ailanthus or this barberry or similar tough plants,
they will perhaps turn the garden into a wasteland.

We have never had three more fastidious gardeners than the
late Reynolds Hole, Gertrude Jekyll, and William Robinson, all of
whom vastly admired this barberry. And the plant's only fault is

that it may be seen anywhere and has no aura of rarity or vogue about it.

There are about 450 species of barberry, and I would guess there are 200 species of barberry grown in gardens of the temperate world. You could make a beautiful garden, I suppose, of nothing but barberries and their relatives, such as nandinas and epimediums and mahonias. Indeed, some people have done it, I am told.

One barberry (among many) that I never see among us is *B. darwinii*, which was discovered by Darwin in southern Chile and Argentina. It is a surprisingly beautiful plant to have come from such a terrible place. Terrible as far as climate is concerned — no doubt the savages were good enough folk, even in Darwin's day. But you hardly expect an evergreen shrub of six feet, with polished leaves like a small holly, to appear at the very end of the world. It is one of the few barberries that are showy in flower (clouds of yellow) in spring. It is said to be hardy in our own climatic zone, and I have talked to a couple of local gardeners who say they have no anxiety about it during our winters.

Barberries illustrate two points at once: there are barberries we do not grow because they are too common and barberries we ignore because they are not common enough, yet both classes of barberry may be finer plants than some creatures we give space to. No barberry — indeed, no other plant on the planet — colors more gorgeously in fall than the plain green Japanese barberry, but there are other garden forms of it that are also splendid, such as *B. thunbergii* 'Atropurpurea', which has reddish purple leaves that turn crimson (occasionally with scarlet leaves here and there) and which also has the same scarlet oval berries as the green form. The purple-leaf form does not color so brilliantly as the green form in the fall, but it is as handsome as anything really needs to be.

There is also a form with rosy and variegated leaves, and a kind with acid-yellow leaves, and there are several variations among the purple sorts, like 'Knight Burgundy', which is a blacker purple than red-purple, and 'Crimson Pigmy', which sits there in a fat little lump like a round cushion and which is therefore popular with some. I have always thought garden designers like this dwarf form because it takes so many of the plants to cover the ground.

But in small sunny gardens it may introduce just the touch of red-dish purple foliage you want.

Some barberries come and go in nursery lists, among them *B. wilsoniae* from Tibet and China, with masses of salmon-colored berries. Seize it when you see it. But there is scarcely such a crea-ture as an ugly barberry or an undesirable one.

❖ *Before You Bring In the Plants, Make Sure Your Rugs Are Clean*

We bring in the houseplants September 30. Sometimes things come up, and we're a day or so late. It may be the dogs rather lost control and the rugs had to go to the laundry after all. (Usually when you think you're going to save $300 this year, it turns out you are wrong.)

The only way the dining room rug gets out is by moving the sideboards, which are solid with stuff, so the drawers have to come out and sit on the living room sofa; then the sideboards and serving table come out (the leg of the table is tricky, and since the tabletop is green stone, you don't want to get too frisky with it); then the main table can be moved to the side, but you want to watch out for the ceiling light, which is just the right height to conk your head with a large crystal ball when you move the dining table. And the chairs have to go, naturally, and the weighty wooden box that holds the tree loppers and electric drill — a box that is supposed to be virtually invisible beneath a sideboard — and Miss Willie C.'s crystal epergne that she rescued from a peddler's cart in Brussels (odd, since it is Irish), and indeed several other things that have to be handled with kid gloves.

Then you roll up the rug. Then you move everything back and put all the living room stuff in the dining room — everything that will temporarily fit, which does not include a ten-ton desk or the sofa that would double for a tank. Then you roll up the living room rug. You then phone the cleaners (your wife must do this, since women can sound more pitiable on the phone) to insist that three men pick up the rugs. Otherwise they send two and you get pressed into service yourself, since the job takes three.

At this point the weather is turning coolish or even nippy at night. You do not want the thirty-seven quite large plants in heavy pots to come in, however, until the rugs get back, because the prospect of moving not only all the furniture but the thirty-seven pots as well is too much to contemplate.

When the rugs get back (assuming they do), the first thing is to get them all unrolled and the furniture back on top of them; then the plants come in to stand all over the place, with a solid phalanx sitting on top of the table that runs along behind the sofa. They do not look good there, and they annoy people who sit on the sofa and who are not used to cycads and palms hanging down around their ears as they sit. The best way to handle this embarrassment is to ignore it. When guests brush away foliage every few minutes, you give no sign of being aware that they feel trapped in a jungle. You get a look on your face (it can certainly be learned; we learned it) that says that everybody's sofa is overhung with leaves.

The orchids do not come in until the temperature reaches thirty-nine degrees — that is good for cymbidiums, they say. But if it gets cold suddenly and falls to thirty-two, it will take two years to nurse the orchids back to health again. We know precisely how long it takes.

Outdoors the big Chinese jar holds the striped sweet flag all summer, but now the sweet flag comes out and rests on the bottom of the big pool, and the jar is emptied of water and is lugged through the kitchen to the dining room. Then the monster rubber plant comes in from another direction and the rubber tree pot goes into the Chinese jar, but you don't want to get into this operation until the rugs are down and the furniture is back in place, because otherwise your wife will scream and say words you didn't know were in her vocabulary.

The fiddle-leaf fig this year cannot sit near the air conditioner because it has got too tall, and the dracaena (raised from a wee thing in the dime store) can no longer be squeezed in by the pier mirror without blocking the door. All these things will fit. They always do. But of course you can't begin till the rugs get back.

They will return at 4:00 P.M. the day the temperature prepares to drop to thirty. This means that everything will be done by flash-light within three hours, after you are properly exhausted from moving the furniture to get the rugs down. The dogs will be shut in a room upstairs, and somebody will go up to the bathroom and down they will charge while you are moving something fragile, with helpful warnings not to drop it, it was Edna's and is priceless. The dogs are put out, where they stay till you go out to bring in the big plants, when you find them as you lug the largest pot up to the kitchen door. What piteous screams, but it was only the tail. But if you would look where you were going — and just how do I do that with this eight-foot rubber tree in my arms?

By 10:00 P.M. everything will be in. A little frost-nipped, possi-bly. No matter. Everything will protest by dropping leaves steadily until spring, when everything will be nearly dead. Then outdoors with everything, where everything will not only recover but will be much larger for coming indoors next year. And you have forgot the aloe, of course, which was hard to see down there by the willow tree, and now it's turned red from the cold. But will be all right by May.

This is how you bring the houseplants in. Always great fun.

OCTOBER

E VEN THOUGH the most beautiful days of the year in Washington are the first eight in November, October is pretty splendid itself, and the gardener should enjoy it. Should enjoy every month, every week, for that matter, and not pay any attention to those "helpful" folk who say that now you must do this, now you must do that. There's no point in doing anything at all if the garden is not the most agreeable and fulfilling thing in life. If it's not a daily wonder (to the gardener alone, of course), why bother?

❖ Room with a View

This morning I peered out the bedroom window and saw things in my own garden that struck me as pretty glorious. Often, as you may know, the gardener may need to climb to the roof or hunch beneath a holly bush or assume some other unusual point of view in order to see the greatest beauty of his garden. I saw, just today, the pyramidal top of my home-built summerhouse, clothed with that wild Japanese clematis that blooms in our alleys — now in seed, and as ornamental as when in September bloom. Beyond it, running into it on one side, is the hundred-square-foot raised pool, with eight large blue tropical water lilies open, along with a few pink and yellow miniature hardy kinds, and scarlet fish moving lazily among them.

To one side of the pool are a couple of horse troughs, iron painted black and covered solid with vines (clipped to keep them from sprawling into the tanks), and a few pale yellow water lilies in them, and just beyond is the brick walk I laid almost the day I moved into the place. Along this walk you see a half-rotting whiskey barrel overflowing with a gray artemisia or dusty miller, touched here and there with bright blooms of the cardinal creeper, then after a space another tub, meant to hold purple-leaf cannas (but they froze to death) and now filled with what are supposed to be wild nasturtiums from the Andes but look like regular nasturtiums to me.

Just beyond this is a double metal arch about eight feet high, surfaced in dull light green. On one side is a big old magenta rugosa rose, clipped back to keep it from intruding through the wall of the arch, which is covered with *Clematis* 'Venosa Violacea', a modest spring-blooming vine with small lavender blooms with big white centers. On the other side is an old white rambler rose, 'Seagull', which nobody ever dreamed of planting except me. (And now I am much gratified to see this old bird is coming up in the world and is to be found in some very fancy gardens indeed.)

Flinging over the arch (because I did not get out there to whack it back in July) is a mass of the fleece vine (*Polygonum aubertii*), now in full flower, and on a stout wooden post (formerly stout, now leaning somewhat) a particularly fine form of what I think is *Actinidia arguta*. This vine does nothing much but have five-inch leaves, every twelfth one being snow white. In the several years since I rooted it from a very soft cutting, it has grown steadily, but it is only after a few years that the spectacular white leaves appear. Next year they will be better, and the year after better still. Or so it says, here in my head.

Opposite this vine and just behind the arch with the roses is an upright yew that I moved there fourteen years ago. A wild grape has wrapped an arm over it, the grape not having been discouraged at my earlier efforts to kill it. It must be got out, but at the moment is pretty enough.

That's about all you see, except beyond my fence in the distance you see a tremendous old star magnolia, as fine as I have ever seen and about twenty feet high and wide, and a splendid old Japanese maple, and in the distance (where I can enjoy them without their roots bothering me) the old oaks and locusts and black walnuts of my neighbors. The garden walk goes on for another hundred feet or so, but you can't see it from the angle I have been speaking of.

The critical thing in this view is simply variation in texture, in height, in mass and the open mirror of the water, and most of all the way in which the light hits the various things. Without lifting a finger to help, the gardener is rewarded by the difference in light on the yew, on the water, on the rose brick, on all the modest plants.

It is true, to an extent no beginning gardener will believe, that the beautiful effects of the garden are those of light falling on wonderful masses and details that come by luck, just in the nature of things. All you do is plant wonderful things — not necessarily rare things — and wait awhile and see what grows and what doesn't, and then just let the light fall, and it will be perfect. Though of course you have to look out the window just so, in just a certain direction, at just the right time of day.

❖ Squills of Delight

Gardeners often would like blue flowers to go with azaleas, and I am fairly horrified that when the Spanish scilla blooms then, so many people ask me what it is. I grew up calling it *Scilla campanulata* and now the name is *Endymion hispanicus,* but whatever the botanists call it in their interminable messing about with names to see how much trouble and confusion they can cause persons who deal with the real world, it is a lovely flower and as foolproof as any plant can be.

You plant it now; the bulbs are available in blue, rose, and white at garden centers or from catalogues of bulb dealers. The blue is best. The one called 'Excelsior' is the best I have run across, though nowadays (when dealers think one thing is as good as another) you may have to settle for just the color blue and forget the particular variety.

I do not know how long the bulbs last outdoors — I know they last for decades and possibly forever. Nothing bothers them. They take any exposure from full sun to medium woodland shade. They are handsome with early garden irises or Kurume azaleas. The Spanish bluebell or scilla is not to be confused with the Siberian squill, which blooms earlier in an intense electric tone of gentian blue. The Spanish squills are nearer sky blue, with a bit of lavender in them, and the dozen or so bells (rather like hyacinths) are borne on somewhat curving stems about a foot high. They multiply to form fat clumps, but do not seed about, staying where you put them.

This is an old plant in gardens and should be in all, I would think. For gardeners who are forever cutting things, this scilla does well in tall wineglasses with a few sprigs of yew, and the clumps soon grow dense enough, with dozens of flower stalks, that half of them can be cut without anyone's noticing.

❖ A Change of Place Has Its Price

I speared a superb lily bulb yesterday, a fact mentioned for no other reason than to remind gardeners prone to distress that everybody does it sooner or later. Unless the garden is a forest of labels and unless plants stay exactly where planted (and some lilies wander considerably), accidents will happen. I dug up the bulb, which had turned into three very large bulbs, and planted them elsewhere.

One notable gardener once wrote of his collection of small bulbs — chionodoxas, crocuses, anemones, snowdrops, and others — that of course he was forever digging them up by accident.

Just plant them back, he said. This advice is so obvious it never occurred to me. Since reading that article, however, I now dig up all kinds of crocuses and scillas and much else and just stick them back. No harm seems to be done.

A thing I noticed some years ago was that patches of crocuses such as 'Ladykiller' and other quite small early varieties kept wandering about, through seeding as well as accidental digging. One of the great colonizers through self-sown seed is *Crocus tomasinianus,* an early light lavender sort. It becomes rather a weed in light sandy soils, but spreads far less rapidly in heavy clay loams. This year I again planted two garden varieties of it called 'Ruby Gem' and 'Whitewell Purple', which have never multiplied with me. This time they are given a spot with more sun and lighter and better soil.

A few years ago, I planted a bush of the single (five-petaled, not the double, multipetaled kind) *Kerria japonica.* For some reason I gave it a handsomely prepared site, with leaf mold, rotted manure, almost full sun. What a mistake. Its stems have spread to a little thicket perhaps eight feet wide, and have encroached on all kinds of things. Recently I dug up some to give away, a backbreaking operation. This shrub, which does surprisingly well in the kind of shade that azaleas grow in, does not need coddling, but produces its long wands of small strong-yellow blooms almost anywhere.

One of the most important things to learn is to leave things alone when they are doing well. This is especially true of plants that are touchy to begin with. Once I had the rich red wild clematis, *C. texensis,* growing in such luxuriance that I moved it in early spring to a "better" spot. It began to die within weeks and at the end of two months was gone forever. Again, I have moved lilies to my sorrow. When they are flourishing, let nothing persuade you to touch them. Even those tough old workhorses the hostas can resent being divided and moved.

Having learned nothing in my years of gardening, I have just moved a flourishing waist-high fan palm, *Rhapidophyllum hystrix.* As all palms are a chancy proposition in Washington (and only one other, *Trachycarpus fortunei,* is a sane choice for outdoor planting up here), it is reckless to move one that has settled down and had pups (small offsets). I should have bought another one if I had to have this palm in a new place. Or at least I should have done the moving in mid-April. My pigheadedness, however, will not prevent my public moans and complaints if I now lose this specimen.

❖ *The Leaves of Autumn*

The coloring of leaves in the fall delights every gardener, though few people seem to think of it when deciding what trees and bushes to plant. It is often said that the fall brilliance is so quickly spent that it's not worth considering, but if brevity of display were to rule plants out, there would be nothing in gardens but grass and yews.

Recently I wandered about in Washington with a friend from Hampshire who is used to the subdued effects of fall foliage in England, and I saw him perk up every time he saw a maple or a sour gum. In fact, however, there are gardens in England celebrated for the glory of fall foliage, such as Sheffield Park.

Much is made of the coloring in New England. They like to say up there that their colors are more brilliant than elsewhere, but I see no basis for the claim. They merely have more sugar maples than other regions, and fewer oaks, beeches, hackberries, and other trees that color less flamboyantly. But a sugar maple colors as brilliantly in Washington as at the North Pole, and the same may be said for swamp maples, sweet gums, tupelos, persimmons, Oriental maples, hickories, ginkgoes, yellow poplars, and sourwoods.

The most dazzling of all American trees for fall color are the sour gums, or tupelos, which are members of the genus *Nyssa*. Their leaves are on the small side, oval and glossy. They turn brilliant crimson and ripen, as you might say, into vermilion. The color is uniform. You may wonder, as I do, why they are so rarely planted.

The sweet gum is more variable. It is our paint-pot tree, and boasts purple and yellow on the same tree, along with tomato red and no telling what else. Individuals vary more than in sour gums or most other trees famous for fall coloring.

One of the commonest trees is the Norway maple, which turns a luminous canary yellow with a hint of green. When sunlight filters through this tree in October, the result is magical. As this tree is often planted near houses, the reflected glow on interior white walls is well known to many.

The hickory is surprising in color, a deep tawny yellow, sometimes with brown streaks. Often if you examine a hickory leaf you will say it is rich in a way but not brilliant, and you would not expect it to show up well in a woodland. But no tree in a forest is more compelling in the fall, and few color effects are richer than hickories mixed with pines.

The ginkgo turns solid yellow and the leaves drop all at once; that is, in two or three days. One afternoon the tree is glorious in golden leaf, and the next morning almost bare. This endears it to people who sweep leaves. The tree remains in beauty for some days before the sudden leaf fall.

Formerly rare in gardens and now relatively common, the sourwood develops its fall beauty slowly. Just now it is rather a subdued crimson, ornamented with six-inch tassels from the faded flower clusters, which are (at least remotely) like lilies of the valley. But these rich dull crimson leaves brighten a great deal and become brilliant, rivaling those of the wild persimmon, which can range into vermilion.

The sassafras, usually thought of as running about in low thickets, though it can make a substantial tree of forty feet or so, has yellow and rosy purple in its mitten-shaped leaves. Again, this is a tree in which individuals vary in coloring (though the individual bears the same colors every fall).

In swamps to the south the bald cypress is beautiful at all times, and turns a kind of rust in the fall, usually not showy at all but agreeable in its way. Its cousin, the metasequoia (from China), turns lighter, a fawn color sometimes with a hint of pink. Some have called it apricot color, but that suggests greater brilliance to me.

Among maples, none is flashier than the sugar maple, which turns yellow and red and which seems to specialize in branches of a fiery tomato color. Equally beautiful is the red or swamp maple, which often colors a week or so later than the sugar maple. The Japanese maples have been selected and propagated in several hundred garden varieties. None is fiercer than 'Osakazuki', which turns solid uniform vermilion. The Japanese like to group these small trees in groves, and so do Westerners if they have the space.

The wild dogwood of eastern America, so famous for its white blooms in April, is crimson in October. If birds have not eaten the fruit, the scarlet berries at tips of twigs are an added brightness.

As far as I can tell, nobody but me loves the common hackberry, usually dismissed as a weed tree. As if we all laid keels of ships where you want white oaks. Once a hackberry about twenty feet tall, a young tree maybe a foot in trunk diameter, went down in a storm. A few days later I propped it up with a large plank. The roots were badly torn, up in the air, but nothing would be lost by propping it up. It took hold again and rewarded me by growing too large for its site. About once every four or five years it turned a luminous yellow-green, as gorgeous as anything to be seen in the fall. More often it turned yellowish, then brown, then bare. But with plants as with people: they have their moments of glory once in a blue moon.

❖ Sometimes Things Just Do Not Go Well

For many years I would not have wanted it generally known that I never had the slightest success or slightest flower from either larkspurs or cornflowers from seed. I never understood that, since other hardy annuals such as California poppies always came up thick as mustard, and while I pretended the birds must have eaten the seeds, I knew in my heart they hadn't.

In my former garden in Tennessee we had plenty of cornflowers and larkspurs that seeded about year after year so you never had to buy new seed and plant it, but up here I never could get them going. As recently as the year before last I planted cornflowers again and surprisingly got a whole row of plants up to about eight inches high, and thought all was well. Not one of those plants ever flowered; they all mildewed and died, though I never saw mildew on cornflowers anywhere else in my life.

A person in the house said the trouble was that I planted everything too close. The bachelor's buttons, for example, were so close to the daylilies that they were simply smothered as the daylily leaves began to lengthen in May.

I mention this for whatever comfort it may give the innocent. Sometimes things simply do not go well. The nadir was twenty-five years ago with nut grass (*Cyperus esculentus*), which is the ultimate vicious weed. I have found its little tubers thirty inches deep. Compared with it, bishop's weed, plantain, chickweed, ground elder, and Johnson grass are mild intruders. Anyway, the nut grass has beautiful polished sedge leaves, and the nuts or tubers are larger than hazelnuts. It is said people eat them in India. One year I had a nice pile of them, rooted out at vast sweat from the rose bed, and planted a lot of them in an ornamental urn. They would be green and handsome and not need fussing with. Every one of them died, and I used to say after that that the best way to kill nut grass was to dig it up and grow it in an urn.

There are whole books devoted to raising things from seed, and I know my trouble has been the usual trouble experienced by gardeners — planting them too deep.

After roughly a century it dawned on me that sterilizing soil is worth the bother, and if one is too lazy to boil or bake the soil, one can use potting soil, which is not sterile but which works better than plain garden soil when seeds are sown. There are so many hazards outdoors, what with birds and beasts and weather, that it is foolish, really, not to start them in flats indoors and then plant them out when they are relatively small plants. Naturally, the garden soil into which the young plants are set should be weed-free.

Many gardeners sow hardy annuals outdoors in fall and winter, but that has not worked well for me very often, though one year I had spectacular success (for me) with sweet pea seeds planted in November. In Washington and north of here there is too often ice that melts and refreezes through the winter, and hardly any young sprouted seedling will take that. Sometimes pansies will, though it is safer to plant youngsters with five leaves (not larger) late in October and give them the slightest of coverings — dustings, really — of straw. Then they bloom like mad with the daffodils in March, while if plants are set out in the spring they bloom only with the irises in May.

Consistency, in the plant world as in the human, is a virtue. This past summer my wax plant (*Hoya carnosa*) bloomed beautifully for the first time in years, after spending the previous winter in an east window of a bedroom kept always on the cool side. Before that, in the years it grew well but never bloomed, it wintered by an east window in a room that was sometimes warm and humid, sometimes chilly and dry. The stephanotis from Madagascar also refuses to flower, so this winter I am trying it in the cool steady room to see if that helps.

You may think the big greenhouse amaryllis is vulgar with its enormous four flowers on a stalk, and admittedly it bears little resemblance to a lily of the valley or Johnny-jump-up or other delicate creature. Still, hardly anything is as cheerfully gorgeous as one of the modern amaryllis in full bloom in January in the living room. I have seven new bulbs and have already started three of them, planting at two-week intervals. That is supposed to ensure a steady production of flowers through the winter. My guess is that they will all bloom more or less together, but it costs nothing to follow directions for a change, and we shall see.

If you stagger your potting dates for these bulbs, keep the unplanted bulbs cool and dry. Not every house has a room that stays at fifty degrees all winter, but mine does. It is perfect for keeping dormant amaryllis happy until potting time.

❖ *Old Duties Before Breaking New Ground*

One reason gardens are so often a mess is the gardener's itch to get on to something new instead of tending to what's already there. I see that the fleece vine has broken its appointed bounds by a good many feet. I had it under perfect control on June 20. Well, I blush at the date, it is so long ago, but it seems only yesterday that I wobbled about, the shears over my head, clipping it into shape.

Of course you should not plant a fleece vine (now in lovely fragile white flower) unless you either can give it a barn to cover or are prepared to keep trimming it back. I knew this when I planted it, but in the enthusiasm of creation, who stops to think of the labor of maintenance? "Oh, I guess ten minutes twice a year will do it," the gardener says, but of course it takes more than an hour three times a year, even if the gardener does not fall backward into the lily pool (when it takes longer).

Now, no gardener in this world is unaware that the instant the wind blows in a seed of dock or bindweed or whatever, action should be taken, the very day the weed is first seen. It is going to have to come out, and the gardener knows it is easier when the thing has three leaves than when it is four feet high and has a root to New Zealand (not quite to China). But I assure you, amazing as this fact is, that there are gardeners who do not get the dock out until it is so large the gardener starts wondering if perhaps he can pretend he grows it deliberately for its bold foliage.

I have at the moment one of the handsomest and largest banana trees I have seen, and I applaud my good sense in siting it where rough winds do not bruise its vast leaves. But I also know from experience that it is better to dig it up early in October and plop it (roots and leaves cut off) in a large plastic tub with about a bushel of its earth still clinging to it. Otherwise a day comes, maybe in mid-November, on which a severe freeze is predicted and is almost certain. On that day the banana certainly has to come in. But that is the day, needless to say, when unexpected crises arise at work and the gardener is home late and it's pitch dark and the flashlight batteries are on their last legs and barely working, and it begins to rain and it turns out two guests are coming for supper and the dogs want to help with the digging and on and on.

Did the gardener not know that this horror could be avoided if he took half an hour in mild October and got the banana in the tub then? Of course he knew. He just didn't do it.

No new project in the garden should even be contemplated until the gardener has done all the things that have to be done. What earthly point is there in mulling over a new place for lilies when the gardener has not even got the grape cut back where it is growing all over a prized climbing rose? Which, by the way, should be tied with tarred string to a post or some support to keep it from whipping about all winter.

One of the truly dumbest things a gardener can do is start building something. I speak with full authority on this, as I am always in the midst of a shed or a summerhouse or a walk when the work of weeding is already neglected and has a higher priority, surely. But some gardeners are cursed with a passion for playing with saws and iron poles and bricks and would rather slop about in mortar than eat.

In all innocence I felt, a few weeks back, that the time had come to do something about the gate that our son bought for five bucks about ten years ago. It is just one of those waist-high iron gates you see all over Capitol Hill, but this one has a double row of curlicues at the middle bar and thus is superior. Anyway, such gates originally had iron posts and little straps that stuck out, with a hole into which you put a prong that sticks out from the top of the side of the gate. If you follow.

One does not so easily march into a store nowadays and get such iron posts. So I decided on short brick posts to hold the gate, and the first thing was to read a dozen books on masonry, gates, and allied subjects. Many of which are interesting (the allied subjects) and substantially delay things.

Then of course the gate must be freed of rust by wire brush and then sandpaper. Now for a can of iron paint, at which point you see (on the paint can warnings) that if you expect the paint to stick, you'd better use Primer No. 7604-B, so you get a can of that and discover (upon reading its label) that the paint will last a lot longer if you use a second coat of Primer 2403-G. So you buy that.

Looks pretty good, by gum. (That is before the cement dust, mixed later, gets all over it.)

One reads a good bit about laying mortar with a mason's trowel. I mean, at my age I should not still be using a garden trowel on the mortar. So I buy one at an incredible price at a rural hardware store. A huge price. I dig holes for the concrete footings. Even though the stubby piers are less than waist high, they need a firm footing. In digging I encounter great roots, which means searching for hatchet and, if that doesn't do it, ax. This concrete must sit a week before the first brick is laid on it, but eventually the first pier, on which the gate hangs from eyebolts, is in. The gate is a quarter-inch crooked, which is infuriating, when I consider how much time I spent on the square and spirit level and so on. But at least it swings free and easy.

The second pier must be built. I have enough sense not to build the second one until the gate is in place; otherwise, it would turn out that the gate would bang right into the bricks of the second pier. But then, again the concrete must be mixed and must sit a further week.

I see the neighbors unobtrusively peering to see what the dickens this fool is doing. Well, don't ask me. Increasingly I see that I don't know. But you, now, don't do it.

❖ When Houseplants Take Over

When our son collected trash and garbage for the city, he had a habit of bringing home houseplants, and the living room and a few other places now resemble Surinam as a result. It seems that this time of year everybody throws out houseplants that have summered outdoors, probably because they are too lazy to bring them indoors for the winter, or maybe because they have some absurd desire to walk about freely inside the house.

The first and critical orphan was a gold-variegated agave of good (but reasonable) size. In several years it has become somewhat gargantuan and has two babies, each the size of a bushel basket. These have also pupped, and a number of them live in six-inch pots.

There are also two smallish palms as well as six banana plants, one of them fourteen feet high (before being whacked back for the winter), a fiddle-leaf fig, a four-foot hibiscus that has decided to come into full bloom just as the year is dying and the light is fading, and a considerable number of oddments like a twisted aloe, some fairly snaky, woody philodendron-type beasts, and what seem to me a vast number of cymbidiums that are always kept too cold to bloom. There is also a red-leaf rubber tree that keeps getting sawed back to fit under the ceiling.

The hearth is solid with plants, as are various tables and any free floor space. We like to think these plants are giving off wholesome oxygen, though we keep our house so cold, in an effort to foil the oil company, that I suspect much of what we call oxygen is simply coldness.

In a fit of folly I actually bought a hoya or wax plant at the All Saints fall bazaar three years ago, and of course it has grown mightily, though it has not bloomed. About the time everybody else's hoya blooms, mine spurts into lavish new growth and has no time for sex, and the same is true of a stephanotis that my wife recklessly ordered by mail several years ago. These live in a bedroom, where they nicely obscure sunlight in the morning.

My wife's bathroom has shelves in the window, occupied by small plants of one kind and another that I have nothing to do with (she also bought several bletillas on her own). My bathroom does not have plants in the window but does have a couple of rubber garbage cans full of water in which I overwinter certain tropical water lilies. There are more water lilies than garbage cans, so every year it is painful to decide which ones will live in water until May and which ones I will have to dry off, storing their tubers in dampish sand in a cake tin that sits atop a bedroom bookcase (where half of them rot).

It is not clear at all how the house got all these plants in it, though I blame the first big agave as the essential break in the dike. Then there was that beautiful cycad I fished out of the trash compactor of a downtown hotel and nursed back to life. I can't recall where the rubber tree came from. Once you start having plants in the house, they just accumulate, without your doing anything at all. Occasionally one will die — one great year all the spathiphyllums did — and make a little room, but others seem to float in on the air.

I did buy, for a dollar, a dracaena eighteen years ago, and don't ask me why. It was about four inches high. Now, though I have always confined it in a pot too small, it is eight feet, with several nodding stems, and it has to spend winters in the living room in a spot with quite poor light. There it languishes and loses most of its leaves by spring, but revives when taken outside in May. Sometimes I wonder if it finds life worth living, but it gets lugged in and out faithfully.

I once knew a night-blooming cereus (an epiphyllum) that was ninety-five years old and had 160 flowers open at once, if my memory is correct; certainly there were more than I ever saw or heard of on such a plant. It occupied a huge wooden tub with metal eyes through which iron pipes could be run. By holding the ends of the pipes, four men could manage, barely, to get it in and out as the seasons progressed.

The owner, who was given the plant (already an old one) as a wedding present, eventually became quite an old woman. For years she would invite the neighborhood to come see it on nights when masses of flowers opened. There would be ice cream and punch. After her death the great plant was left out through a sharp freeze, and that was that.

My wife keeps African violets in an east window in a bedroom. Someone recently gave her two fine young plants, and she said how nice that was, as her old ones had gotten ratty and worn out. Then she checked them in their summer quarters, and behold, they were in fine fettle and blooming their heads off. It is in such ways that the gardener winds up with houseplants, though he never intended to.

All of this would be understandable except that I have always disliked houseplants. I would hate to see any of them go, however. They are like a rabbit that you wish you didn't have (we had a vicious one for years and years) but that you get used to feeding and watering every day forever and ever and therefore miss when it dies at twice the usual age of rabbits. And these plants are much like the Vietnam War — once you have invested enough labor and woe, you are strangely unwilling to acknowledge that it was a stupid mistake to begin with. You just go on and on.

Still, it surprises me that I am as incompetent in harboring these plants as the government was in managing that war. And at least the government (with a little help from many of us) finally proclaimed triumph and called it quits. But I see no tunnel, let alone light at the end of it, for the plants of my house. So there probably was no harm done when we bought fifteen narcissus bulbs to force. At the moment they are in relative darkness beneath a sideboard, but soon they will have to come out and sit on some table or other. Perhaps we can start eating standing up, balancing plates. That way the dining table could start doing its share of protecting the tropical flora of three continents.

NOVEMBER

ANY SPARE PART of the garden that is not being used for something quite marvelous should be dug up now, even if you have no firm idea what to use it for, and even if it is no larger than six feet square. Most gardeners, within two or three years of commencing life as a gardener, begin to notice that few plants can just be stuck any which way in ground that for years has been compacted.

I speak now of clay or clay and silt loams, on which most of us garden in Washington, thanks to a marvelous bit of luck. But there is one great drawback: these soils compact to the point of concrete if not handled sensibly. Spring here is often too wet to dig the soil right, and in winter the soil is too wet and is often frozen. Summer is no good, partly because the gardener has been inspired to plant petunias and partly because enthusiasm wanes as the thermometer rises. Fall is the time.

I suppose I like digging, since I find myself digging year after year, but apart from liking it, I know that at my place there is no point in planting a peony, iris, or rose, say, without turning the earth to a depth of sixteen or twenty inches. I have a narrow spade with a blade fourteen inches long. I dig its full depth, toss the soil to the side, then dig down another few inches but leave that lower soil in place. Then, with my hands, I break the great clod that has been set to the side. It is wonderful the number of weed roots I pick out from the crumbled earth.

❖ Turning Over a New Leaf

Sometimes the gardener wearies of the same old thing and would like a plant or two that may not be the most gorgeous plant in the world but that is new to him and that doesn't look like everything else. Too many plants have leaves that are quite worthless, except for keeping the plant alive, of course. Just green dabs. Think of roses, phlox, zinnias, petunias, erigerons, and endless others — apart from the flowers, they are nothing to look at.

You will also notice that the gardens people get most excited about have plenty of flowers, perhaps, but the main thing is the leaves. This makes sense, since the leaves are there to admire for months on end, the flowers only a week or two in most cases.

I would not chop down an old lilac, if I had one, because a heady air of sentiment surrounds it in almost every garden in which you find a lilac, and there is much to be said for beloved old plants. But if you think of it, the lilac has rather dull leaves and the flowers last only a few days, and they sometimes manage to arrive in the worst weather of the year.

In contrast, the fern-leaf tansy, the rue, the lad's love, and some other humble herbs have no flowers worth speaking of, yet their foliage is handsome at all times (except in winter), and they often make the garden seem rich and well furnished. So does the plume poppy (*Macleaya cordata*). And few things are handsomer in the way of fat low glossy leaves than the bergenias. How often a clump of bergenias is set against an expanse of stone or masonry with fine effect, and the casual viewer who remembers the beauty of a garden supposes it was the brilliant poppies or roses he so admired, when in most cases the critical effect of the garden depended less on that brilliant color than on leaves handsome in themselves, such as those of the bergenias, artfully contrasted with other leaves or with water, brick, and so on.

We largely ignore the rodgersias, which at first blush seem a trifle like some vigorous ground elder or maypop. *Rodgersia sam-*

bucifolia likes damp conditions and makes knee-high to waist-high mounds of leaves very like those of the horse chestnut, or the fingers of a hand. It does not do much except look luxuriant.

The same is true of *Peltiphyllum peltatum,* also a damp-lover, with leaves a foot across, somewhat pleated in the spring. I have never been able to keep it alive, though any fool can; it is not a difficult thing.

The meadow rues, with leaves like maidenhair ferns, have pretty flowers somewhat like clouds of extremely small butterflies, but their leaves are the best thing about them. *Thalictrum speciosissimum* has leaves almost as blue as the rue, but with handsomer yellow cloud-tuft blooms, and there is a lovely lavender meadow rue, too. I have never met a meadow rue I didn't like.

Bugbanes (*Cimicifuga*) have beautiful ferny leaves in the spring and ultimately tall, tight, narrow, feathery white spikes of bloom in late summer or fall. Bugbanes do not look just like everything else but are distinct, though one critic once said the bugs they are supposed to chase off all live in Siberia.

The ordinary garden daylilies (*Hemerocallis*) have leaves beautiful to see in April and May, when their lime-green luxuriance is telling, even before the flowers in June and July.

Few, if any, plants have better-looking leaves than the hostas, or plantain lilies. There is now a great vogue for them, and dozens of varieties are on the market. One of the handsomest is 'Frances Williams', with wide pointed leaves of green edged with yellow. Equally handsome in spring (though it becomes plain green in summer) is *Hosta fortunei* 'Albo-Picta'. A fat patch of this by a fish pool or old box bush or tall yew will give endless pleasure. One good thing about hostas is that while they differ in leaf size and leaf color, still there is a strong family resemblance to all of them, and clumps may be used along a walk to give a sense of unity. There might be clumps of ten or twelve different hostas, satisfying the gardener's common itch to grow one of everything but not exacting the usual penalty for a passion for variety, namely, formlessness and blur.

Often you see small gardens in shade, maybe no bigger than a small living room, sensibly planted with azaleas. In front of them you often see rather sad grass. It might be easier and better to stop fighting for grass in shady spots, and in front of the azaleas to use several kinds of hosta, maybe contrasted with a few clumps of day-lilies, maybe with an edging of barrenwort (*Epimedium*) along the walk, and possibly a few auratum or superbum lilies rising in July from beneath the hostas.

A plant of great beauty is the mullein, often found in fissures of cliffs or in waste places, with basal tufts of leaves and shoulder-high spikes of flowers that are not very showy but distinct and noticeable. One of the handsomest of all mulleins is *Verbascum bombyciferum,* the name probably referring to bumblebees, but which I call the bomb-carrying mullein. Its basal rosette is two or three feet across and the spike is up to nine or ten feet. The main thing is that the whole plant is silver-white. The leaves always get stolen by people who want to stroke them against their faces to see if they're as soft as they look.

There are dozens — hundreds — of other marvelous plants not commonly seen that pay full rent for their space, as you might say, simply because of their beauty of leaf. The gardener may not want to stuff all or even many of them into his small paradise, but I am sure that trying two or three will give pleasure and add more than you might think to the excitement of wandering about when the roses and irises look pretty sad.

❖ High Crimes Against a Rambling Rose

People who have flowering plants out in front of their houses where everybody passing by can see them have an unacknowledged duty to refrain from heedless slaughter.

My route home from the subway takes me past a very neat place that boasts a rambler rose, 'American Pillar', near the sidewalk. Its owners want it to occupy a space about four feet high and ten feet long, but of course the poor rose does not understand that. This rose is a good one for growing up a rather dull forty-foot-high conifer, and it can also be made to grow on a six-foot fence if it has thirty feet or so to stretch out to the side.

The managers of the rose in question have in all innocence and wholesomeness cut it back to knee height, so that it looks like a floribunda trimmed back for the winter. As a result, it will not bloom next spring and its owners will probably snarl at it.

I was not present at the butchery, or I would have risked protesting such enthusiasm with knives. Even though that rose is not a good choice for so restricted a site, it could still have been managed. What you do is let it flower in spring, and the minute the flowers fall you cut out every single stem that has borne flowers, right to the ground, or down to where new shoots are arising from the old stems. And of these new shoots, which will grow with astonishing speed to ten feet or so, you tie down four or five to the rustic fence behind them. If there are too many new shoots, you just cut them out — a pity, but it must be done if the rose is not to outgrow the allotted space.

These new shoots are allowed to bloom the next spring, then they are cut completely away. In other words, with 'American Pillar' and ramblers of that sort, you keep a continuing supply of vigorous new shoots every year, and every year you cut away all the wood that has borne flowers. If you do that, you will have a mass of flowers every spring so solid you can't stick your hand in without touching some.

One reason 'American Pillar' is almost a rarity (it was everywhere from World War I to World War II) is that a terrible amount of cutting is necessary in May or June, just when the gardener wants to take it easy and enjoy the warm weather. Another thing against the rose is its assertive rose-pink coloring (which, however, fades to a lovely softer color after the sun has hit it a day or so) and its lack of scent and its thick thorny canes and its somewhat coarse leaves. But disease does not bother it, and it takes rain and drought and heat and cold in its stride and is pretty unfailing in its spectacular display every spring.

'American Pillar' does not give even a stray flower or two after its big spring show, so gardeners on city lots often prefer a less vigorous climbing rose that blooms off and on in summer and fall, and one that requires no pruning except occasionally to cut out dead wood or wood that seems worn out (that no longer produces very many flowers) and whose flowers are perfumed and good for cutting. Yet no rose makes a more striking display in its two weeks of glory than 'American Pillar'. I love to see it, and I hope those gardeners who have it out front will follow these suggestions and prune it only at the end of its flowering, not in the fall or winter.

❖ The Vine of Subtle Pleasures

No plant received from a nursery in the fall looks quite so desperate as a clematis. The leaves turn brown, shrivel up, and hang on. The stems are like brittle black wire. Nothing looks so dead as a dormant clematis. One year I imported some from England, and when they arrived in December (a good time in our zone for planting many dormant shrubs and vines) I never expected to see green, let alone flowers, from any of them. But not one of them died, and I still have them years later.

Even though the garden-variety clematis, the ones with saucer-size flowers, are so popular that they dominate gardeners' attention, there are several wild American kinds that have charm and beauty of a subdued sort. The most beautiful of our wild clematis is *C. texensis,* with fleshy, nodding, urn-shaped flowers of glowing cherry red. It goes up to eight feet or so and often dies to the ground in winter, shooting up stronger the next spring. It blooms for many weeks. I once grew it against a wall of white marble blocks, and it grew so easily and vigorously I recklessly moved it one year. It died. Almost any large, established old clematis is hard to move — it is better to start with a young plant.

The sad news is that I do not know of any source for this clematis, which is one of the most beautiful of all vines. I have seen plants that people tell me they bought as *C. texensis,* but they were not handsome and not *C. texensis.* In the last century a number of hybrids of this Texan were raised, and a few are still in commerce. I grew 'Sir Trevor Lawrence' a few years, and have seen the others. They are nice enough but far from the beauty of their wild Texas parent. It is to me unthinkable, or at least outrageous, that American nurseries cannot pull themselves together sufficiently to propagate this plant.

A related native is *C. viorna,* which has solitary urn-shaped flowers (like an old-fashioned child's top) of purplish blue. One clematis authority, Christopher Lloyd, observed of *C. viorna* that he had always liked it but had to admit that its subfusc small flowers were not calculated to make anybody gasp or leap about. I did not see much progress in this plant when I grew it some years ago, and was surprised one spring to see its small modest flowers hanging out from an evergreen photinia bush. Although I like it, I admit it is not showy, even in full bloom, and should be planted where it will be seen closely.

The same is true of *C. crispa,* another one I planted and forgot, and it too peered out of a photinia. It is blue, not a gorgeous blue like a gentian but rather milky-murky blue. It is fragrant. Another one, with even smaller flowers, *C. versicolor,* is purplish blue. All these are pretty growing over a granite boulder, if you happen to have one in your garden, as I, thank God, do not.

Sometimes I suspect it takes years for the gardener to notice that native wildflowers such as these clematis are indeed beautiful in their modest way. It is permissible — I say this to reduce guilt feelings — for the gardener to confine his interest to big roses, big daylilies, big lilacs, big irises, big clematis, and to have all of these in the most vibrant or gaudy colors available. Why not? A bright scarlet rose five inches across is certainly something to see.

But then, so is a clematis flower no larger than a butter bean, or a wild American wisteria with flowers less than half the size of its gorgeous Chinese brother. The flashy garden-variety clematis such as 'Nelly Moser' and the richly perfumed, elegant lavender Chinese wisteria are striking, eminently worth growing. It's just that some of their more modest relatives have a quieter beauty, equally elegant.

❖ Cues for Minding Your Peas

Success is sweet and (in gardening) relatively easy; indeed, the simple make the best gardeners because they pay attention to simple instructions and do not go sailing off in their minds to the Himalayas when the topic at hand is sweet peas. Failure with this queen of annual plants is guaranteed if, in early May, the gardener trots out with a pack of seed and scratches like a hen and covers the seed a little and sits back. And yet this is the way many people handle sweet peas, possibly in order to have something to complain about for years.

Here is how to grow them — not utterly superbly, but well enough to knock the average gardener off a chair. Find a sunny patch of land that perhaps gets broken shade on summer afternoons. It may be as narrow as two feet. One foot, even. It should be as long as can be managed, maybe twelve feet, maybe twenty or sixty.

Dig this earth to a depth of eighteen inches. There will yet be good days in December for this, but do it immediately if the soil is not sloppy wet. Do not try to pulverize it. The idea is to open it up deep.

For each foot of row sprinkle a handful of ground limestone (not powdered lime) along the bottom, cover it maybe an inch, and spread a shovelful of rotted manure every foot or two along the row. Leave the earth in lumps as large as half a cantaloupe. If larger, whack them with the spade. Early in March, when the earth is dry enough to work without turning into taffy, go over this with a spading fork, breaking it up well but not disturbing it deep down.

It probably goes without saying that if the soil is heavy, as it usually is in Washington, it should be made lighter by incorporating black woods earth (fully rotted leaves, which you collect in the fall) or dampened crumbly peat moss and sand. The addition of the shovelfuls of manure, however, will go far to tend to the soil for sweet peas. If you have no manure, then you must use peat moss or thoroughly rotted leaves or whatever other humus you can provide. It is fairly imbecilic to say that one has no peat, no sand, no manure, no compost. Get some. You should have had it years ago, and unless you want to settle for pokeweed (which adores us just as we are), you need to produce a soil that is brown and crumbly.

Order the seeds now or in January. I am considering the tall Spencer sweet peas, which grow more than six feet, but there are other kinds that grow shorter, so suit yourself.

On Washington's Birthday, plant one seed to one three-inch pot. It is a good idea to soak the seeds overnight in a glass of water before planting them. They will swell up surprisingly. If they do not swell up, leave them longer, until they do. Virtually all will swell overnight, however, and you do not want to leave them in the water once they swell.

The dirt in the pot should be moderately light, such as you get by digging up the lawn, salvaging the four inches of earth just below the grass, and mixing it with about a fourth its volume in sand and a fourth its volume in humus. I do not say you should dig up the lawn to do this, but this gives you the right idea of the dirt you should have in the pot. You could also use commercial potting soil, which I am generally suspicious of but which is better than heavy, soggy clay dug from the garden in February.

If you have twenty feet of row, use twenty three-inch pots, each one with one sweet pea seed buried a half-inch to three-quarters of an inch deep. Firm the soil and water it. Cover the pots with a sheet of paper, and once the seeds sprout, remove the paper forever.

When the seedlings have their second pair of leaves, lug the pots outdoors to a sheltered place. You want them to get sun and air, but bring them in if the temperature falls below freezing. A large tray or cardboard box obviously makes this easier than trotting back and forth with one pot at a time.

You want the young plants to be "hard"; that is, with firm and not spindly growth. You do not want plants with soft eight-inch sprouts flopping about the ground. If they are grown too soft — with too little sun and too much heat — they will be ruined by a cold snap, or else provide a small feast for vermin such as slugs.

Now, our spring can vary from tropical to frozen. Usually by March 10 the daffodils are in bud well above their leaves, and the early ones may be in bloom. Choose a good dry day, which need not be sunny, and take the young plants out of their pots and set them in the outdoor bed you have been preparing, off and on, since December. If the soil is fairly dry, press hard in planting the seedlings — not by applying a battering ram, and not by stomping with your feet, but by pressing firmly with your hands. Thanks to your December digging and early March forking over of the bed or row, the soil will be fine and crumbly.

Water the seedlings. If it snows or sleets, prudence suggests a little protection in the way of crumpled newspapers or evergreen branches or something of the kind. You want the sweet peas to start out cold, airy, and sunny. Watering is no problem as a rule in a Washington March. The rain around here is not to be believed. If, through perversity, the season should turn dry, then of course you water.

You also provide pea sticks. These are simply thin branches, about eight feet long and as twiggy as possible, stuck about a foot or a foot and a half into the ground. They can be crooked and they can be set at an angle, tied with cord where they meet, since there will be winds in summer storms and you don't want them to keel over when clothed with the growth of the plants.

Some gardeners use nets instead of sticks, or fence wire. It makes no great difference to the sweet peas. What you want is support up to six feet above the ground, and you want this support to be twiggy enough for the delicate (and strong as iron) tendrils of the plants to cling to.

At this point you have done what is required of you. You may sit back. Of course, you may find the young plants reaching vainly the first few inches for something to cling to; if so, provide them with little twigs to get them started up the main sticks.

Usually the main stem of the little plant you have set out will wither away and two buds beneath the lowest leaves will sprout, and these will be the real plant, which grows to six or eight feet. Some people worry about pinching off the end of the main stem, but as a practical matter the plant will send out these side shoots itself. If it makes you feel better, however, pinch the main stem off just above the second pair of leaves in March.

Thanks to your good, well-prepared soil, you will not have to worry much about watering, but if the weather turns dry in late June, then water deeply. The little vines should never suffer drought. Once they start growing well — they will mark time for a few weeks in March and early April — you can give them a mulch. Late April is soon enough. An inch and a half or two inches of shredded rotted leaves or bark will do. The idea is to keep the soil cool and moist.

The sweet peas will begin to bloom in late May or early June. Keep the flowers picked. If they are not picked, they will set seed and flowering will decrease and stop. If they are picked every other day they will keep flowering, sometimes into October.

Purists like to keep the colors separate. I like bunches of them in which the colors are all mixed up, the blue-mauves, pale raspberries, off-scarlets, whites, and so on. The colors are delicate. So is the scent, not nearly as strong as it should be but better than nothing. Sweet peas will be found a good bit more exciting than marigolds, and not really any more trouble, once you catch on to the routine.

In places farther south and west, sweet peas fling up their hands in July, unable to bear hot dry winds or sauna sweats. Here, despite murmuring about our excellent summers, it does not get very hot, except maybe around Labor Day, and I have had sweet peas blooming beautifully right through July and August. If I had treated them better (as I propose to do this year, following my instructions to you, for a change), I do not doubt I'd have had them almost to Thanksgiving.

❖ *In for the Winter*

Everything should be in the house now, everything subtropical and everything that will perish in our winters. My great treasures, the *Typhonodorum lindleyanum,* are safe in east and west windows.

They grow in five-gallon buckets with three inches of water over the dirt. They are fourteen inches high from seed planted in May. Eventually they should form trunks like bananas, only with elephant-ear leaves.

The finest one, growing in the great bucket all by itself, arrived indoors a few weeks ago. As it was heavy, I feared the wire handles might give way. I set the bucket in a large tin pan with handles, and two of us lugged it upstairs. Near the top the bucket leaned over and fell right out of the pan and went head over heels. Many pounds of mud were scraped off the stair carpet. It takes more hours than you would think to get a few gallons of mud off carpeted stairs. For some reason the true hazards of gardening, of which the mud bucket is perfectly typical, are not dealt with in gardening books.

There are some plants that pull through outdoors in mild winters (gardeners call mild winters "normal winters") but die in bad ones, or that survive when planted against a wall and given heavy mulch but die in the open garden. Among these are the night jasmine, *Cestrum nocturnum,* which is grown for the intense perfume of its inconspicuous flowers in late summer, and the potato vine, *Solanum jasminoides,* which is grown for its pretty glossy leaves and clusters of thumbnail-size white flowers with yellow centers (no fragrance). Both plants grow madly in hot weather and look so tough you cannot imagine anything ever happening to them. But they are not hardy.

As I grow the night jasmine in a wooden barrel, in which it would suffer more from cold than if it were planted in the open garden, I propose to dig it up and keep it in the basement till April. It is about six feet high and has five or six half-woody stems. I'll cut it back to knee height, lift its roots with a good ball of dirt, and set it in a plastic bag with all the leaves exposed to air and light. The bag is tied about the root ball at the base of the stems. The leaves will fall, the stems will shrivel a bit, and I shall make sure the dirt does not get bone dry.

The potato vine grows in a five-gallon bucket, is eight feet high, and now winters atop a steel file cabinet that is atop an old wooden bookcase. All its growth has simply been bent down toward the floor and leans into an east window. A huge saucer is under the bucket, and it gets two teapots full of water each week.

This vine, which commonly grows to eight or ten feet by August from a five-inch-high plant set out in May, is of uncertain hardiness. Books say it is not hardy north of St. Augustine, Florida. One nursery says it is hardy in Zone 7 — they imply it would do well outdoors up to Baltimore.

I got two little plants last spring. One is indoors, as I have described; the other remains outside, growing up a post and onto a little roof. It is about ten feet high and is in the middle of the garden, far from any protecting wall. It will get a few bags of dry leaves over its roots, and maybe some burlap or ragged old blue jeans tied around its stems where they emerge from the ground. The top will be left alone and will almost certainly die back. I hope the root and basal stem protection will keep it alive so that next spring it can again shoot up.

Naturally, such tropical plants as fiddle-leaf figs and tropical palms have to come indoors, as no amount of leaves and sacking will preserve them through a Washington winter. There are two palms, vastly hardier than those of the tropics, that are reasonable risks outdoors in the capital. The best known is a Korean fan palm, *Trachycarpus fortunei,* and the other is also a fan palm, with a gray-green leaf and painful spines on the trunk, *Rhapidophyllum hystrix.* Even in a hard winter in which the leaves are browned, they can be expected to produce new leaves in spring. It is well to wrap the trunks with burlap or pile Christmas-tree branches about them, removing the stuff gradually in late March and early April. Nobody is quite sure what is meant by "gradually removing" the protective burlap and evergreen branches. You guess and hope you're right. Under no circumstances would I enclose the whole plant in plastic. Any plant that cannot pull through with its base protected and its top uncovered is best brought indoors or else not planted in the first place.

Other plants not quite hardy but not so tender either include the beautiful glossy smilax or Jackson vine, without which no wedding or banquet in the South is legal. This is *Smilax smallii,* named for a Dr. Small, not for its size, as it grows to any height you can think of, or give it support for. It has tendrils tough as steel and will hold on to a trellis. It is best given support up to eight feet or so, then allowed to flop sideways, as over an arbor. It is too big to bring indoors.

A similar creature is the kadsura vine, *Kadsura japonica,* which has drooping oval evergreen leaves four or five inches long. It twines on a pole or wire fence and bears dime-size white flowers like magnolias (to which it is related). The new growth is salmon-red, and the whole plant is elegant without looking feeble.

Once I recommended it to a gardener in south Mississippi who wanted an evergreen vine of restrained habit to grow over a tin shelter at the kitchen door. Through error the gardener acquired a kudzu instead of a kadsura. The kudzu promptly twisted the tin like a stomped-on beer can and was threatening to take off the house roof. I never wanted to know.

❖ *Not a Monument, Just a Garden*

The main cost of a garden, for most gardeners, is simply the cost of the land and the endless taxes paid on it. Many would-be gardeners, having broken their backs to acquire a house with a bit of land around it, are in no position to spend thousands of additional dollars on a garden. And of course that is not necessary.

Often I have mentioned out-of-the-way plants merely as a matter of interest, knowing that hardly any gardener will wish to try them. It is possible, after all, to be interested in things we do not want to own. I am an architecture buff, but would not accept Norwich Cathedral if you gave it to me. In the same way we can be interested in Japanese gardens, or vast French formal gardens, or Italian hill gardens, without wanting them for ourselves and without wanting to copy them. So I defend my occasional enthusiasm for odd plants that few gardeners will wish to possess. But in gardening, along with rarities, there is certainly a place for very common things, and in garden design there is a place for quite inexpensive treatments of garden land.

Take a row house or a house on a small city lot. Let's say the front is taken care of, either because the house sits right on the street or because the small patch of land is paved or is grassed over or for some other reason is not available for gardening. Suppose that out the back of the house there is a rectangular or square or irregular plot, maybe no larger than an average living room, or maybe ten times that size. Say there are no fine trees, no beautiful old pink bricks, no inherited features worth focus or preservation. Suppose also that the new owner has no money worth speaking of to develop this into a garden, and not much time or even interest, yet wants a place that looks good.

First, enclose it. This may be done with shrubs, fences clad with vines, or whatnot, and the result can be quick. Posts with wires, covered with such climbers as akebia, ivy, and honeysuckle, might be used as temporary enclosure while slower-growing plants like hollies are reaching great enough size to screen out the world.

Such a plot could have a canal down the middle, with arbors of grapes on both sides. This could be very costly, if executed with marble copings to the pool, stone columns supporting the arbors, and bronze fountains. There is usually a way to spend a lot of money on almost anything. But it might be done for practically nothing. The canal could be shallow, maybe a foot deep, with a separate deeper spot to comfort the fish over winter. It could be lined with plastic, and could be devoted to lotus, which grow in shallow water. Or small water lilies.

To reduce labor, all grass could be abolished and the land paved with concrete, stone, brick, or gravel. To reduce cost further, it could be covered with weed-discouraging plastic and topped with gravel or shredded bark or even leaves collected in the fall. (Later, if there is more labor and more money, this surface can be replaced with brick or stone.)

The arbors could have columns built of concrete rubble covered with stucco, or of brick. Cheaper than that, they could be supported by steel pipes painted dark green or black, or prefabricated arches could be lined up to form the arbor. Or wood posts like fence posts could be used, with wire between them. And on these arbors there would be grapevines. Many varieties would do. My favorite is perhaps 'Villard Blanc', as it is the only variety I have that I consider edible, but 'Concord' or 'Buffalo' or anything else would do. Even if the vines are never sprayed, a good many edible grapes are produced, and various birds will eat enough that the dropped fruit is not too messy.

Later, the strip of land in which the parallel rows of grapes are grown could be further embellished by adding daffodils and tulips for spring, tuberoses or anything else for summer, while still keeping the design almost brutally simple — the canal or pool down the middle, with grape arbors at the sides.

There would be no grass to mow. Which almost justifies the whole thing right there.

❖ Go with the Seasonal Flow

The way it works is this: summer is hot and winter is cold and the other seasons fall in between. Gardeners who every year go off the deep end at the first slight variation in mean temperature should try to get that sentence fixed in their heads.

The last week of November finds the usual tag-end flowers blooming in Washington. Still a few roses, still begonias and early pansies and late larkspurs and snapdragons, and as always a few lilacs are trying to bloom, and a few azaleas, along with pear trees, are testing the waters by opening an occasional floret.

I guess if one never noticed such a thing before, it would cause comment. Just as this winter you can be sure some excited gardeners will notice some daffodils coming through the ground in January, some crocuses in bloom in that month (though March is their great month), and somebody will certainly discover the ice in his fish pool is "ten inches thick, I measured it, and it's never been more than four inches before." Which means, of course, he never noticed such a thing before, and he expects the climate (and everything else) to fit his perhaps limited experience of it.

It's safe to say we won't have a glacier this winter, nor will we have a ten-day spell of hundred-degree afternoons. We also will not have twenty-below-zero temperatures. I expect the low in my garden to be eight above zero, though it may be seventeen above or four above or even hit five below, in which case the gardener is entitled to snarl for a week.

We know pretty much what to expect, and we are reasonably sure that crape myrtles will not freeze and that pittosporums and gardenias will. Something else we know and the beginning gardener should know: there are going to be disasters aplenty in the garden during a year, whatever the weather is. Things long cherished or long hoped for will fail, just as things we never dreamed of, wonderful things, will happen.

It is far more true of the garden than of the stock market that you shouldn't put all your eggs in one basket. Don't pin all your hopes on camellias when sooner or later a winter is certain to cut them to the ground or kill them outright. Don't set your heart on daffodils or peonies when a blast of spring heat will collapse them both just as they come into bloom. Not every year, thank God, but one horrible year in five or ten or fifteen.

Concentrate if you please on some favorite flower, but avoid monoculture. I can say that, who had 560 varieties of irises in my old town garden and not much else. Still, I had cyclamen and roses and chrysanthemums and tithonias and daffodils and azaleas and hollies and osmanthus and viburnums and pink locust and a grand oak from Burma, zub, zub, zub. There was no year in which everything was a disappointment and no year in which something wasn't.

Would you say that is why we gardeners as a group are so wise and even-tempered and generally delightful? We have taken our lumps. We have passed to the other side of misery and have discovered (not simply read somewhere) that where there's a warp there's a woof, and taken all together the game is worth the candle. Ten of them.

❖ *A Gardener's Thanksgiving*

Gardeners, as a caste, are usually grateful for blessings. Indeed, it is wonderful how little it takes to make a gardener happy. A rooted sprig of some uncommonly pretty goldenrod will do it, or a start of Jacob's ladder, or a tuft of soldiers-and-sailors. A rooted sucker of Jew's mallow or some seeds of willow herb. An old out-of-date iris that the connoisseur would sneer at will bring joy to nine gardeners in ten, whether they have room for it or not.

I am grateful first of all for my little cat-run garden, too small for grand effects. I do not envy those gardeners (or not much) who have pink walls of Tudor brick, or a cathedral tower at the back, or a crystal stream or a black moss-hung bayou running through the place. No. Like almost every gardener I have met, I am enchanted at what has fallen to me, my 40-by-185-foot town lot, with a big red maple and a big pin oak in front and sun in the back.

You wouldn't know it to look at me, but almost every day I thank God for my Italian arum, which sends up its arrow leaves to perfection in October and dies down in May. All winter it is green, with white marblings, and I never tire of it.

A few years ago I bought a box bush. It has trebled in bulk. I feel like a dog with two tails when I see it, though other people would not even notice it.

I am grateful indeed for my modest iron gate, which I sanded and painted and hung, and the little brick piers (one lopsided, despite great care with the masonry) my wife and I built. I like the slate walk and remember the day we widened it by two feet with rectangular flags. The epimediums or barrenworts we planted along it are a considerable joy. Now the leaves are bronze-red. They will be cut to the ground on a mild day in February, so the tender, elegant, feathery new growth and flowers can rise unobstructed at the end of March.

Nothing pleases me more than my roses, though they are out of date to the point that most rose fanatics would not give them space.

DECEMBER

WE'RE IN THE DARKEST TIME of the year, and if the gardener were an animal of the long June afterglows, he would think — he would see — that the light is getting worse and not better, and wonder what possible future could be worth waiting for. We have one advantage, at least, over the average bug: we know that once we get past Christmas, if we can only hold out till March, the blessed sun will be born again.

I love to look at my garden in the winter, not because it is beautiful (a garden can be at its best in winter; mine is not) but because it is so bare and so ruined and will be once more so soft and so sweet. The tall yews that I look at now I never look at except in winter. Only gardeners, I guess, understand how it happens that yews and willows were thought good substitutes for palms. The yews are very much contained, very little given to expansive gestures, but when you see them in the winter, powdered with snow or bent down with sleet, they speak promises; and no gardener ever lived who was sorry he planted them.

❖ *Where Have All the Poppies Gone?*

Birds, I think, are fond of poppy seeds, and this may be why I never have any poppies. Other people have poppies (I whine piteously), but I never get any. This year I hope I am on the right track.

I only planted the seeds at Thanksgiving, on top of some newly dug earth. The new digging was to accommodate some daffodils that had been sitting about in the garage since June.

The thing I hope for is that the poppy seeds fell down the interstices of the dirt, for I was careful not to bring the surface to too fine a tilth. Thus the birds would have to poke around in the dirt to find a seed, not simply harvest a seed sitting up there on top. The birds at my place are so lazy they will not hunt for anything; the woodpeckers and flickers drill holes, but all the rest simply glower about on the branches until the seeds, fruit, or suet is put out for them.

The best way to have poppies (as in wheat fields in France) is simply to have them to begin with. Then they seed in such abundance that you have them forever after, provided you dig up the ground once a year.

But suppose you have a nice stand of Shirley poppies or other kinds that grow readily from seed. There are so many seedpods, you think, *Ha, now I've got 'em and won't ever have to plant again.* And this is true as long as the earth is disturbed every year or two, but there comes a time when the earth is undisturbed for a couple of years, and presto, the poppies vanish.

You can't believe it. There were hundreds of them, and now not one. I am not sure how this works, because poppies love to seed themselves into gravel or between stones, and the earth is certainly not disturbed there. A friend of mine used to grow opium poppies between big clumps of irises, but they died out except between the stone blocks used for edging the beds, and this rather defeated the plan.

It is interesting that poppies, like many another garden creature, will come up where they were never intended to grow. Indeed, this phenomenon sheds light on two kinds of gardeners — those who say they always put their plants in just the right places, and those who notice that they never do. It makes for happier gardening if one is the first sort, and thinks that every volunteer has sprouted up precisely where it looks best.

Oriental poppies are usually planted not from seed but by root division. I have grown Oriental poppies off and on for a half-century now and never yet had a good clump. That is because it takes them a couple of years to settle in well, and before that time I have thought it good to plant something else "so it will flop over and conceal the bare spot when the poppies die down." Since I am never quite certain just where the Oriental poppies are, I usually plant things on top of them. My Oriental poppies always stagger into bloom eventually, but they do not like being smothered and soon give up. There is a clear orange Oriental poppy, however, that I have often noticed, which seems slightly more vigorous than a dandelion, and possibly that is the one I should try.

A poppy relative I am fond of is *Macleaya cordata,* formerly called *Bocconia cordata,* the plume poppy. There are supposed to be two forms of this in cultivation, one that runs all over the place and one that just makes clumps. The one I have is supposed to sit there in great dignity, but I began to lose faith in its nonexpansionist attitude the year it burrowed underground six feet and came up on the other side of the walk.

Nothing is easier, of course, than to chop it out if it comes up in the wrong place in April. Except, of course, it is clever at surfacing in a new clump of irises that one does not wish to disturb, or a quarter-inch from a rather fragile clematis. In these cases one cannot whack freely and must simply slice off the crown of the plume poppy, and it will make several efforts at surviving before giving up. Naturally, having performed surgery twice, one then forgets about it, and within a few weeks the plume poppy has reared itself six feet high and is handsome, and the clematis has bid a long goodnight. This has happened to me twice.

The point of the plume poppy is its superb leaf, about the size of a cantaloupe (only flat, naturally) with indentations like a mitten for a giant. The flowers, in a kind of plume, are agreeable though not showy, but the reason to grow it is that it makes a six-by-five-foot mound of glaucous leaves. When well sited it is a dramatic plant, utterly foolproof.

I have had to dig out all the ones I sited carefully for drama, since they started choking out miniature daffodils, irises, and roses and almost did in a good-sized dwarf plum tree. But the plant is so handsome that I settled it between a ravenous maple and a fence. There it can grow up to eight feet if it pleases and run as it likes. Being somewhat hidden, however, it hardly fulfills its role as a plant of high drama, rising above the plain of lesser vegetation.

It is an important art to do one thing at a time and do it well. In a garden it means deciding that here we shall have that, and then allowing the necessary space and care for everything to do well in its season. It is an art I no longer hope to master.

❖ *Turn Down the Noise*

I am glad to see that the American holly is not so despised as formerly. It used to be the case that gardeners wanted only English or Chinese hollies, with their admirable glossy leaves. I think it may take sophistication, or at least age, to come round to the beauty of our wild holly with its dull mat leaves.

When I was a young man and poor and worked on a cotton farm one winter, I was proud to have a Jeep, my own car and my first. It didn't have a top; you sat there behind the wheel with the rain beating down on you. Getting back to the farm, I always got cold. I used to stop sometimes in a holly grove that had once been around a house, I think, but the house was no longer there. You could drive in, and there were maybe a hundred old hollies.

Once inside, you found that the grass was green, though the fields were withered and there weren't any birds. The wind could howl, but inside that grove it was quiet as a temple, and it was always soft in there, the air was, no matter what the weather was outside. I fell in love then with the wild green holly. I think that to love it, you have to give it some time to get to you. I think it helps to have an open Jeep and to stop at a holly grove and get out and let the magic work.

Sometimes I think that's the worst fault of America: we don't get out enough and sit still enough for the magic to work. That the magic is there I know with all sureness. But if the volume of "music" is turned to Deafening and the speed of the car is pushed to

Suicidal, you can't hear it or see it; you could fairly say it doesn't exist.

Turn down the noise. Reduce the speed. Be like the somnolent bears, or those other animals that slow down and almost die in the cold season. Let it be the way it is. The magic is there in its power. The holly and the ivy and the yew and the box and the nandina and the rest — the photinias, cleyeras, certain azaleas, cunninghamias, red cedars, deodars, arums, cyclamens — are in suspended life. They are not shooting out leaves or flowers, they are marking grave and stately time, but they are flamboyantly alive all the same, and they show it.

No gardener would want an endless summer. Many think so, but the trains back from Florida are filled with homesick gardeners who get to the point that they would give every flash of scarlet in this world for the frozen ivy. It's all right for fancy people to head for lush places, but a gardener should stay steady and stay home. Let it come, whatever comes. The gardener walks always with the unseen crown of oak leaves, the invisible rush of roses, the tuberoses and the cestrums in his nostrils through all decay of the year.

Hold on to it, I say. It will come again. But far more than that, it has already been and the gardener has been through it and in it. It was him. So is this winter him, this sleeted ivy, which was sacred, all the same, to the god.

❖ Yewing and Strewing

Not that I've finished, of course, but my two-pronged attack on the garden problems of winter is extremely sensible. First, I actually got out there on a ladder and cut the bejibbers out of some yews. These are upright columnar beasts that ten years ago were just mid-thigh in height and were moved (in the very nick) from under some windows. In their new place they have grown to fifteen feet or so, and present substantial griefs during heavy snowfalls. Though they grow upright, the branches rise up parallel, and the weight of snow and ice makes them sprawl apart. The usual treatment for this consists of swatting them vigorously with a broom or, if that doesn't work, a long wooden pole.

If you're out of town, you may be in trouble. The yew is strong enough that it never breaks (it is, after all, the classic wood for bows), but it also never snaps back straight after a few days of being bent. It then starts growing in an increasingly open and spreading pattern, so succeeding winters become even greater problems. The thing to do is tie the ascending branches with great loops of rubber-coated wire or anything else strong enough to keep them from sprawling. I used rope but found it rotted out within four years.

Even with this support (and you tie loosely enough that there is still room for some spreading), the yews need attention at least every other year, else the new growth bushes out instead of growing straight up. So this year, before the snows, I lopped off vast amounts of foliage, especially on one side, so the plants look a bit naked. It will take them two years to green out properly. Yew is one of the few plants that will endure being cut back to the main stems, and will send out new growth along the entire length. But you can do this only on one side. If you cut the whole tree back to bare trunk, it will die, so you do one side this year and the other side two or three years later. In this way even huge ancient overgrown hedges can be brought back to very narrow shapes.

With all the yew trimmings I shall mulch things that appreciate protection from freezing and thawing. There is a new seedling tree peony I am excited about, the gift of a friend who grows them superbly. I shall strew several yew branches about it, partly to temper the wind on its still-small stems and partly to insulate the earth from sudden thaws and freezes, for the plant has only been in place a couple of weeks and its root system is not yet very strong.

I have found mulches good for tall bearded irises as well. Although evergreen branches are grand, I have used plain oak leaves, though it is a nuisance to get them off the plants when new growth starts in late winter.

Once a thoughtful reader in Delaware wrote saying that she has some tea roses (forerunners of today's hybrid teas) more than thirty years old. She found they suffered more from cold winds than anything else, and therefore planted them with shelter from the northwest. Taking a tip from her, I shall protect my valued Noisette rose, 'Jaune Desprez', by weaving some yew branches among its basal stems. I would never dream of wrapping it in plastic, as I know some people do in the case of tender plants, because I consider that an invitation to overheating and death.

This rose (thought to be a cross between 'Blush Noisette' and 'Parson's Yellow Tea', about 1830) is probably at least as hardy as any of our common hybrid teas. In the last century there were huge plants of it around Philadelphia, I have read. But while I cannot coddle it (it is already about twelve feet, and will probably double or triple that), I am keen to give it shelter from wind. Burlap on the windy side would be good, but since I shall never get around to that, I hope the yew branches will help. I will not mulch the ground with yew, however, until after Christmas or whenever the earth is too frozen to dig.

In the meantime, the yew branches cover some feet of the garden walk. It seems silly to pick them up until they can go in their permanent winter place. Neither the hound nor the terrier approves, and they make a great show of pussyfooting through the greenery, which is better now that I have fished out the rose prunings (which in a fit of energy I whacked off the rugosas and temporarily threw on the walk with the yew). They still mutter when they use the walk, but really, you cannot do everything at once, you know.

❖ *Bananas*

Humans' first home must have been tropical, as so many gardeners yearn for year-long summer. In fact, the tropics are not nice to garden in — the storms, the winds, the monotonous drudge of one perfect day after another, and (worst of all) the failure of irises, daffodils, peonies. All the same, I know there are gardeners like me who (and never mind the blunt reality that we lack time or energy to keep our temperate gardens in fine order) are continually seduced by some tropical plant or other.

The great triumph, naturally, is to grow a tropical plant outdoors and keep it alive through the winter. Few joys equal that of a buddy of mine in Connecticut who grows and flowers his ginger lilies outdoors, year after year. And to keep a night jasmine (*Cestrum nocturnum*) year after year under a south wall (with a considerable mulch of hay or branches over it) is wonderful.

I have known gardeners determined to keep banana trees outdoors over winter. In November they cut the great leaves off and surround the eight-foot stump with hog wire in a cylinder four feet in diameter, into which they pack leaves. It takes a billion bags of leaves. Their reward comes in the spring, when the banana sprouts out again.

Of course, it is easier to dig the stem up with a water-pail-size ball of earth, plop it in a bucket, and store it in a cold but frost-free spot indoors, planting it outdoors again in May. I have known gardeners who just pulled up their bananas in fall and laid the great stems horizontally across water pipes in the basement. One woman, who knew no better, had a crawl space (quite open to the elements at the sides) beneath part of the house, and she simply dumped the trunks on the dirt there. On winter nights that went to zero, she did nothing and didn't even worry — not knowing enough to — and was rewarded for her faith as the old stems grew beautifully when she planted them out the next spring.

Some people loathe bananas in a garden. To me they are one of the great good plants, regular princes of the vegetable kingdom. Usually I restrain myself — I have only one at the moment, and I love those hot days when it flaunts its six-foot-long leaves fourteen feet in the air. You understand that there is a difference between an innocent quirk of introducing a tropical banana amid the dogwoods and roses and a full-blown insanity in which the gardener starts collecting different banana trees and has them all over the place.

Among the most dangerous catalogues issued in this nation is the one sent out by the Banana Tree, 715 Northampton St., Easton, PA 18042. Gardeners who are not seriously interested in buying banana trees really should send a dollar or two to defray the cost of the modest twenty-page list. The bananas begin on the first page, where you learn that there are 450-odd varieties. Thirty-odd varieties are offered for sale, from corms, which you plant in an eight-inch pot. Ideally, you then give them a temperature of seventy-five, and twelve to sixteen hours of light a day. And you want to keep the humidity at 75 percent. Still, there can be lapses from the ideal without disaster.

Recently I have debated at length which bananas would be best. The little six-foot Cavendish is easy to manage; the giant Cavendish, at twenty feet, would take more doing. So would the giant Pisang, no doubt, which can reach eighty feet. It takes a stronger hold on reality than most gardeners possess to pass over the French Horn, Grand Nain, Hua Moa, Dwarf Jamaican Red, Mysore, Rajapuri, and Pink Orinoco.

Often, the gardener will learn over the years, the passion and longing abate somewhat. Most gardeners go through dreadful yearnings — weeks on end of desperate desire — for some plant or other. Old codgers can look back on their Peony Period, Daffodil Fanaticism, Iris Psychosis, Rose Neurosis; and gardeners with high thresholds of pain usually have also endured the Oleander Attack and Arum Moratorium (in which nothing seems real but arums).

I have had banana fits before, and know that in time they will pass. Still, it is not unreasonable, surely, to have just one little Cavendish? And there is a good west window on the stair landing — a good-size tub on the living room floor and a slight bending of the stem over the stair rail, with plenty of light from the window, and the stem could continue up to the height of the upstairs hall. Let's see, seventeen feet. Well, upon my word, I see I really could have the Mysore banana, which often stops at fourteen feet.

❖ Happiness Is a Hummingbird

Forget poinsettias, if you don't mind, and turn your thoughts to hummingbirds, which surely are far more festive and delicate and marvelous. I do not mind poinsettias, though mine have a dismal way of lasting until March, so that one gets rather weary of them. But hummingbirds are one of the glories of eastern America, and although we have only one kind, the ruby-throated, that one is abundant and should suffice.

Gardeners love hummingbirds — I cannot think of ever hearing anybody complain of "those damned hummingbirds," though gardeners complain of everything else. On hot June days it is a delight to everybody to behold the hummingbirds hovering about, and there is no reason that every garden should not be attractive to them.

A friend of mine recently sawed down a huge old mimosa tree. Before he did so, I had often admired the hummingbirds. It was no rare thing to see as many as thirty hummingbirds at a time working the nectar-laden flowers. The mimosa (*Albizia*) is scented, though most flowers loved by the hummers have no fragrance. Thomas Jefferson, you may recall, planted thirty-two seeds of this tree on his birthday in 1809, and while that is the only reference to it I can find at the moment, I think this was one of his favorite trees at Monticello. Hummingbirds, if not Jefferson, consider the mimosa a veritable prince of the vegetable kingdom, and sometimes visit it in a regular cloud of tiny wings so that the entire flowering canopy seems to be vibrating. A mistake to cut down a mimosa, needless to say, but there you are.

Another great favorite of these little fowl is the trumpet vine (*Campsis*) in several varieties. I was uneasy that they might not like the yellow trumpet vine, as red is their favorite color, but was happy to see that they worked the yellow flowers as well as the others. We were proud last year when hummingbirds built a nest in a wild trumpet vine on our fence. The nest, which I have not found despite diligent searching, is so cleverly disguised that it resembles a mere swelling on a stem or twig. I did not want to go poking about until cold weather, and although I knew just where the nest was, within a margin of five feet or so, and though I know how cleverly the birds patch it about with lichens, I have not been able to find it. I have read that usually two white bean-size eggs are laid, but we saw three infants feeding, we thought, unless one of them was a small adult, after all.

The usual way of feeding these birds is with sugar water. People used to use honey and water, but this was said to cause a fungus bad for the birds. Nowadays you use a solution of sugar and water (put four ounces of sugar in a pint jar and fill with water — do not use more sugar, as too rich a solution is bad for the birds' livers, I have been told). It is, of course, a nuisance to feed the birds this artificial mixture, which should be changed every day in hot weather lest it ferment. It should be dispensed in one of those glass tubes (usually with something red, like an artificial flower, to attract them), and the feeder should be kept free of ants and bees. This is sometimes hard to manage, but if you suspend the feeder from a wire coated with vegetable oil, the ants are supposed to be discouraged. There are endless numbers of hummingbird feeders on the market, but I believe the main thing is to put them where it is easy to take them down and wash them out with hot water at least every other day.

A garden well stocked with flowers that hummingbirds like is the best way to attract them. A plant famous for its popularity with the birds is bee balm, *Monarda didyma,* and you might as well grow a red one, such as 'Cambridge Scarlet'. Cannas are not always considered outstanding hummingbird flowers, but in my garden the birds like the wild cannas we grow. Red zinnias do very well, especially the ones that have few petals and big yellow centers, and verbenas. Columbines are better than either of these, and I used to grow them with heucheras or coral bells, also visited by the birds. The heucheras kept up till July, so there were flowers for more than three months.

Many campanulas are said to be great favorites, though I have never seen hummingbirds on them myself. Other flowers the birds like are clematis, delphiniums, pinks and sweet Williams, daylilies, petunias, lobelias, trout lilies (they never visit mine, or if they do I never see them), sweet peas, catmints, four o'clocks, poppies, honeysuckles, sages, geraniums (the subtropical ones planted out for the summer), and viburnums.

❖ *A Good Time for Pleasant Chores*

The north wind doth blow and we shall have snow. EEEEEeee-ee-e!

We may be wrong, you know, ever to have fooled with a garden. Though of course we have pleasant little tasks that keep us amused. This is the ideal time to clean the leaves from the lily pool. You rake neatly from the sides, bringing up the corruption from the bottom — deposited by Norway maples, needless to say. After an hour and a half of this, you notice that you are not getting many leaves on the rake. You must therefore lower the water level. After some hours you go out again and get a lot more leaves. There is no known way to perform this operation without getting soaked. But you cannot do it sooner, because the leaves have not all fallen. And you must do it or the leaves will decompose and noxious gases will kill the fish.

Now then, having enjoyed this wholesome task, you examine the oak. Also the red maple — both great forest trees that some thoughtful predecessor planted on the small lot. There is considerable dead wood in the oak. It should be cut out. It is 5,396 feet above the ground and you, as it happens, get dizzy at 7.2 feet. Well, you work it out.

The wild clematis that got into the climbing roses, into the flowering plum, must be pulled out and cut out now. It will not do to leave it till spring. Yank, yank, yank (as they say in dreams). In the real world, three hours in the wind, cutting more than pulling and filling a number of bean baskets that are trundled out to the alley, all the dogs excited and making egress and ingress great fun for the man with the bean baskets.

The post supporting the akebia (or rose or clematis or honeysuckle, or even the post just sitting there) has veered from plumb. When better to straighten it? Do you really think you'll do it in the spring, as delicate new growth emerges like an emerald veil? Or do you, perhaps, think January 13 will be a better day than today?

It is great fun to straighten posts, especially when they are set in concrete.

Certain wild elms, wild mimosas, have sprung up outside the fence. Many new mulberries have been born. Why, anybody can whisk through these in ten minutes, surely? A full Saturday morning will as a rule suffice to clear them out.

Other plants — the thorniest of climbing roses, for example — should be tied in. Awfully merry times are spent doing this. The fastigiate (columnar) yews should be pulled together (the various upright stems) with chains encased in heavy canvas or rubber hose. Just try it. Just try it.

❖ *Singular Sensations*

It's all very well to "paint pictures" with plants. The great Edwardian gardener Gertrude Jekyll always said that's what she did, and there never was a handsomer garden than hers at Munstead Wood. So I have nothing against the idea of treating a garden as a picture in three dimensions, working out the colors with various flowers. But a word needs to be said for the occasional glory of an individual plant. Sometimes you don't need to paint a picture, but should just stand there amazed at one plant.

I well remember the great *Amorphophallus titanum* at the New York Botanical Garden. It flowered in 1937. It sat in sullen sinister beauty in a greenhouse. This plant is an arum, like the calla, jack-in-the-pulpit, and so on, with a circular collar and a spike, or spadix, in the center. The amorphophallus, however, had a flower forty-nine inches across, and the spadix rose to 101 inches. The New York newspapers at the time spoke of its terrible stench, but I did not notice it. After a few days, I think, it more or less disappears. And in any case I am fond of the smell of skunks at a distance.

These great tropical arums rarely produce huge flowers, because

it takes years for the bulb to reach a size to produce truly giant flowers. It was a miraculous thing to behold, and it didn't paint any picture, it just sat there by itself.

I read somewhere that in tiresome times you should have a mental picture of great beauty that you can conjure up, and the article suggested a seashore or a forest or anything else that reminds you of the world's harmony and grace. For some, I suppose, a chocolate cake will do. For me, it is the image of a single blue iris.

I had never thought of it before and was a bit surprised that after trying out many mental images I hit on the single iris. Greedy by nature, I would have guessed I'd hit on a whole field of irises or a pond full of water lilies or a long pergola of roses. But when you are quite alarmed and frustrated and worried about a dozen things at once, you need to keep your baggage light. The blue iris has served me well in war and peace.

By the front steps there is a single plant of *Dasylirion texanum*. I look at it with some care every day of the year. It looks like a yucca on some weird diet, with leaves only half an inch wide and toothed or spined their whole length. The rosette of these leaves is now five feet high. I would be no happier if I had a field of them.

In the middle of November I saw a foxglove in perfect bloom. It was one of the common purplish sort, and only twenty inches high. It was not strikingly beautiful, just striking. And not a field of them. It did nothing for the "garden picture," but was dandy for all that. The same is true of the old nasturtium 'Golden Gleam', of which this one plant sulked all year and did nothing except try to survive a terrible infestation of aphids. Then after a harsh freeze it opened one defiant flower.

Once near Tallahassee I saw in the distance what looked like a rose blooming in the middle of a rapidly running stream. On investigating, I found it was a six-foot-high plant of *Rosa palustris*, which is able to stand a bit of waterlogging, but I never knew it could grow in a running stream with eight inches of water above the crown.

I have a little clump of merrybells against a tile of the raised fish pool. Every year it sends up its nodding pale yellow flowers. It does not increase or diminish in size. The same is true of a guinea-

hen flower (*Fritillaria meleagris*) that you can't see until you bend down the branches of a box bush, then there it is, with its three dull purple inverted cups on a fourteen-inch stem. Just one, and one every year. I used to have, for many years, a single plant of *Iris reticulata* that grew jammed up against a piece of concrete. I had planted drifts of this and other small bulbous irises elsewhere, but they all petered out after two or three years. Except this one, all by itself. It was worth the contortion of getting my nose four inches off the ground to relish its violet perfume.

My baby of the moment is a tropical arum, not the great stinky one from Sumatra (as in New York) but *Typhonodorum lindleyanum,* from Madagascar. As I've mentioned, it grows in a five-gallon bucket of mud with four inches of water over the crown, and the plant is twenty-two inches high with just three leaves. But I have seen no plant more beautiful in the arc of its spear leaves. It sits in front of an east window at the head of the bed. I suppose the bucket will spring a leak one of these days and it will be awful. This is the same plant that was dropped on the stair carpet coming in from outdoors a while back. Down eleven steps, flinging mud on each. Heh-heh.

In gardens there are wonders to be seen in plants boldly grouped, and in masses of peach and pear trees, and in whole valleys full of California poppies, and in ponds surrounded by masses of jacarandas. There are also many individual wonders to be seen, from the vast amorphophallus in a hothouse to a stray viola blooming against a wall in the snow.

❖ Nights When the Chickens Sing

I have never raised chickens and I don't much like them, but I do love to hear them cackle and crow, the rooster being a melodious animal. This time of year, "wherein our savior's birth is celebrated," as Shakespeare puts it, "the bird of dawning singeth all night long." It was some years before it registered with me that the

bird of dawning is simply your good lusty farmyard cock. It should be singing all night long now, but thanks to various asinine laws there are no roosters in the capital, so we do not get to hear them.

Even so, the gardener can recognize the season by the long nights. From now on the days get longer, though it is only in March that you notice any great difference. In the rest of this month and in January it is mainly the intellectual assurance of increased daylight that we rely on. All the same, we have some of the most richly colored sunsets of the year right now, and many a gardener admits that his town garden never looks finer than when covered with rounded blankets of snow.

Every year for Christmas I see to it that the house has at least a small bunch of the traditional Christmas greens. There seems to be no full agreement about these, but I think five are generally accepted, namely, rosemary, bay, holly, ivy, and mistletoe. I consider yew, box, and juniper equally necessary. The only one not in the garden is the bay, so I used a dried bay leaf from the kitchen, and they all go out of the house on January 6.

I've read that it's unlucky not to have those greens somewhere in the house for Christmas, and while I am not so superstitious as the idiots who go in for astrology, still there is no point in bucking old custom. Besides, I've had as much luck as anybody deserves in this life, and the rosemary, juniper, and so forth at Christmas may account for it.

One of the agreeable gardeners of the world is Peter J. Hatch, director of gardens at Monticello. For some years I have watched with increasing admiration the development of the gardens, and have shared Hatch's eagerness to acquire the Taliaferro apple and other fruits Jefferson spoke highly of. I take with much salt Jefferson's enthusiasm for any particular plant. When he records in his notes or correspondence that a certain cherry or fig or peach is utterly utter, it reminds me of those easy, quick passions to which young gardeners (those under ninety) are susceptible. Even so steady a fellow as myself has gone through near psychotic passions for pomegranates, oleanders, the Burmese oak, the cork oak, the American persimmon, Perny's holly, and a number of irises, from

'Purissima' and 'Alta California' onwards, and — but the list is endless.

One of Jefferson's heated assertions concerns the 'White Marseilles' fig. When the fruit plants of Monticello were replanted in restored gardens and orchards, various figs called by that name were offered, but some of them differed, and it was not certain which, if any, was the true variety. Fortunately, an elaborate importation scheme got the variety from France. The French, who are of course quite thorough, have (I believe) a subminister of figs, and very likely the French Academy has something to say about any fig bearing a French name. Anyway, the 'White Marseilles' is back, and is the genuine variety insofar as human effort can get anything fully correct.

And now the great 'Breast of Venus' peach has been imported for Monticello, after years of mishap and quarantine. Jefferson thought well of this variety. He had virtual hedgerows of peaches separating parcels of land, including thirty-eight named varieties. In 1802 Jefferson planted some pits of this variety. The resulting trees were not the true variety. They might or might not have resembled their parent closely.

It is partly from this habit of gardeners of planting seeds that we are in heavy doubt about many old garden plants. I have eaten peaches grown from seed that were every bit the equal of their parent. In my former garden was a huge pecan tree planted by my mother from seed during World War I, and it was the equal of good commercial varieties. I have a rose I grew from seed that I consider excellent, and another rose from seed dropped probably by a bird that is pretty in its way but not worth growing.

Anyway, back to the goddess's anatomy: Jefferson first got it from a farmer neighbor, Philip Mazzei. Peter Hatch found what is supposed to be the true variety in a garden in Tuscany. The first budwood was sent in 1981 and there were the usual mishaps along the way, but now 'Breast of Venus' is growing both at Monticello and at Burford Bros. Nursery in Monroe, Virginia. It is hoped that within the next three years this old variety will again fruit at Jefferson's farm.

I hope it will be as glorious as everybody hopes, but knowing quite well how gardeners go off deep ends on behalf of various plants they happen to possess, I am not laying any money on the outcome.

❖ *Gifts for the Gardener*

Peat moss is a safe gift for a gardener. I once knew a woman who had fifty bales, along with wooden bins full of rotted manure and leaf mold. She also planted a dozen gold-banded lilies every fall just for cutting. Most gardeners have half a bale, and they dole it out by the trowelful. If the gardener lives in an apartment, a bag instead of a bale is better and, of course, cheaper. Other useful gifts are a bale of hay, a batch of burlap, some rabbit wire (or hardware cloth, as it is known up here), and a bag of unchopped sphagnum moss.

If a tool is contemplated, be sure the gardener needs it, and get the best quality possible. For the rich giver, a pair of loppers that will cut through branches two inches thick is an ideal gift, but most fanatical gardeners already have them, especially if, like me, they are plagued by mulberries that birds sow here and there. Something most gardeners can use and rarely possess is a short curved pruning saw, in which the blade retracts into the wooden handle.

A load of manure is regarded by all gardeners as a sign of almost divine favor. There is plenty of it around, but the trouble is transporting it. A stout plastic bag of manure is a splendid gift. I think a whole load is too much like giving emerald cufflinks — a bit much, and rather improper, unless you know the gardener well. But a good sackful does not exceed the bounds.

It's risky to give a gardener a plant unless you know he lusts for it. Many gardeners would go wild with joy if you gave them a box bush, but many others would have no use for it.

Someone recently gave me four seeds of *Euryale ferox,* a water plant like a water lily that has leaves three feet across and flowers that look like nothing much. Before the introduction of *Victoria amazonica,* the great platter-leafed water lily of the Amazon, the euryale had the biggest leaves of any water plant. The seeds came in a jar of water. They will sprout, God willing, in the spring and will go into a pool (too small for them, of course) in late May. This is an example of a perfect gift for a somewhat odd gardener. All gardeners tend to be odd, but before getting them a Christmas present, it's well to pin down the oddity.

Almost any gardener would like amaryllis or paperwhite narcissus bulbs for blooming in the house. Almost anybody, gardener or not, would like a pot of blooming cyclamen. Many gardeners are lukewarm toward poinsettias. The main trouble with them is they stay in bloom till March, but I suppose it's Scroogesque to complain of a pot plant that behaves so well.

Nowadays the Christmas cactus comes in a variety of pastel colors. I feel you should give a Christmas cactus only to the sort of gardener who will take care of it for decades. I had an aunt whose Christmas cactus lived in a brass pot for almost a million years and sat out the hot summer on a shelf in the garage, and was glorious indoors in winter. Any cactus strikes me as rather like a puppy — something to be given or received only with due thought and, of course, sobriety. My wife once won a golden barrel cactus as a door prize and she hated it, but she was able to disguise it as a gift to me, and I have valued it for several years now. Its only fault is that grass creeps up in it during the summer, when its pot sits on the rim of a pool, and it is delicate surgery to get the grass out once it creeps under fierce curved spines.

Here is what to buy for a guy like me, and other men, I imagine, who are equally sensible:

Weathercocks. When properly mounted, they turn in the least hint of wind. I have two, one an eagle and one a carp. They are copper. I need two because they point in different directions usually, because of things like trees that deflect the wind. When they point the same way, as they do in a gale, it is very reassuring.

Sheet copper. An ideal gift. You can look at the sheet for some months before deciding just what to do with it. It is good to keep under the bed so from time to time you can pull it out and dream.

Sheet lead is grand. I once made a twenty-foot fish pool out of it. It bends easily and is hammered to shape in no time. You can also hammer it around a wastebasket, put the wastebasket away, and strengthen your lead vessel with a lining of concrete, and then you can plant valerian in it for the garden.

Horse troughs. These are called stock tanks nowadays. They are galvanized steel. You paint them black outside and set them on the ground near where you sit outdoors. Goldfish or any carp do well in them if you put in enough seaweed, which you get at an aquarium or out of a stream.

Lath. Not lousy lath (though that is better than nothing) but one-by-two-inch clear pine. You can nail it together in squares and paint it black and it will last forever.

Dowels. I have never known anybody who used dowels and never known anybody who did not long for some. You can sometimes get a whole bag of them in different sizes and lengths. You never know when you will need one urgently.

Two-inch plank, a foot wide and as long as you can afford. In my time I have had several such planks. Few things have given me more joy.

Telephone wire. This may not be the right name for one of the world's most desirable objects, but what I mean is copper wire covered with rubber, about a quarter-inch in diameter and usually gray. It is ideal for tying things outside. Once some linemen left about thirty feet of it in the alley, and I parcel it out like sapphires on various jobs. I am now out. There must be someplace you can buy it.

Tarred twine. The place I got mine was at Wisley, Ripley, Surrey, England. Not much is used but it has a smell rather as I suppose heaven smells. It could be kept in a bureau drawer to confine the fragrance.

Rat poison. I asked the president of an internationally celebrated humane outfit the best way to kill rats. You can't shoot them in town, though I imagine that is the most humane way. He said he didn't really know and took my address, but never wrote. I am not going to put up with rats; on the other hand, I don't want to dispatch them with agony. You are going to have rats if you have bird feeders or tomatoes or an empty garage. I get the kind of poison that comes six boxes to a package and spend roughly $20,000 a year for it. A most useful gift.

Bricks. They used to cost two cents each, now more. I had a friend who once bought 10,000 to play with, but his wife looked at them and hired a man to lay a new front walk and cover the floor of the front porch, with none left over. My friend was too embarrassed to buy any more. Except when one comes loose from the walk, he has none to carry around the yard on Saturdays.

Buckets. Few things raise the heart like a shiny new pail, but the ones I covet (they are not all that cheap) are black rubber. You can feed calves from them.

Cedar shavings. You have to pay for this stuff now, a clear sign of collapse at the foundation of the state. If you get a small bale, you can take some out and stuff something with it for the dog and keep the rest in your clothes closet with church shoes.

Four-by-four posts ten feet long. Has anybody ever had enough of these? They are much better than those little Erector sets kids used to get. Be sure they are pressure treated.

Cut stone. I have rarely met a stone I didn't love, provided it's cut clean. How disgusting random paving is. My front walk is great hunks of slate in random sizes, but when I am rich I shall buy rectangular slabs of fieldstone. Sometimes I buy just a one-square-foot piece of particularly nice color and personality and mortar it atop a small brick pier (you see how valuable bricks are; they go with everything).

Lanterns. I go fairly to pieces for lanterns, as I do for hinges, rabbit wire, and Persian tiles. They all make me feel that God is up there. I have a Coleman that needs a new mantle. How wonderful a Dietz is. When I was a kid they had Aladdins at the farmhouse Aunt Marie spent the summer at. You can blow yourself up if you don't know what you're doing, but what else is new? Miners' lanterns of brass can sometimes be got for peanuts in England, where, alas, many miners have been thrown out of work and mines closed down. I already have one and need no more, but there is not a man alive who wouldn't steal for one.

I never knew anybody easier to please than myself or the guys I know. Somebody once gave my wife and me an old Meissen soup tureen that thrilled my wife witless for a month. It is lovely and was most generous and I like to see people happy, but my God, do you have any idea how much rabbit wire you could buy?

INDEX